SECOND EDITION
TOUCHSTONE

STUDENT'S BOOK

D1554671

MICHAEL McCARTHY
JEANNE McCARTEN
HELEN SANDIFORD

CAMBRIDGE
UNIVERSITY PRESS

CAMBRIDGE
UNIVERSITY PRESS

University Printing House, Cambridge CB2 8BS, United Kingdom

One Liberty Plaza, 20th Floor, New York, NY 10006, USA

477 Williamstown Road, Port Melbourne, VIC 3207, Australia

314–321, 3rd Floor, Plot 3, Splendor Forum, Jasola District Centre, New Delhi – 110025, India

79 Anson Road, #06–04/06, Singapore 079906

Cambridge University Press is part of the University of Cambridge.

It furthers the University's mission by disseminating knowledge in the pursuit of education, learning and research at the highest international levels of excellence.

www.cambridge.org
Information on this title: www.cambridge.org/9781107661523

© Cambridge University Press 2005, 2014

First published 2005
Second Edition 2014

20 19 18 17 16 15 14 13 12 11

Printed in Great Britain by CPI Group (UK) Ltd, Croydon CRO 4YY

A catalogue record for this publication is available from the British Library

ISBN 978-1-107-68043-2 Student's Book
ISBN 978-1-107-62430-6 Student's Book A
ISBN 978-1-107-63748-1 Student's Book B
ISBN 978-1-107-68275-7 Workbook
ISBN 978-1-107-62708-6 Workbook A
ISBN 978-1-107-69602-0 Workbook B
ISBN 978-1-107-66152-3 Full Contact
ISBN 978-1-107-67936-8 Full Contact A
ISBN 978-1-107-66763-1 Full Contact B
ISBN 978-1-107-68151-4 Teacher's Edition with Assessment Audio CD/CD-ROM
ISBN 978-1-107-61272-3 Class Audio CDs (4)

Additional resources for this publication at www.cambridge.org/touchstone2

Touchstone Second Edition has benefited from extensive development research. The authors and publishers would like to extend their thanks to the following reviewers and consultants for their valuable insights and suggestions:

Ana Lúcia da Costa Maia de Almeida and Mônica da Costa Monteiro de Souza from **IBEU**, Rio de Janeiro, Brazil; Andreza Cristiane Melo do Lago from **Magic English School**, Manaus, Brazil; Magaly Mendes Lemos from **ICBEU**, São José dos Campos, Brazil; Maria Lucia Zaorob, São Paulo, Brazil; Patricia McKay Aronis from **CEL LEP**, São Paulo, Brazil; Carlos Gontow, São Paulo, Brazil; Christiane Augusto Gomes da Silva from **Colégio Visconde de Porto Seguro,** São Paulo, Brazil; Silvana Fontana from **Lord's Idiomas**, São Paulo, Brazil; Alexander Fabiano Morishigue from **Speed Up Idiomas**, Jales, Brazil; Elisabeth Blom from **Casa Thomas Jefferson**, Brasília, Brazil; Michelle Dear from **International Academy of English**, Toronto, ON, Canada; Walter Duarte Marin, Laura Hurtado Portela, Jorge Quiroga, and Ricardo Suarez, from **Centro Colombo Americano**, Bogotá, Colombia; Jhon Jairo Castaneda Macias from **Praxis English Academy**, Bucaramanga, Colombia; Gloria Liliana Moreno Vizcaino from **Universidad Santo Tomas**, Bogotá, Colombia; Elizabeth Ortiz from **Copol English Institute (COPEI)**, Guayaquil, Ecuador; Henry Foster from **Kyoto Tachibana University**, Kyoto, Japan; Steven Kirk from **Tokyo University**, Tokyo, Japan; J. Lake from **Fukuoka Woman's University**, Fukuoka, Japan; Etsuko Yoshida from **Mie University**, Mie, Japan; B. Bricklin Zeff from **Hokkai Gakuen University**, Hokkaido, Japan; Ziad Abu-Hamatteh from **Al-Balqa' Applied University**, Al-Salt, Jordan; Roxana Pérez Flores from **Universidad Autonoma de Coahuila Language Center**, Saltillo, Mexico; Kim Alejandro Soriano Jimenez from **Universidad Politecnica de Altamira**, Altamira, Mexico; Tere Calderon Rosas from **Universidad Autonoma Metropolitana Campus Iztapalapa**, Mexico City, Mexico; Lilia Bondareva, Polina Ermakova, and Elena Frumina, from **National Research Technical University MISiS**, Moscow, Russia; Dianne C. Ellis from **Kyung Hee University**, Gyeonggi-do, South Korea; Jason M. Ham and Victoria Jo from **Institute of Foreign Language Education, Catholic University of Korea**, Gyeonggi-do, South Korea; Shaun Manning from **Hankuk University of Foreign Studies**, Seoul, South Korea; Natalie Renton from **Busan National University of Education**, Busan, South Korea; Chris Soutter from **Busan University of Foreign Studies**, Busan, South Korea; Andrew Cook from **Dong A University**, Busan, South Korea; Raymond Wowk from **Daejin University**, Gyeonggi-do, South Korea; Ming-Hui Hsieh and Jessie Huang from **National Central University**, Zhongli, Taiwan; Kim Phillips from **Chinese Culture University**, Taipei, Taiwan; Alex Shih from **China University of Technology**, Taipei Ta-Liao Township, Taiwan; Porntip Bodeepongse from **Thaksin University**, Songkhla, Thailand; Nattaya Puakpong and Pannathon Sangarun from **Suranaree University of Technology**, Nakhon Ratchasima, Thailand; Barbara Richards, Gloria Stewner-Manzanares, and Caroline Thompson, from **Montgomery College**, Rockville, MD, USA; Kerry Vrabel from **Gateway Community College**, Phoenix, AZ, USA.

Touchstone Second Edition authors and publishers would also like to thank the following individuals and institutions who have provided excellent feedback and support on **Touchstone Blended**:

Gordon Lewis, Vice President, Laureate Languages and Chris Johnson, Director, Laureate English Programs, Latin America from **Laureate International Universities**; **Universidad de las Americas**, Santiago, Chile; **University of Victoria**, Paris, France; **Universidad Technólogica Centroamericana**, Honduras; **Institut Universitaire de Casablanca**, Morocco; **Universidad Peruana de Ciencias Aplicadas**, Lima, Peru; **CIBERTEC**, Peru; **National Research Technical University (MiSIS)**, Moscow, Russia; **Institut Obert de Catalunya (IOC)**, Barcelona, Spain; Sedat Çilingir, Burcu Tezcan, and Didem Mutçalıoğlu from **İstanbul Bilgi Üniversitesi,** Istanbul, Turkey.

Touchstone Second Edition authors and publishers would also like to thank the following contributors to **Touchstone Second Edition**:

Sue Aldcorn, Frances Amrani, Deborah Gordon, Lisa Hutchins, Nancy Jordan, Steven Kirk, Genevieve Kocienda, Linda-Marie Koza, Geraldine Mark, Julianna Nielsen, Kathryn O'Dell, Nicola Prentis, Ellen Shaw, Kristin Sherman, Luis Silva Susa, Mary Vaughn, Kerry S. Vrabel, Shari Young, and Eric Zuarino.

Authors' Acknowledgments

The authors would like to thank all the Cambridge University Press staff and freelancers who were involved in the creation of *Touchstone Second Edition*. In addition, they would like to acknowledge a huge debt of gratitude that they owe to two people: Mary Vaughn, for her role in creating *Touchstone First Edition* and for being a constant source of wisdom ever since, and Bryan Fletcher, who also had the vision that has led to the success of *Touchstone Blended Learning*.

Helen Sandiford would like to thank her family for their love and support, especially her husband Bryan.

The author team would also like to thank each other, for the joy of working together, sharing the same professional dedication, and for the mutual support and friendship.

Finally, the authors would like to thank our dear friend Alejandro Martinez, Global Training Manager, who sadly passed away in 2012. He is greatly missed by all who had the pleasure to work with him. Alex was a huge supporter of *Touchstone* and everyone is deeply grateful to him for his contribution to its success.

Touchstone Level 4 Contents and learning outcomes

	Learning outcomes	Language		
		Grammar	Vocabulary	Pronunciation
Unit 1 **Interesting lives** pages 1–10	• Ask questions to get to know someone • Tell interesting stories about my life • Highlight key moments in a story • Highlight important information in a story • Understand a conversation about an accident • Understand a podcast about an athlete's life story • Read about a person who overcame an obstacle • Write an anecdote about facing a challenge	• Simple and continuous verbs (review) • Verb complements: verb + *-ing* or *to* + verb ***Extra practice***	• Verbs followed by verb + *-ing* or *to* + verb	***Speaking naturally*** • Reductions of auxiliary verbs and the pronoun *you* in questions ***Sounds right*** • Word stress
Unit 2 **Personal tastes** pages 11–20	• Talk about my tastes in clothes and fashion • Compare how people look different over time • Describe patterns, materials, and styles of clothing • Show I understand by summarizing what people say • Use *Now* to introduce follow-up questions • Understand people discussing food, music, and movies • Understand people discussing trends • Read an article about how to develop a personal style • Write interview questions and answers	• Comparisons with *(not) as . . . as* • Negative questions ***Extra practice***	• Colors, patterns, materials, and styles of clothing	***Speaking naturally*** • Linking words with the same consonant sound ***Sounds right*** • Are the sounds the same or different?
Unit 3 **World cultures** pages 21–30	• Talk about my country's cultural traditions • Talk about manners, customs, and appropriate behavior in my country • Use expressions like *to be honest* to sound more direct • Use *of course* to show I understand or agree • Understand a conversation about living away from home • Understand people explaining proverbs • Read an article about proverbs • Write an article about a favorite proverb	• The simple present passive • Verb + *-ing* and *to* + verb • Position of *not* ***Extra practice***	• Cultural items, icons, and events • Manners, customs, and culturally appropriate behavior	***Speaking naturally*** • Silent syllables in which unstressed vowels are not pronounced ***Sounds right*** • Matching vowel sounds

Checkpoint Units 1–3   pages 31–32

	Learning outcomes	Grammar	Vocabulary	Pronunciation
Unit 4 **Socializing** pages 33–42	• Talk about going out and socializing • Talk about things I am *supposed to* do, things I think will happen, or plans that changed • Check my understanding with "statement questions" • Use *so* in different ways • Understand people discussing their evening plans • Understand someone talk about his social style • Read an article about introverts and extroverts • Write an article about my social style	• *be supposed to; was / were going to* • Inseparable phrasal verbs ***Extra practice***	• Expressions with *get*	***Speaking naturally*** • Intonation of sentences when you are sure vs. when you are checking ***Sounds right*** • Pronunciation of *get* before vowels and consonants
Unit 5 **Law and order** pages 43–52	• Talk about what the legal age should be • Discuss rules, regulations, crime, and punishment • Use expressions to organize what I say • Show someone has a valid argument • Understand a conversation about a crime • Understand a class debate about changing the law • Read an article about privacy issues with smartphones • Write a comment responding to a web article	• The passive of modal verbs • *get* passive vs. *be* passive • *catch* + person + verb + *-ing* ***Extra practice***	• Rules and regulations • Crimes and offenses, the people who commit them, and punishments	***Speaking naturally*** • Saying conversational expressions ***Sounds right*** • Which sound in each group is different?
Unit 6 **Strange events** pages 53–62	• Talk about coincidences and superstitions • Order events in the past and say why things happened • Show things I have in common • Repeat ideas in other words to be clear • Use *just* to make what I say softer or stronger • Understand someone talking about a coincidence • Understand conversations about superstitions • Read an article about identical twins • Write about a family story	• The past perfect • Responses with *so* and *neither* ***Extra practice***	• Strange events • Superstitions from around the world	***Speaking naturally*** • Stressing new information ***Sounds right*** • Vowels with consonant sounds /y/ and /w/

Checkpoint Units 4–6   pages 63–64

Interaction	Skills				Self study
Conversation strategies	Listening	Reading	Writing	Free talk	Vocabulary notebook
• Use the present tense to highlight key moments in a story • Use *this* and *these* to highlight important people, things, and events in a story	***A lucky escape*** • Listen for details in a story, and retell it with a partner ***Facing a challenge*** • Listen to a true story and answer questions	***Blind Chef Christine Ha Crowned "MasterChef"*** • A news story about a woman who lost her vision and how she won a prize as a TV chef	***Facing a challenge*** • Write a story about a time in your life when you faced a challenge • Format for writing an anecdote or a story	***An interview with . . .*** • Pair work: Complete interesting questions to ask a classmate; then interview each other and note your partner's answers	***Mottoes*** • Write down the verb forms that can follow new verbs, and use them in sentences
• Show understanding by summarizing things people say • Use *now* to introduce a follow-up question on a different aspect of a topic	***Broad tastes*** • Listen for details and answer questions; then listen and choose the best responses ***Keeping up with trends*** • Listen to four people talk about trends, identify the topics they discuss, and answer questions	***How to develop your personal style*** • An article about developing a personal style	***Style interview*** • Write questions to interview a partner on his or her personal style; write answers to your partner's questions • Punctuation review: comma, dash, and exclamation mark	***What's popular?*** • Group work: Discuss questions about current popular tastes and how tastes have changed	***Blue suede shoes*** • Find and label pictures that illustrate new words
• Use expressions like *in fact* to sound more direct when you speak • Use *of course* to give information that is not surprising, or to show you understand or agree	***Away from home*** • Listen to a woman talk about being away from home, and choose true statements ***Favorite proverbs*** • Listen to people talk about proverbs; number and match them with English equivalents	***Proverbs: The wisdom that binds us together*** • An article about the study of proverbs	***Explain a proverb*** • Write an article about your favorite proverb and how it relates to your life • Useful expressions for writing about proverbs or sayings	***Traditions*** • Pair work: Ask *yes-no* questions to guess traditional cultural items	***Travel etiquette*** • Find examples of new words and expressions you have learned in magazines, in newspapers, and on the Internet

Checkpoint Units 1–3 pages 31–32

• Check your understanding by using statement questions • Use *so* to start or close a topic, to check your understanding, to pause, or to let someone draw a conclusion	***Going out*** • Listen to a couple discussing their evening plans ***Extrovert or introvert?*** • Take a quiz; then listen to a woman describe her social style, and answer the quiz as she would	***Examining the "Extrovert Ideal"*** • A magazine article about a book on introverts living in an extroverted society	***Extrovert or introvert?*** • Write an article about your own social style as an extrovert, an introvert, or a little of both • Uses of *as*	***Pass on the message*** • Class activity: Play a game where you pass a message to a classmate through another classmate, and then tell the class about the message you received	***Get this!*** • Expressions with *get* in context
• Organize your views with expressions like *First (of all)* • Use *That's a good point* to show someone has a valid argument	***We got robbed!*** • Listen to a conversation; answer questions and check true sentences ***Different points of view*** • Listen to a debate, answer questions, and respond to different views	***Is your smartphone too smart for your own good?*** • An article about online invasions of privacy	***Posting a comment on a web article*** • Write a comment responding to the online article about privacy issues • Use *because*, *since*, and *as* to give reasons	***Do you agree?*** • Pair work: Discuss controversial topics	***It's a crime!*** • Write down new words in word charts that group related ideas together by topic
• Repeat your ideas in another way to make your meaning clear • Use *just* to make your meaning stronger or softer	***It's a small world!*** • Listen to a story, and answer questions ***Lucky or not?*** • Listen to people talk about superstitions; decide if things are lucky or unlucky; write down the superstitions	***Separated at birth, then happily reunited*** • An article about the true story of twins who found each other after growing up in different adoptive families	***Amazing family stories*** • Write a true story from your own family history • Prepositional time clauses	***What do you believe in?*** • Group work: Discuss unusual beliefs and strange events in your life	***Keep your fingers crossed.*** • Use word webs to group new sayings or superstitions by topic

Checkpoint Units 4–6 pages 63–64

Interaction	Skills				Self study
Conversation strategies	Listening	Reading	Writing	Free talk	Vocabulary notebook
• Speak informally in "shorter sentences" • Use expressions like *Uh-oh!* and *Oops!* when something goes wrong	**Wedding on a budget** • Listen to people plan a wedding; check what they agree on and what they'll do themselves **Fix it!** • Match conversations with pictures; then check which problems were solved	**Developing your problem-solving skills** • An article about an interesting problem-solving technique	**A good solution** • Write a proposal presenting a solution to a problem at work • Format for presenting a problem and its solution	**Who gets help with something?** • Class activity: Ask and answer questions to find out who gets help	**Damaged goods** • Find out if new words have different forms that can express the same idea, and use them in sentences
• Use expressions such as *That reminds me (of)* . . . to share experiences • Use *like* informally in conversation	**Similar experiences** • Listen to two people share experiences, and number the incidents in order; then answer questions **Good and bad apologies** • Listen to conversations; match the people to the apologies; then decide if they were effective	**Apologies: The key to maintaining friendship** • An article about the importance of apologizing and suggesting ways to do so	**A note of apology** • Write an email apologizing for something • Expressions for writing a note of apology	**How did you react?** • Group work: Tell a story about an incident, and listen and respond to classmates' stories	**People watching** • Learn new vocabulary by making a connection with something or someone you know, and write true sentences
• Report the content of conversations you have had • Quote other people or other sources of information	**Who's materialistic?** • Listen to someone answer questions, and take notes; then report his answers **I couldn't live without . . .** • Listen to four people talk about things they couldn't live without, and complete a chart; then listen and write responses to opinions	**This Stuff's Gotta Go!** • A blog post about a woman who declutters her home	**I couldn't live without . . .** • Write an article about your classmates and things they feel they couldn't live without • Use of reporting verbs for direct speech and reported speech	**Material things** • Pair work: Ask and answer questions about material things	**Get rich!** • When you learn a new word, notice its collocations – the words that are used with it

Checkpoint Units 7–9   pages 95–96

• Use tag questions to soften advice and give encouragement • Answer difficult questions with expressions like *It's hard to say*	**Great advice** • Listen to a conversation and answer questions **Success is . . .** • Listen to four conversations about success, and complete a chart	**Three Child Stars Who Beat the Odds** • A magazine article about actors who have managed to avoid "Child Star Syndrome"	**A success story** • Write a paragraph about someone you know who has achieved success, and explain why that person became successful • Topic and supporting sentences in a paragraph	**Quotations** • Group work: Define success	**Do your best!** • Learn new idioms by writing example sentences that explain or clarify meaning
• Refer back to points made earlier in a conversation • Use more formal vague expressions like *and so forth* and *etc.*	**Trends in the workplace** • Listen to conversations about trends, and identify advantages and disadvantages **Trends in technology** • Listen to four people talk about trends, and write notes on their views	**The Internet – The new pathway to success?** • An article about the recent trend of using the Internet to become successful	**Trends in technology** • Write a comment on a web article about trends in technology • Expressions for describing trends	**What's trending?** • Group work: Discuss trends	**Try to explain it!** • Write definitions in your own words to help you learn the meaning of new words and expressions
• Introduce what you say with expressions like *The best part was (that)* . . . • Use *I don't know if* . . . to introduce a statement and involve the other person in the topic	**An interesting job** • Listen to a personal trainer talk about her job; write notes **A fabulous opportunity!** • Complete a job ad, and listen to check and answer questions	**Ace that Interview!** • An article about how to answer the most common questions in job interviews	**A fabulous opportunity!** • Write a cover letter in response to an ad • Format for writing a cover letter for a job application	**The best person for the job** • Group work: Interview the members of your group for a job	**From accountant to zoologist** • When you learn a new word, learn other words with the same root as well as common collocations to expand your vocabulary quickly

Checkpoint Units 10–12   pages 127–128

Useful language for . . .

Working in groups

We're ready now, aren't we?

Are we ready? Let's get started.

Haven't I interviewed you already?

I've already interviewed you, haven't I?

Where are we?

We're on number _____.

We haven't quite finished yet.

Neither have we.

We still need more time – just a few more minutes.

So do we.

One interesting thing we found out was that _____.

_____ told us that _____.

Checking with the teacher

Would it be all right if I missed our class tomorrow? I have to _____.

I'm sorry I missed the last class. What do I need to do to catch up?

When are we supposed to hand in our homework?

Excuse me. My homework needs to be checked.

I'm sorry. I haven't finished my homework. I was going to do it last night, but _____.

Will we be reviewing this before the next test?

"_____" means "_____," doesn't it? It's a regular verb, isn't it?

I'm not sure I understand what we're supposed to do. Could you explain the activity again, please?

Could I please be excused? I'll be right back.

Interesting lives

 Can Do! In this unit, you learn how to . . .

Lesson A
- Get to know your classmates using simple and continuous verbs

Lesson B
- Tell your life story using verbs followed by verb + -ing or to + verb

Lesson C
- Highlight key moments in a story with the present tense
- Use *this* and *these* to highlight information

Lesson D
- Read an article about a person who overcame an obstacle
- Write an anecdote about facing a challenge

Before you begin . . .

- In what way are these people's lives interesting?
- Do you know anyone who does things like these?
- Do you know any interesting people? Why are they interesting?

---

http://www.englishdept...

English Department News

Student of the month – MELIDA CORTEZ

How long have you been living here?
I've been living in Mexico City for five years. I came here to go to school originally. It's a great place to live.

Have you ever lived in another country?
No, I haven't. But my brother has. He's been living in Bogotá, Colombia, for almost a year now. I'm going to visit him later this year.

What kind of music are you listening to currently?
Well, of course I love Latin music. I'm listening to a lot of Latin jazz right now. I like to listen to music when I paint.

What's your favorite way of spending an evening? What do you do?
I like to go out with my friends – we go and eat someplace and then go dancing all night!

When did you last buy yourself a treat?
Last week, actually. I was at a friend's art studio, and I fell in love with one of her paintings. So I bought it.

What did you do for your last birthday?
I went home and had a big party with my family.

What's the nicest thing anyone has ever done for you?
Actually, about six months ago, I was complaining to my dad that I didn't know how to drive, so he paid for some driving lessons. I was thrilled.   *excited*

Who or what is the greatest love of your life?
Oh, chocolate! I can't get through the day without some.

What were you doing at this time yesterday?
I was sitting on a bus. We were stuck in traffic for an hour!

You should really get to know **Melida Cortez**, a graduate student in our English Department. Also a talented artist, she spends her free time painting, and she started a sculpture class last month. She hopes one day to have an exhibition of her work.

1 Getting started

A Do you know someone that other people should get to know? Tell the class about him or her.

"You really should get to know my friend Frank. He's . . ."

B 🔊 1.02 Listen and read. Do you have anything in common with Melida? Tell a partner.

Figure it out **C** Choose the best verb form to complete the questions. Use the interview above to help you. Then ask and answer the questions with a partner.

1. What book **do you read** / **are you reading** currently?

2. What **did you do** / **were you doing** for your last birthday?

3. Have you ever **been living** / **lived** in the United States?

2 **Grammar** Simple and continuous verbs (review) 🔊 1.03

Extra practice p. 140

Simple verbs are for completed actions or permanent situations.	Continuous verbs are for ongoing actions or temporary situations.
Present	What kind of music **do** you **listen** to? I **love** Latin music. I **listen** to it a lot.	What kind of music **are** you **listening** to currently? I'm **listening** to a lot of Latin jazz right now.
Present Perfect	**Have** you ever **lived** in another country? No, I've never **lived** anywhere else.	How long **have** you **been living** here? I've **been living** here for five years.
Past	What **did** you **do** for your last birthday? I **went** home and **had** a big party.	What **were** you **doing** at this time yesterday? I **was sitting** on a bus.

A Complete the conversations. Use the simple or continuous form of the verb in the present, present perfect, or past. Sometimes more than one answer is possible. Then practice.

> ❌ **Common errors**
>
> Use the simple past for completed events, not the past continuous.
>
> *My birthday was great. My friends came to visit.*
> (NOT *My friends ~~were coming~~ to visit.*)

1. A What _____have_____ you _____been doing_____ (do) for fun lately?

   B Well, I've been tak___(take) kickboxing classes for the past few months. It's a lot of fun, and I've been gett___(get) in pretty good shape.

2. A Who's the most interesting person you know?

   B Well, I _____think_____ (think) my best friend is interesting. She _____lived_____ (live) in Europe for three years when she was growing (grow up).

3. A _____Have_____ you ever _____met_____ (meet) anyone famous?

   B No, but last year, I _____saw_____ (see) a TV star on the street. We _____were_____ both _____waiting_____ (wait) in line for ice cream.

4. A When _____did_____ you last _____exercise_____ (exercise)?

   B Actually, I haven't exercised (not exercise) in months. I've been (be) really busy at work, so I haven't had time.

5. A What _____do_____ you _____do_____ (do) for a living?

   B Actually, I'm not workin (not work) right now. I've been lookin (look) for a job for six months, but I haven't found (not find) anything yet.

About you **B** **Pair work** Ask and answer the questions above. Give your own answers.

3 **Speaking naturally** Reductions in questions

*How long **have you** been learning English?*	*Why **are you** learning English?*
*What **do you** like to do in your English class?*	*What **did you** do in your last class?*

A 🔊 1.04 Listen and repeat the questions. Notice the reductions of the auxiliary verbs (*have, do, are, did*) and *you*. Then ask and answer the questions with a partner.

About you **B** **Pair work** Interview your partner. Ask the questions in the interview on page 2. Pay attention to your pronunciation of the auxiliary verbs and *you*.

1 Building vocabulary and grammar

A 🔊 **1.05** Listen to Dan's story. Answer the questions.

1. Where did Dan live before he moved to Seoul?
2. Why did he want to go to South Korea?
3. How did he get his job there?
4. What did his new company offer him?

LIVING ABROAD: **Dan's story**

Dan Anderson was born in the U.S.A. He's now living in South Korea.
We asked him, "How did you **end up** living in Seoul?"

Dan: Well, it's a long story! Before I came here, I **spent** three years working for a small company in Tokyo while I **finished** doing my master's in business. To be honest, I wasn't **planning on** leaving or anything. But one day, I **happened** to be in the office, and one of the salespeople was looking at job ads online.

He knew I was **considering** going to South Korea someday – you see, my mother's South Korean, and I've always been interested in the culture and everything – and anyway, he leaned over and said, "Dan, this **seems** to be the perfect job for you. Check this out."

I looked at the ad, and I **remember** thinking, "Should I **bother** to apply?" But I **decided** to go for it, even though I didn't **expect** to get it, and to make a long story short, I got the job!

The company **offered** to transfer me to Seoul, and they **agreed** to pay for my Korean language lessons. I **started** working here two months later. And the rest is history.

I mean, I **miss** living in Japan, but you can't have it both ways, I guess. Actually, I can't **imagine** living anywhere else now!

Word sort **B** Can you sort the verbs in bold above into the correct categories in the chart? Which verbs are followed by *to* + verb, verb + *-ing*, or a particle or preposition + verb + *-ing*?

Verb + *to* + verb	Verb + verb + *-ing*	Verb + particle / preposition + verb + *-ing*
happen (to be)	*spend (three years working)*	*end up (living)*
decided to go	*remember thinking*	
expect to get	*started working*	
seems to be	*miss living*	
	imagine living	
	finished doing	

Vocabulary notebook p. 10

Figure it out **C** Complete the sentences with the correct forms of the verbs given. Use Dan's story to help you.

1. I considered *studying* (study) electronics, but I ended up *doing* (do) math.
2. I expected *to graduate* (graduate) in three years. Then I decided *to change* (change) my major.

4

2 Grammar Verb complements: verb + -*ing* or *to* + verb ◄)) 1.06

Extra practice p. 140

Verb + verb + -*ing*: consider finish imagine miss mind spend (time)	I **finished doing** my master's in business. I **spent** three years **working** in Tokyo.
Verb + particle / preposition + verb + -*ing*: end up keep on think about plan on	How did you **end up living** here? I wasn't **planning on leaving** Japan.
Verb + *to* + verb: agree decide happen offer seem intend expect	They **agreed to pay** for Korean lessons. I didn't **expect to get** the job.
Verb + -*ing* or *to* + verb with the same meaning: begin bother continue start like love hate	Should I **bother applying**? Should I **bother to apply**?
Verb + -*ing* or *to* + verb with a different meaning: remember stop try	I **stopped talking** to him. (We don't talk now.) I **stopped to talk** to him. (I stopped walking.)

A Complete the conversations with the correct forms of the verbs given. Then practice with a partner.

1. A How did you end up _studying_ (study) here?

   B My friend recommended this school. I remember
   to think (think) his English was good, so I decided
   to sign up (sign up) for this class. How about you?

   A Well, I wasn't planning on _learning_ (learn) English,
   but my company offered _to pay_ (pay) for my classes.
   I agreed _to come_ (come), and here I am! I want to
   keep on _taking_ (take) classes if I can.

2. A What are you thinking about _doing_ (do) next summer?

   B Well, it depends. I just started _working_ (work) in a new job, so I don't expect _to get_ (get)
   much vacation time. I intend _to take_ (take) a couple of long weekends off, though. You have
   to stop _working_ (work) occasionally! Anyway, I love _to surf_ (surf), so I hope I can spend a
   weekend _visiting_ (visit) my cousins at the beach, too.

About you **B** Pair work Take turns asking the questions. Give your own answers.

> **In conversation**
>
> *Begin, bother, continue, like, love,* and *hate* are followed more often by *to* + verb. *Start* is followed more often by verb + -*ing*.

> ✖ **Common errors**
>
> Don't use *to* + verb after these verbs.
>
> *I finished reading the ad.* (NOT . . . ~~to read~~)
> *I considered applying.* (NOT . . . ~~to apply~~)
> *I don't mind working hard.* (NOT . . . ~~to work~~)

3 Talk about it Why did you stop doing that?

Pair work Take turns asking each other questions using the ideas below. Ask follow-up questions.

Can you think of someone you . . . ?
- ► don't miss seeing
- ► expect to see next week
- ► happened to run into recently
- ► intended to see but didn't
- ► keep on calling
- ► love to hang out with

"I don't miss seeing my old math teacher."

Can you think of something that you . . . ?
- ► agreed to do recently
- ► are considering doing soon
- ► can't imagine doing in the future
- ► finished doing recently
- ► never bother to do
- ► stopped doing recently

"Why's that? Were you bad at math?"

(((Sounds right p. 137

We're both getting scared....

1 **Conversation strategy** Highlighting key moments in a story

A Think of a time when you got lost. What happened? Tell the class.

B 🔊 1.07 Listen. How did Mateo and Bryan get lost?

Mateo	Remember that time we were hiking in Utah?
Bryan	When we got lost? That was funny.
Kim	Why? What happened?
Mateo	We were on this trail, and it was getting dark. Then Bryan says, "Where are we?"
Bryan	Yeah, we couldn't see a thing, and we walked off the trail. It was that bad.
Mateo	Yeah, there were all these trees around us, and we were so lost. And we're thinking, "Oh, no." And we're both getting kind of scared. We just wanted to get out of there.
Kim	I bet.
Mateo	And Bryan says, "Should we jog a little?" And I go, "Yeah. I was thinking the same thing. Let's go."
Bryan	So we started jogging, . . .
Mateo	And we said to each other, "We've got to stick together, in case anything happens."

C Notice how Mateo changes to the present tense at key moments in his story. It makes them more "dramatic." Find more examples in the conversation.

"We're both getting kind of scared."

D 🔊 1.08 Read more of their conversation. Change the underlined verbs to the simple present or present continuous to make the story more dramatic. Then listen and check your answers.

hear

Bryan Yeah. And all of a sudden, we ~~heard~~ this noise.

Mateo And I <u>looked</u> over at Bryan, and I <u>saw</u> his face <u>was</u> white, and he <u>was starting</u> to run fast.
I'm looking *see* *is* *is starting*

Bryan Well, yeah. I <u>mean</u>, it was a weird noise.
I'm thinking

Mateo So, I <u>was thinking</u>, "Wait a minute. What happened to our plan to stick together?" So I <u>started</u> to run with him.
start

Bryan Yeah, we <u>were running</u> through the trees, scared to death. It was hilarious! It was just like in a movie.
are running

6

2 Strategy plus *this* and *these* in stories

When you tell stories, you can use *this* and *these* to highlight important people, things, and events.

We were on this trail, . . .

There were all these trees . . .

A Replace *a, an,* and *some* with *this* or *these* in the story below. Then take turns telling the story with a partner.

this

these

"I have **a** friend who's always getting into funny situations. One time she was invited to **a** going-away party, and she ended up getting totally lost and wandering around a neighborhood she didn't know. Anyway, she finally sees **a** house with **some** cars outside, and **some** people were barbecuing in the backyard. So she knocks on the door, and **a** nice guy lets her in. He thought she was one of his wife's friends. Anyway, she spent about an hour talking to **some** people before **some** guys bring out a big birthday cake and candles and everything. Then she finally realized it was the wrong party!"

this
these

these
this
these

these

About you **B** **Pair work** Tell about a time you or a friend got into a funny situation.

3 Listening and strategies A lucky escape

A You're going to hear a story about a skiing accident. Aaron was skiing with friends when one of them fell down the mountain. Circle four questions you want to ask Aaron.

1. Where were you skiing?
2. How far did your friend fall?
3. What did you do when he fell?
4. How badly was he hurt?

5. Did you get help? How?
6. Did he have to go to the hospital?
7. When did this happen?
8. Is he OK now?

B 🔊 1.09 Listen. Write answers to the questions you chose. Then share answers with a partner. Can you remember the entire story together?

About you **C** **Pair work** Think of a time when something went wrong or when you or someone you know had an accident. Tell a partner the story.

". . . And suddenly she falls off the climbing wall and lands next to this guy. And all these people run over to see if she's hurt. She was OK. A little embarrassed, but OK!"

1 Reading

A What kinds of competitions are there on TV shows? Do you ever watch them?

B Read the article. What was Christine Ha's disadvantage in the MasterChef competition? What advantage did she have?

📖 **Reading tip**

Read the quotes in a news story first. They often give you a quick summary of the article.

Blind Chef Christine Ha
Crowned "MasterChef"

From the moment she took those first tentative steps onto the national stage, amateur chef Christine Ha captured America's heart.

During the season 3 "MasterChef" finale, Ha won the title, $250,000, and a cookbook deal, beating out about 100 other home chefs. But that's not what makes her so inspiring. Ha is blind – the first blind contestant on the show.

"I think there are a lot of people who completely discounted me," Ha said. "People will say, 'What is she doing? Is she going to cut her finger off?' But I cooked at home for years without vision, so if I can do it at home, I don't see why I can't prove to everyone else I can do it on national TV."

Week after week, the 33-year-old, who lives in Houston, Texas, managed to whip up culinary masterpieces with only her senses of taste, smell, and touch to guide her.

"I couldn't see what anyone else was doing, I was solely focused on myself, and I think that helped me. It gave me an advantage," she said. "When I came out of it, it was the most stressful, intense experience of my life, it was amazing."

Ha lost nearly all of her eyesight about five years ago after being diagnosed with an autoimmune disease that attacks the optic nerves.

"When I lost my vision, there was one time I tried to make a peanut butter and jelly sandwich," she said. "I recall getting it all over the counter. I just started crying and was wondering if I would ever cook again."

But she did more than pick herself up off the counter. She started her own blog, which is how the producers of "MasterChef" discovered her.

Now an official "MasterChef," Ha said, "I just want people to realize that they have it in themselves if they really want to. If they have that passion, that fire, that drive, that desire . . . you can overcome any obstacle and any challenges to really achieve what you want and prove yourself to the world. Everyone is very capable. Much more capable than they think they are."

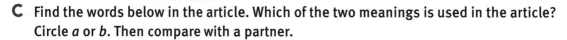

C Find the words below in the article. Which of the two meanings is used in the article? Circle *a* or *b*. Then compare with a partner.

1. tentative
   a. not final
   b. not certain or confident

2. a cookbook deal
   a. the chance to publish her own cookbook
   b. free cookbooks

3. beating out
   a. mixing rapidly in a bowl
   b. winning against

4. discounted
   a. reduced the price
   b. did not consider seriously

5. whip up
   a. make quickly and easily
   b. mix quickly until light and fluffy

6. pick herself up
   a. stand up after falling down
   b. recover from a difficult situation

7. drive
   a. determination
   b. use a car

8. overcome any obstacle
   a. beat or solve a problem
   b. climb over something that's in the way

D Read the article again and answer these questions. Compare your answers with a partner.

1. Why do you think Ha "captured America's heart"? Has she captured yours from your reading of the article?

2. After losing her vision, what did Ha try to do in the kitchen? In what way is this anecdote significant?

3. What do you think Ha means by "people have it in themselves"? Do you agree with her view?

2 Listening and writing Facing a challenge

A 🔊 1.10 Listen to a podcast about Bethany Hamilton. Complete the sentences with the correct information. Choose *a*, *b*, or *c*.

1. As a child, Bethany surfed almost every day with __*b*__ .
   a. her parents   b. her friend Alana   c. Alana's father

2. Bethany decided to return to surfing _____ after the shark attack.
   a. a couple of weeks   b. a month   c. three months

3. Bethany managed to stay on her surfboard because _____ added a handle.
   a. her mother   b. her father   c. Alana's father

4. In the World Junior Championship, Bethany took _____ place.
   a. first   b. second   c. fifth

5. Since Bethany lost her arm, she has _____ .
   a. written a book   b. starred in a movie   c. received help from a charity

6. Bethany is described above all else as a great _____ .
   a. athlete   b. role model   c. traveler

About you **B** **Pair work** Think about a time in your life when you faced a challenge. How did you feel? Did someone help you? How did you feel afterward?

C Read the story and the Help note. Then write a story about your challenge.

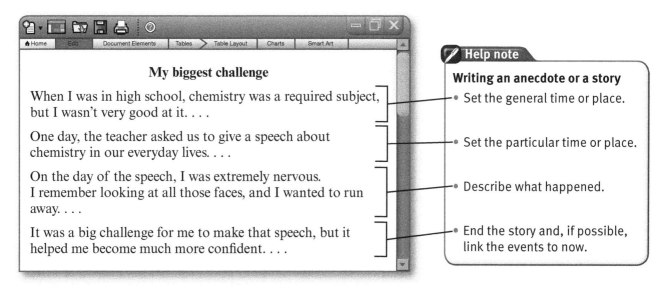

My biggest challenge

When I was in high school, chemistry was a required subject, but I wasn't very good at it. . . .

One day, the teacher asked us to give a speech about chemistry in our everyday lives. . . .

On the day of the speech, I was extremely nervous. I remember looking at all those faces, and I wanted to run away. . . .

It was a big challenge for me to make that speech, but it helped me become much more confident. . . .

Help note

Writing an anecdote or a story
- Set the general time or place.
- Set the particular time or place.
- Describe what happened.
- End the story and, if possible, link the events to now.

D **Pair work** Read a partner's story. Then ask questions to find out more about the story.

Free talk, p. 129

Learning tip *Verb patterns*

When you learn a new verb, write down the verb form(s) that can follow it.
Then use it in a sentence. For example:

imagine verb + -ing	*I can't imagine having lots of money.*
decide to + verb	*I've decided to be a doctor.*
start verb + -ing	*I'm going to start saving money.*
start to + verb	*I'm going to start to save money.*

1 Write down the form(s) of the verbs that can follow the verbs below. Then complete the mottoes. Use the correct form(s) of the verbs given.

1. agree ___*to + verb*___   "Never agree *to lend* (lend) money to strangers."
2. intend ___*to + verb*___   "If you don't intend *to do* (do) something properly,
   bother *+ing or to + V*   don't bother *starting* (start) it!"
3. stop *+ing or*   "Never stop *doing* (do) the things you
   enjoy *to + V*   enjoy *to do* (do)."
4. keep on *+ing*   "Keep on *trying* (try) until you find success."
5. consider *+ing*   "Consider *taking* (take) every opportunity you get in life."
6. seem *to + V*   "Things aren't always what they seem *to be* (be)."

2 **Word builder** Find out the meanings of these verbs, and write down the verb form(s) that can follow them. Then make up your own motto for each verb.

give up   promise   put off   refuse

On your own

Make a flip pad for the new verbs you have learned in this unit. Write each new verb in a sentence. Every time you have a spare minute, learn a verb!

 Can Do! Now I can . . .

✓ I can . . .   ? I need to review how to . . .

- [ ] ask questions to get to know someone.
- [ ] tell interesting stories about my life.
- [ ] highlight key moments in a story.
- [ ] highlight important information in a story.

- [ ] understand a conversation about an accident.
- [ ] understand a podcast about an athlete's life story.
- [ ] read an article about a person who overcame an obstacle.
- [ ] write an anecdote about facing a challenge.

Personal tastes

2

 Can Do! In this unit, you learn how to . . .

Lesson A
- Talk about fashion and makeovers
- Make comparisons with *(not) as . . . as*

Lesson B
- Ask negative questions when you expect someone to agree
- Describe clothing

Lesson C
- Show understanding by summarizing what people say
- Use *Now* to introduce follow-up questions

Lesson D
- Read an article about how to develop a personal style
- Write questions and answers for an interview about personal style

1

2

3

4

Before you begin . . .

What kind of . . .

- music do you like?
- hairstyle looks good on you?
- clothes do you wear?
- car would you like?

Do you and your classmates have similar tastes?

11

Would you let a friend give YOU a makeover?

before

We gave Cindy and Scott, two very good friends, the chance to choose a new look for each other. How did they do? Here's the verdict!

before

What do you think about your new look, Cindy?

I love it! I don't usually wear these colors, but this dress is really nice. I like it. I wouldn't usually wear this much makeup – I try to get ready as quickly as I can in the morning – but it looks good. I'm really pleased.

Scott, you chose a completely different look for Cindy. How do you like it?

I like it a lot. I tried as hard as I could to find a style that suits her personality better. Her hair looks great. I mean, I don't usually like short hair as much as long hair, but it looks good on her, I think. And I like the dress on her. She looks great.

How do you like your new look, Scott?

Well, I kind of like it. I'm not used to wearing pants like these, but they're just as comfortable as my jeans. And Cindy made a good choice with the suede jacket. It's cool. Yeah, I don't look as scruffy as I did!

Cindy, do you like Scott's new look? He looks very different!

Yes, I really like it. He doesn't pay as much attention to his appearance as he should. Actually, the pastel shirt I chose doesn't look as good on him as the bright colors he usually wears. I don't think I like pastels that much, after all. But overall, he looks a lot better! I like his hair short like that.

after

after

1 Getting started

A Look at the "before" and "after" pictures of Cindy and Scott. What has changed?

B 🔊 1.11 Listen. What do Cindy and Scott think about their makeovers? Do you agree with their comments?

Figure it out **C** How do Cindy and Scott actually say these things? Find the sentences in the article above. Compare with a partner.

1. Scott   These pants and my jeans are equally comfortable.
2. Scott   I used to look scruffier.
3. Cindy   He should pay more attention to his appearance.
4. Cindy   I try to get ready quickly in the morning – I can't get ready faster.

2 Grammar Comparisons with *(not) as . . . as* ◀》 1.12

Extra practice p. 141

You can make comparisons with *(not) as . . . as* **with adjectives, nouns, and adverbs.**

Adjectives	The pants are just **as comfortable as** my jeans. (They're the same.)
	The pants are **not as comfortable as** my jeans. (They're less comfortable.)
	I **don't** look **as scruffy as** I did. (I was scruffier before.)
Nouns	She spends **as little time as** possible on her makeup.
	She **doesn't** wear **as many bright colors as** she should.
	He **doesn't** pay **as much attention** to his appearance **as** he should.
Adverbs	I tried **as hard as** I could to find the right style for her.
	I **don't** like short hair **as much as** long hair.

✖ Common errors

Don't forget the first *as*.

*Jeans aren't **as** nice as pants.*
(NOT *Jeans ~~aren't nice as~~ pants.*)

A Complete the sentences. Use the words in parentheses and *as . . . as.*

1. Older people ___*don't care as much as*___ (not care / much) younger people about their appearance.

2. Makeover shows _____ (not be / interesting) other reality shows on TV.

3. Men _____ (spend / much) money on themselves _____ women do.

4. When I choose clothes, looks _____ (be / important) comfort.

5. I _____ (not have / many) clothes and shoes _____ I'd like.

6. I _____ (spend / little time) possible shopping for clothes.

7. Today's styles _____ (not be / attractive) the styles of ten years ago.

8. Women _____ (get haircuts / often) men.

About you **B Pair work Do you agree with the statements above? Explain your views.**

3 Speaking naturally Linking words with the same consonant sound

big glasses	wear red	dark colors	some makeup	stylish shoes

A ◀》 **1.13 Listen and repeat the expressions above. Notice that when the same consonant sound is at the end of one word and at the start of the next, it is pronounced once, but it sounds longer.**

About you **B** ◀》 **1.14 Now listen and repeat these statements. Are they true for you? Discuss with a partner.**

1. I think men loo**k c**ool in shirts and ties.

2. I don't like bi**g g**lasses. They're le**ss s**tylish than small glasses.

3. I li**ke c**asual clothes. I can't stan**d d**ressing up for anything.

4. I think women should always wear so**me m**akeup.

5. I own a lot of bla**ck c**lothes. I ha**te t**o wear bright colors, and I never wea**r r**ed.

6. There are a lot of styli**sh sh**ops in my neighborhood. They sell some goo**d d**esigner stuff.

1 Building language

A 🔊 **1.15** Listen. Why doesn't Ben like the jacket? Practice the conversation.

Yoko   Oh, don't you just love this jacket? I mean, isn't it great?

Ben   Hmm. I don't know.

Yoko   Don't you like it? I think it's really nice.

Ben   It's OK. It's kind of bright.

Yoko   But don't you like the style? It'd look good on you, don't you think?

Ben   Well, maybe.

Yoko   Well, don't you want to try it on, at least?

Ben   Not really. And anyway, isn't it a little expensive?

Yoko   Oh, isn't it on sale?

Ben   No. It's full price. The sale rack is over there. Hey, look at those jackets. Aren't they great?

Figure it out   **B**   How does Yoko actually say these things? Underline what she says in the conversation.

1. I love this jacket!   2. I think you should try it on.   3. I'm surprised you don't like it.

2 Grammar   Negative questions 🔊 1.16

Extra practice p. 141

When you want or expect someone to agree with you, you can use negative questions.

To express an opinion	To suggest an idea	To show surprise
Isn't this jacket great?	**Aren't** they a little expensive?	**Isn't** it on sale?
Don't you think it's great?	**Don't** you think it's too bright?	**Don't** you like it?
Doesn't that look good on him?	It'd look good, **don't** you think?	**Doesn't** she like it?

Look at the rest of Yoko and Ben's conversation. Rewrite the underlined sentences as negative questions. Then practice with a partner.

Ben   Look at these jackets. I think they're nice.

Yoko   Well, I'm not sure about the color. They're kind of plain.

Ben   Really? I'm surprised you don't like them. Look. This one looks good.

Yoko   Um . . . it's a little tight. It looks kind of small.

Ben   No, it's just right. I think I'll get it!

Yoko   *And* it's not as cheap as the other jackets.

Ben   Oh, it's not the same price. Well, maybe we should look around a bit more.

Aren't they nice? / Don't you think they're nice?

3 Building vocabulary

A **Pair work** Read the product descriptions on the website. What do you think about each item?

"Those rubber boots are cool."   *"Aren't they a bit bright?"*

OUTERWEAR
SHIRTS
PANTS
FOOTWEAR
ACCESSORIES
ACTIVEWEAR
KIDS
GIFT CARDS
FREE SHIPPING OVER $50

1 Choose from our huge selection of men's and women's **leather** and **suede** jackets.

2 Luxury **cashmere** scarves and **silk** ties make perfect gifts.

3 Men's **wool turtleneck** and **V-neck** sweaters will keep you warm all winter.

4 Women's **long-sleeved cotton** tops are available in a range of **solid colors**. Shown here in **neon** green, **dark** green, and **light** green.

5 Looking for **denim** jeans? Whether you want **boot-cut** or **flared, fitted, skinny,** or **baggy** – we have jeans to fit you!

6 Women's **short-sleeved striped** shirts in **polyester**. **Floral-print** and **plaid** shirts also available.

7 Our **rubber** boots come in a variety of patterns. Shown here in **turquoise** with a **polka-dot** pattern.

 Word sort **B** Complete the chart with the words in bold above, and add your own ideas. Then compare with a partner. Do any of these words describe clothes that you and your classmates are wearing?

Colors	Patterns	Materials		Styles	
neon green	striped	leather		V-neck	

Vocabulary notebook p. 20

4 Talk about it Different styles

Group work Discuss the following questions. Use negative questions where possible.

▶ What styles are in fashion right now? What colors? What fabrics? Do you like them?

▶ What kinds of styles look good on you? How about your friends?

▶ What colors are the clothes in your closet? What materials are they made of?

▶ Are there any colors you won't wear? Why?

▶ Would you buy any of the items on the website above? Why? Why not?

"Well, skinny jeans are in fashion, but don't you think they look kind of ugly?" **◀·Sounds right** p. 137

1 Conversation strategy Summarizing things people say

A Pair work Who do you buy gifts for?
What do you usually buy? Tell the class.

B 🔊 1.17 Listen. What do you find out
about Don's sister?

Janet	What do you want to get for your sister? What kind of things does she like?
Don	Well, she likes to read. She likes music. She likes to cook, sew . . .
Janet	She seems to have a lot of different interests.
Don	Yeah. I'm not sure what to get her. She has hundreds of books already.
Janet	She has a big collection, then.
Don	Yeah. And she has a ton of music and as much stuff for the kitchen as she could ever want.
Janet	Sounds like she has everything she needs.
Don	Yeah. She doesn't really need anything.
Janet	Now, doesn't she travel a lot? Because you could get her an e-reader or a tablet or something.
Don	Actually, that's a great idea. She's always complaining about carrying her books everywhere. I think I'll do that.

C Notice how Janet summarizes the things Don says.
It shows she's involved in the conversation and is
following what Don is saying. Find more examples.

*"She seems to have a lot of
different interests."*

D Match each statement with the best response. Write the letters *a* to *g*.
Then practice with a partner.

1. I only download free books or go to the library. _____
2. I've downloaded thousands of songs. _____
3. A friend of mine never seems to like the gifts I give her. _____
4. It's hard to buy gifts for my dad. He never wants anything. _____
5. My mom reads a lot. She knows everything. _____
6. My boyfriend remembers the lyrics of every song he hears. _____
7. I read all kinds of stuff, from romance to science fiction. _____

a. Sounds like she's a walking encyclopedia.
b. Yeah. What do you buy the man who has everything?
c. Wow. He has a fantastic memory.
d. Gosh. You have really broad tastes.
e. Sounds like she's really choosy.
f. You have a huge collection, then.
g. Right. You don't buy books, then.

2 Strategy plus *Now*

Now is often used to introduce a follow-up question. It shows that you want to move the conversation on to a different aspect of a topic.

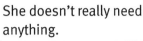
In conversation

Now is one of the top 100 words. About 20% of the uses of *now* are to introduce questions.

She doesn't really need anything.

Now, doesn't she travel a lot?

Find two follow-up questions for each conversation. Write the letters *a* to *f*. Then practice with a partner. Ask the questions again and give your own answers.

a. Now, do you have an idea before you start looking?
b. Now, do you like to do all the tourist things?
c. Now, does she have a background in design?
d. Now, do you have similar tastes?
e. Now, do you usually go alone?
f. Now, do you ask what people want?

1. A Do you like to shop for gifts?

   B Yeah. I like to look for something really unusual. You know, something different.

   A So you put some thought into it. _____ _____

2. A So, are you good at decorating your home? Like choosing colors and fabrics?

   B No, not at all! My wife does all that stuff. She loves buying cushions and things like that.

   A So you're not interested in that. _____ _____

3. A So, I heard you like to travel a lot?

   B Yeah, I really like going to a new city and seeing the sights.

   A So you like exploring. _____ _____

3 Listening and strategies Broad tastes

A ◀)) 1.18 Listen to three conversations. Who has broad tastes? Write the name or names. Then listen again and answer the questions below.

1. What happens in the cooking show? How did Mary learn to cook?
2. What is Nick listening to? How did Nick get into that kind of music?
3. Why is James exhausted? How did James get into sci-fi?

B ◀)) 1.19 Now listen to three excerpts from the conversations. Circle the best response.

1. a. So you don't do it much anymore.   b. Wow. You know what you're doing.
2. a. Really? You play everything.   b. So you gave it up.
3. a. You think anything's possible, then.   b. Right. It doesn't seem real at all.

About you **C** Pair work What kind of tastes do you have in movies, food, and music? Discuss with a partner.

   A *I love classic movies. I think they're just as good as the movies they make these days.*
   B *Really? So you're into old movies. Now, what genres do you like? Sci-fi or . . . ?*

1 Reading

A Can you think of some ways to dress well without spending a lot of money? Tell the class.

B Read the article. Does it mention any of your ideas? Which ideas are the best? Which ideas have you tried?

Reading tip

Read the first sentence of each tip to see what the article covers.

HOW TO DEVELOP YOUR PERSONAL STYLE

Do you ever worry that you don't look as great as you could? Maybe you don't have as much time – or money – as you'd like to spend on yourself. But dressing well is important because knowing you look good makes you feel more confident.

Developing your own personal style is not as hard (or as expensive) as you might think! Even jeans and a T-shirt can look as stylish as a dressy outfit – if you know how to put them together. Here are some quick, inexpensive tips to help you create your own fabulous personal style.

① Don't wear clothes that are too "old" or too "young" for you, and choose styles that are appropriate for your lifestyle. _____ You want to feel as comfortable as possible.

② Flip through a magazine to find styles you like. Use the photos as a guide. _____

③ Look at photos of yourself wearing a variety of outfits. Which ones look good on you? Which ones aren't particularly flattering? Notice what you like and dislike about different outfits. Is it the fabric? The color? The style?

④ Think about your life goals. Are you looking for a job? To impress potential employers, liven up your professional look by adding some accessories to the suit you already have. How about a scarf? A colorful new tie?

⑤ Call attention to your best features. Choose colors that bring out the color of your eyes. _____ If you're not as slim as you'd like to be, buy tailored clothes that fit well. Don't just wear baggy outfits to cover up those few extra pounds. Choose the best fabrics for your shape. Silk may feel nice, but be careful – shiny fabrics can make you look heavier. Cashmere, on the other hand, can make you look slimmer and looks especially good on muscular men.

⑥ Clean out your closet. _____ Get rid of stained, out of shape, torn, faded, or out-of-style clothing and scuffed shoes. Sell them at a consignment store, and use the extra cash to jazz up your wardrobe.

⑦ Update an outfit you already have. Add a new belt. If your jeans are worn at the bottom, cut them off to make a pair of capris.

⑧ Make sure you have a few essentials. Men need a well-fitting sweater with a pair of casual but well-cut pants. For women, a classic black dress and a pair of simple pants that you can dress up or down are must-haves. _____

C Where do these sentences fit in the article? Write the correct letters in the spaces.

a. If you want to look taller, wear clothes with vertical stripes.
b. Bring the pictures with you when you go shopping.
c. And for both men and women, a pair of classic black shoes is a necessity.
d. Take out everything that doesn't fit you anymore.
e. If you walk everywhere, be sure to buy shoes that are comfortable as well as stylish.

2 Listening and speaking Keeping up with trends

A 🔊 1.20 Listen to four people talk about trends. Number the topics 1 to 4.
There is one extra topic.

☐ hairstyles   ☐ fashion   ☐ technology   ☐ cars   ☐ sports and fitness

B 🔊 1.20 Listen again. Do the people keep up with trends? Circle *Yes* or *No*. Write one thing they do
or don't do.

		Keeps up with trends?	What do they do or not do?
1.	Maddy	Yes / No	
2.	Frank	Yes / No	
3.	Laura	Yes / No	
4.	Nate	Yes / No	

About you **C** Pair work What are the current trends in each area in Exercise A? Do you keep
up with the trends? Why? Why not?

3 Writing Style interview

A Read the question and answer below and the Help note. Add commas (,) where needed and a
dash (–), and change one period to an exclamation mark (!).

How would you describe your tastes in clothes?

*I like to wear fashionable clothes when I go out
with my friends. I get ideas from men's clothing stores
magazines and from my friends. At home I like to wear
something more comfortable my old jeans a T-shirt and
sneakers. I look completely different.*

> **Help note**
>
> **Punctuation**
> - Use commas (,) in lists.
>   *My clothes are fun, colorful,
>   and unusual.*
> - Use a dash (–) to add or
>   explain more about something.
> - Use an exclamation mark (!)
>   for emphasis.
>   *I wear every color under the
>   sun – sometimes all at once!*

About you **B** Write three questions about personal style. Then exchange papers with a partner. Write answers to
your partner's questions.

C Pair work Read your partner's answers to your questions. Check the punctuation.

Free talk p. 129

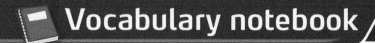

Learning tip *Labeling pictures*

When you want to learn a new set of vocabulary, find and label pictures illustrating the new words. For example, you can use a fashion magazine to label items of clothing, styles, colors, patterns, and materials.

In conversation

Shades of blue

The top ways of describing *blue* in conversation are:

1. *navy* blue   4. *bright* blue
2. *dark* blue   5. *light* blue
3. *royal* blue   6. *deep* blue

1 **What styles of clothing, colors, and patterns can you see in the picture? What materials do you think the clothes are made of? Label the picture with words from the box and other words you know.**

✓baggy	polka-dot
dark brown	short-sleeved
fitted / skinny	silk
flared	striped
floral-print	✓suede
leather	turquoise
light blue	turtleneck
long-sleeved	V-neck
neon orange	wool

baggy

suede

2 **Word builder** **Find out what these words mean. Then find an example of each one in the picture above, and add labels.**

ankle-length	gold	navy blue
beige	maroon	plastic
crew-neck	mauve	tweed

 On your own

Find a fashion magazine and label as many of the different styles, materials, patterns, and colors as you can in ten minutes.

✓ Can Do! Now I can . . .

✓ I can . . .   ? I need to review how to . . .

- ☐ talk about my tastes in clothes and fashion.
- ☐ compare how people look different over time.
- ☐ describe patterns, materials, and styles of clothing.
- ☐ show I understand by summarizing what people say.
- ☐ use *Now* to introduce follow-up questions.

- ☐ understand conversations about food, music, and movies.
- ☐ understand people discussing trends.
- ☐ read an article about how to develop a personal style.
- ☐ write interview questions and answers.

World cultures

✓ **Can Do!** In this unit, you learn how to . . .

Lesson A
- Talk about your culture using the simple present passive

Lesson B
- Talk about customs and manners using verb + -ing and to + verb

Lesson C
- Use expressions like *to be honest* to sound more direct
- Use *of course* to give information that is not surprising, or to agree

Lesson D
- Read an article about proverbs
- Write an article about a favorite proverb

Before you begin . . .

What are some of the cultural traditions in your country? Think of a typical . . .

- dish or drink.
- type of music or dance.
- symbol.
- festival.
- item of clothing.
- handicraft.

21

What not to miss . . .

SOUTH KOREA

"Oh, Korean food! We have so many different dishes. One typical dish is *kimbap*. It's made with rice and vegetables and wrapped in dried seaweed. And it's eaten cold. It's delicious." –Min-hee Park

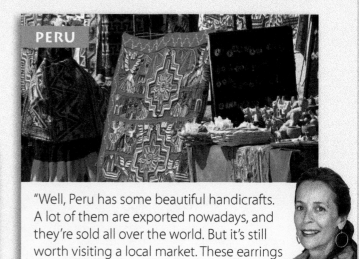

PERU

"Well, Peru has some beautiful handicrafts. A lot of them are exported nowadays, and they're sold all over the world. But it's still worth visiting a local market. These earrings are made locally. They're made of silver."
–Elena Camacho

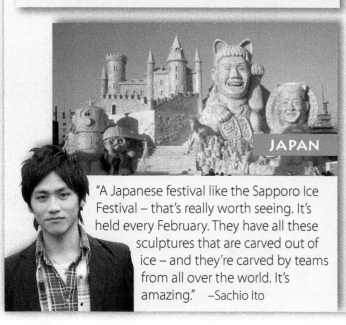

JAPAN

"A Japanese festival like the Sapporo Ice Festival – that's really worth seeing. It's held every February. They have all these sculptures that are carved out of ice – and they're carved by teams from all over the world. It's amazing." –Sachio Ito

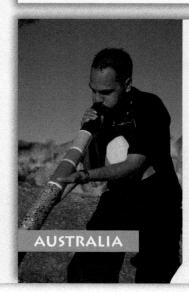

"Oh, you should go to a performance of traditional Aboriginal music. They play this instrument – it's called a *didgeridoo*. It's made out of a hollow piece of wood and painted by hand. It makes a really interesting sound."
–Robert Flynn

AUSTRALIA

1 Getting started

A Look at the countries above. What do you know about each country? Make a list of ideas.

B 🔊 1.21 Listen. What aspect of their country's culture does each person talk about?

Figure it out **C** Rewrite the sentences below, but keep the same meaning. Use the comments above to help you.

1. You eat *kimbap* cold.
2. People make earrings like these locally.
3. They export a lot of handicrafts.
4. Teams from all over the world carve the sculptures.

Kimbap _____ cold.

Earrings like these _____ locally.

A lot of handicrafts _____ .

The sculptures _____ by teams from all over the world.

2 Grammar The simple present passive ◀)) 1.22

Extra practice p. 142

Use the passive when the "doer" of the action is not known or not important.

Active

How do they make *kimbap*?
  They make it with rice and vegetables.

Do they eat it hot or cold?
  They eat it cold. They don't eat it hot.

They carve the sculptures out of ice.

Passive

How **is** *kimbap* **made**?
  It**'s made** with rice and vegetables.

Is it **eaten** hot or cold?
  It**'s eaten** cold. It**'s** not **eaten** hot.

The sculptures **are carved** out of ice.

> **In conversation**
>
> The most common passive verbs are *made*, *done*, and *called*.

If the "doer" of the action is important, you can introduce it with *by*.

The sculptures **are carved by** teams from all over the world.

> **✖ Common errors**
>
> Be sure to use the verb *be* in the present simple passive.
>
> The sculptures **are** carved out of ice. (NOT ~~The sculptures carved out of ice.~~)

About you **A** Rewrite the questions about your country. Then write true answers. Use the simple present passive.

1. When do people sing the national anthem?
   When is the national anthem sung? It's sung . . .
2. How do you make your favorite traditional food? Do you serve it cold?
3. Do both men and women play your country's national sports?
4. When do people celebrate your most important festivals? Does everybody celebrate them?
5. When do people wear the national costume? Do people wear it a lot?
6. Do people play traditional folk music?
7. Do people make traditional handicrafts? Where do they sell them?

About you **B** Pair work Compare your answers with a partner. Can you add more ideas?

3 Speaking naturally Silent syllables

> ev~~e~~ry   diff~~e~~rent   int~~e~~resting   veg~~e~~table

A ◀)) 1.23 Listen and repeat the words. Notice that the unstressed vowels are not pronounced.

B ◀)) 1.24 Listen to people talk about their cities. Cross out the vowel that is not pronounced in the underlined words. Then read the sentences to a partner.

1. Broc, Switzerland: We're known for our <u>chocolate</u>, which is sold all over the world. If you're really <u>interested</u>, you can visit a factory to learn about the <u>history</u> of <u>chocolate</u> and how it's made.
2. Coober Pedy, Australia: The <u>average</u> <u>temperature</u> here in summer is almost 40°C, so it's much cooler to live underground. It's definitely something <u>different</u> for <u>travelers</u>!
3. Akihabara, Japan: If you want a <u>camera</u>, then you have to shop here. <u>Practically</u> <u>every</u> brand of electronic and computer goods is displayed here!
4. Boyacá, Colombia: <u>Emeralds</u> are mined all over the world, but our region has some of the best and most <u>valuable</u> stones. They're mostly exported and made into <u>jewelry</u>.

About you **C** Choose a city, region, or country, and tell the class what it's known for. Guess the places your classmates talk about.

"This place is known for its wooden dolls. They're painted by local artists."

23

1 Building vocabulary and grammar

A 🔊 **1.25** Listen. Are these statements true in your country? Check (✓) True or False.

	True	False
1. Eating food on a subway or bus is bad manners.	☐	☐
2. It's rude to **cut in line**.	☐	☐
3. You should try to **keep your voice down** in public.	☐	☐
4. You can offend someone by not **bowing** or **shaking hands** when you meet.	☐	☐
5. People might **stare** at you for **walking around barefoot**.	☐	☐
6. **Having an argument** in public is considered bad manners.	☐	☐
7. It's impolite to walk into someone's home without **taking off your shoes**.	☐	☐
8. **Showing affection** in public – **holding hands** or **kissing** – is inappropriate.	☐	☐
9. You should try not to **stand too close** to people. It's considered rude.	☐	☐
10. It's acceptable not to **tip** cab drivers.	☐	☐
11. You should be careful not to **point at people**.	☐	☐
12. It's customary to **bargain** with street vendors to get something cheaper, but it's not acceptable to do this in a store.	☐	☐

B Word sort What behaviors are considered acceptable in your country? Complete the chart with ideas from above. Add your own ideas. Then compare with a partner.

It's acceptable to . . .	It's not acceptable to . . .
take your shoes off in the house.	*stand too close to people.*

C Figure it out Circle the correct choices. Are the sentences true in your country? Discuss with a partner.

Vocabulary notebook p. 30

1. **Cut** / **Cutting** in line is bad manners.
2. You might offend someone by **standing** / **stand** too close.
3. You can offend your host by not **taking** / **to take** off your shoes.
4. It's polite **bow** / **to bow** when you meet someone.
5. It's customary not **to tip** / **tip** cab drivers.

2 Grammar Verb + *-ing* and *to* + verb; position of *not* ◀)) 1.26

Extra practice p. 142

Verb + *-ing* as a subject
Eating in public is bad manners.
Not shaking hands is impolite.

Verb + *-ing* after prepositions
You can offend people by **eating** in public.
People might stare at you for **not shaking** hands.

***to* + verb after *It's* . . .**
It's bad manners **to eat** in public.
It's impolite **not to shake** hands.

Position of *not*
Not comes before the word it negates.
Be careful **not** to point at people.
You can offend people by **not** bowing.

Notice the difference in meaning:
It's acceptable **not** to tip cab drivers.
(It's optional.)
It's **not** acceptable to tip cab drivers.
(You shouldn't do it.)

A Complete the sentences about eating at restaurants. Use verb + *-ing* or *to* + verb.

1. If a friend invites you out to dinner, it's inappropriate _____ (take) another friend with you.

2. It's bad manners _____ (not /call) the restaurant if you have a reservation and you decide to cancel your plans.

3. _____ (arrive) a little late when you meet a big group of friends at a restaurant is acceptable. _____ (not / show) up at all is impolite.

4. If you get to the restaurant before your friend, it's fine _____ (sit) down at the table.

5. It's not acceptable _____ (complain) to your server if you don't like your meal.

6. People might be upset with you for _____ (not / pay) your fair share of the bill.

7. _____ (talk) with your mouth full is considered rude. _____ (take) phone calls during dinner is also bad manners.

8. You can offend the server by _____ (not / leave) a tip. But _____ (give) a smaller tip is fine if the service is bad.

9. _____ (ask) the server for a box to bring your leftover food home is acceptable.

10. It's bad manners _____ (not thank) the person who paid afterwards. _____ (not say) thank you is really impolite.

About you **B** **Pair work** Discuss the statements above. Which ones do you agree with? Can you add more etiquette advice?

A Yeah. Taking another friend with you is rude – especially if you're not paying.
B But it's not rude to invite another friend if it's a casual evening out.

About you **C** **Pair work** What etiquette advice can you think of for the following situations? Make a list and then share with another pair.

visiting someone's home   going to a birthday party   going to an interview

"Well, when you visit someone's home, you might offend the host by not bringing a gift."

Sounds right p. 137

1 Conversation strategy Sounding more direct

A What kinds of things do people miss about home when they move abroad? Make a list.

B 🔊 1.27 Listen. What would David miss if he left Brazil?

Hilda	So, when you're living here, do you miss home?
David	Um, I don't miss too much, to be honest. Um, I miss my family, of course. . . .
Hilda	Right.
David	But I definitely don't miss the food! Um, I miss my family. That's about it.
Hilda	So, if you went back home, would you miss lots of things about Brazil?
David	Oh, yeah. I'd absolutely miss the food here. Yeah. But actually, I think the biggest thing would be . . . it would be weird for me to live in a country where I knew the language already, where all I have to do is work. I just don't see a challenge in that. You know, here every day is a challenge, speaking the language.
Hilda	Uh-huh.
David	In fact, living back home would be boring, I think. I honestly don't know what I'd do.

C Notice that when David wants to sound more direct or assertive, he uses expressions like these. Find examples in the conversation.

> *absolutely, definitely, really,*
> *actually, certainly, honestly, in fact,*
> *to be honest, to tell you the truth*

About you **D** Make these statements about living in another country more direct. Use the expressions given. Then discuss each statement with a partner. Do you agree?

1. I'd miss my friends. (definitely) I'd miss everyone. (in fact)
2. I wouldn't miss the weather. (certainly) But I'd miss the food. (really)
3. I'd enjoy living in a different culture. (actually)
4. Learning the language would be a challenge. (to be honest)
5. I wouldn't miss the lifestyle here. (to tell you the truth)
6. I think I'd be scared to go abroad on my own. (honestly)

    A If I lived in another country, I'd definitely miss my friends!

    B Well, yes, but to be honest, it's good to make new friends too.

2 Strategy plus *of course*

Of course usually means, "This idea is not surprising. It's what you expect."

You can also use *Of course* in responses to show you agree or understand.

A *I really miss my family.*
B *Of course.*

> I miss my family, of course.

i Note

Be careful when you use *of course*. It can sound abrupt or rude as an answer to a question.

A *Do you miss your family?*
B *Oh, yes, I really do.*
(NOT ~~Of course.~~)

In conversation

Of course is one of the top 50 expressions.

A Read the conversations. Which response is more polite? Circle *a* or *b*.

1. Do you think living in another country would be exciting?
   a. Of course it would.
   b. Absolutely. Of course, I'd probably feel homesick at times.

2. Would you learn all about a country before you went?
   a. Well, I guess I'd like to know all about its culture. And, of course, its traditions.
   b. But of course. You really should learn something.

3. Would you take something with you to remind you of home?
   a. Of course.
   b. Probably. Maybe a photo of my cat. Of course, I couldn't take the cat with me, but . . .

About you **B Pair work** Ask and answer the questions above, giving your own answers. Use *of course* in your answers, but be careful how you use it.

3 Listening and strategies *Away from home*

A 🔊 **1.28 Listen to Val talk about her experience. Answer the questions.**

1. Why is she living away from home?
2. What has been challenging for her?
3. What has been going well?
4. How does she keep in touch with family? When?

B 🔊 **1.28 Listen again. What would Val's friend say about her experience? Check (✓) the sentences.**

1. ☐ To tell you the truth, Val's host sister is pretty unfriendly.
2. ☐ To be honest, she hasn't gotten to know many people.
3. ☐ She's definitely learning about the culture.
4. ☐ Of course, she doesn't like having to be home at ten.
5. ☐ She's certainly homesick. In fact, she wants to go back home right now.

About you **C Group work** Think about a time you were away from home. Who and what did you miss? How did you keep in touch? Talk about your experience.

"When I was an exchange student, I missed my friends. Of course, I missed my family, too."

1 Reading

A Think of a proverb in your language. When is it used, and why?

B Read the article. Do you have similar proverbs in your language? Are proverbs used in the same ways?

📖 **Reading tip**

Read the first sentence of each paragraph. What do you think each paragraph will be about?

PROVERBS: The wisdom that binds us together

Proverbs exist in every language and culture and are a way of passing down folk wisdom, or "common sense," from generation to generation. Who doesn't remember a time when they were struggling with a problem or dilemma, and someone quoted a proverb that aptly summed up or explained the situation? "All's fair in love and war" describes the injustice that is often encountered in a romantic relationship and may help some of us accept it. "Absence makes the heart grow fonder" is meant to give hope when a loved one is far away. When that same relationship is brought to an end by distance, we hear, "Out of sight, out of mind."

Proverbs have lasted for thousands of years, probably because they're so memorable. Some are short and concise, like "Practice makes perfect" and "Haste makes waste," while others use a poetic language such as metaphors, repetition, and rhymes. The metaphor "Out of the frying pan and into the fire" is easy to visualize when you are faced with a difficult situation that just got even worse. The repetition of the consonant "t" makes it easy to remember "It takes two to tango." The rhyme "When the cat's away, the mice will play" comes to mind as soon as the boss leaves on vacation, and the repetition of the structure in "Once bitten, twice shy" makes this an extremely catchy phrase.

Some scholars who study proverbs look for examples that are unique to a particular culture as a key to understanding cultural differences. Others focus on the proverbs that appear in almost every language as a way of defining a common wisdom that binds all humans together.

Proverbs don't always offer up universal truth, however, and they are frequently contradictory. People say, "Clothes make the man," to reflect the importance of appearance as part of one's personal identity. On the other hand, they also say, "You can't judge a book by its cover," to point out that appearances can be deceptive. And with "Handsome is as handsome does" they stress the value of good behavior over good looks.

So while proverbs can help us grasp some universally shared wisdom, they also force us to recognize that life is complex and that there are no easy answers. The complexity of the human condition as reflected in proverbs is yet another thing that is shared by people around the world.

C Read the article again. Can you find these things? Compare with a partner.

1. a function proverbs serve in different languages and cultures
2. two different ways scholars look at proverbs
3. two proverbs that are memorable because they use rhyme
4. three proverbs that are memorable because they repeat consonants, words, or structures
5. two pairs of proverbs that are contradictory
6. two things we can learn when we study proverbs from different cultures

2 **Listening and speaking** Favorite proverbs

A Can you guess the meaning of the proverbs below? Discuss with a partner.

Every Tuesday has its Sunday.
—SPANISH

If you're afraid of the wolves, don't go into the woods.
—RUSSIAN

Hard bread is better than nothing.
—PORTUGUESE

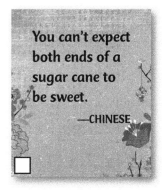

You can't expect both ends of a sugar cane to be sweet.
—CHINESE

B ◀))) 1.29 Listen to four people talk about their favorite proverbs. Number the proverbs above 1 to 4. What do they mean? Did you guess the meaning correctly?

C ◀))) 1.30 Match each proverb above with a similar English proverb below. Write the numbers. Then listen again as someone comments on each proverb, and check your answers.

a. You can't have your cake and eat it, too. _____

b. Every cloud has a silver lining. _____

c. If you can't stand the heat, get out of the kitchen. _____

d. Beggars can't be choosers. _____

About you **D** **Pair work** Which of the proverbs above is your favorite? Why? When would you use it?

"'Beggars can't be choosers' is used a lot in our house. My mom is always saying it. It's great because . . ."

3 **Writing** Explain a proverb

A Read the article below. Find the useful expressions from the Help note, and underline them.

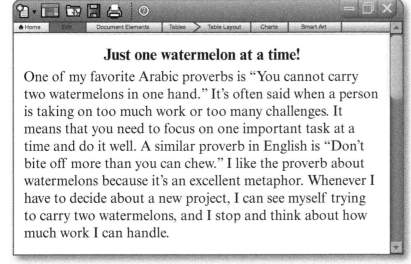

Just one watermelon at a time!

One of my favorite Arabic proverbs is "You cannot carry two watermelons in one hand." It's often said when a person is taking on too much work or too many challenges. It means that you need to focus on one important task at a time and do it well. A similar proverb in English is "Don't bite off more than you can chew." I like the proverb about watermelons because it's an excellent metaphor. Whenever I have to decide about a new project, I can see myself trying to carry two watermelons, and I stop and think about how much work I can handle.

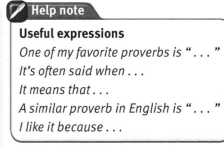

Help note

Useful expressions
One of my favorite proverbs is " . . . "
It's often said when . . .
It means that . . .
A similar proverb in English is " . . . "
I like it because . . .

B Write a short article about your favorite proverb. Say why you like it and what it means. Then read your classmates' articles. Did anyone choose the same proverb?

Free talk p. 130

Vocabulary notebook / Travel etiquette

Learning tip *Finding examples*

When you learn a new expression, find examples on the Internet. Type the expressions into an Internet search engine with quotation marks (" ") around it.

> **Search**
>
> Web Images Groups News Local
>
> **Search** 🔍 "don't point your foot"
>
> **Web**
> **Dos and Don'ts in Thailand**
> . . . when sitting opposite someone , **don't point your foot** at . . .
> www.thailand.com - 12k - Cached - Similar pages
>
> **drills - racquetball**
> **Don't point your foot** in the direction . . .
> www.racquetballdrills.com - 12k - Cached - Similar pages

1 **Complete the sentences using the words and expressions in the box.**

bowing	having an argument	kissing	to take off	walking around barefoot
eating	to keep your voice down	to cut in line	to shake hands	

1. In Japan, _____ is customary when two people introduce themselves.
2. In the United States, it's polite _____ firmly when you are introduced to a colleague.
3. In South Korea, _____ food on the subway is considered rude.
4. In many places of worship in Asia, it's polite _____ your hat and shoes.
5. In Chile, people often say hello by _____ each other on the cheek.
6. In Australia, _____ is acceptable at beach resorts, but not in public buildings.
7. In Taiwan, _____ in public is considered impolite. It's better _____ .
8. In Great Britain, it's considered rude _____ . You should always wait your turn.

2 **Word builder** **Find the meaning of the words and expressions. Write a tip for each one.**

blow your nose   burp   offer your seat to someone   swear

Be prepared for a kiss on the cheek.

On your own

Find a travel guide for a country you'd like to visit. Find six things you should or shouldn't do if you go there.

✓ Can Do! Now I can . . .

✓ I can . . .   ? I need to review how to . . .

- ☐ talk about my country's cultural traditions.
- ☐ talk about manners, customs, and appropriate behavior in my country.
- ☐ use expressions like *to be honest* to sound more direct.

- ☐ use *of course* to show I understand or agree.
- ☐ understand a conversation about living away from home.
- ☐ understand people explaining proverbs.
- ☐ read an article about proverbs.
- ☐ write an article about a favorite proverb.

1 Is it polite?

A Complete the questions with the correct forms of the verbs.

1. Would you ever consider __*not tipping*__ (not tip) a server in a restaurant?
2. Do you remember _____ (stare) at people when you were little?
3. Do you feel it's rude _____ (not say) hello to your neighbors?
4. Is _____ (hold hands) OK on a first date?
5. Do you bother _____ (bargain) with street vendors when the items are already very cheap?
6. Do you ever offer _____ (help) people with their bags on the bus or subway?
7. Have you and a friend ever ended up _____ (argue) in public?
8. Have you ever offended someone without _____ (intend) _____ (be) rude?

B **Pair work** Ask and answer the questions. Show that you understand your partner's answers by summarizing what he or she says.

"I'd never consider not tipping – I used to be a server myself."   *"So you always tip the server."*

2 Think, Bob, think!

A Complete the conversation with the correct forms of the verbs.

Officer _____*Have*_____ you _____*seen*_____ (see) these people before?

Bob Yes, they're my neighbors. They _____ (live) upstairs.

Officer How long _____ they _____ (live) there?

Bob I guess I _____ (know) them for six months.
They _____ (move) here in August.

Officer When _____ you last _____ (see) them?

Bob Um, about a week ago, I think. Last Tuesday.

Officer What _____ they _____ (do) when you _____ (see) them?

Bob Well, as I _____ (come) home, they _____ (carry) a big suitcase to the car.

Officer _____ you _____ (speak) to them?

Bob I _____ (say), "Hi! Where _____ you _____ (go)?" And they _____ (reply), "On vacation."

Officer What time _____ they finally _____ (leave)?

Bob Oh, um, it was pretty late, around 11 at night, I guess.

Officer Can you remember what they _____ (wear)?

Bob Let me think. . . .

B Write Bob's answer to the police officer's last question. How much detail can you give? Compare with a partner.

3 Can you complete this conversation?

A Complete the conversation with the words and expressions in the box. Practice the conversation.

> ✓definitely   don't you think   now   of course   these   this   to be honest

Anna   Bella used to live in Japan. You loved living there, right?

Bella   Oh, ___definitely___ . I lived there for nine years, working for a Japanese advertising company.

Chris   Nine years? Wow! Didn't you ever get homesick?

Bella   Occasionally. But, _____ , I didn't really miss living at home. I was too busy. I mean, _____ I missed my family.

Chris   Oh, I bet you did. _____ , how did you get that job? Did they hire you over here, or . . . ?

Bella   Actually, I was already in Japan on an exchange program, staying with _____ family. And the father starts bringing home all _____ documents from his work to translate into English. Anyway, I started helping him, and his company ended up hiring me.

Anna   And they transferred her here. It's a cool story, _____ ?

B Pair work Choose a topic below and have a conversation. Ask and answer questions.

- something difficult you did once
- an interesting experience you had
- a time you missed someone
- an unusual person you once met

A   *Can you think of a time you missed someone?*

B   *Yes. My mom went on a trip when I was five. I wanted to go with her.*

4 As bad as that?

Pair work   Compare these things using *(not) as . . . as*. Try to use negative questions to give opinions or to suggest ideas.

- folk music / rock music
- baked potatoes / fries
- old buildings / new buildings
- cheap watches / expensive watches

A   *Folk music isn't as popular as rock music. You don't hear it as much.*

B   *But don't you think it's just as good? I like folk as much as rock.*

5 Guess the dish!

A Write questions in the simple present passive, using the words below. Then think of a traditional dish, and answer the questions.

1. eat / hot or cold
2. When / eat
3. How / cook
4. What / make / with
5. What / serve / with
6. What / call

B Pair work   Take turns asking and answering the questions. Can you guess your partner's dish before question 6?

Socializing

4

 Can Do! In this unit, you learn how to . . .

Lesson A
- Say what should happen with *be supposed to*
- Talk about weekend plans using *was / were going to*

Lesson B
- Talk about going out and formal events using *get* expressions

Lesson C
- Check your understanding with "statement questions"
- Use *so* to start or close topics, pause, or check understanding

Lesson D
- Read an article about introverts and extroverts
- Write an article about your social style

1

2

3

4

Before you begin . . .

- Who do you usually socialize with?
- Do you usually go out in small groups, large groups, or with just one person?
- Where are some good places to go out with friends in your town or city?

33

Marco: Are you going to Brad and Gayle's party?

Anna: Well, I wasn't going to go, but maybe I will. I'm supposed to be studying for an exam. Are you going?

Marco: Yeah. The party's at their house, right? Do you know where they live?

Anna: Not exactly. Brad was going to call and give me the address, but he didn't. Maybe Ellen knows.

Ellen: What kind of party is it?

Phil: I think it's supposed to be a barbecue.

Ellen: That'll be fun. Have you heard the weather forecast?

Phil: Yeah. I heard it's supposed to be a really nice evening.

Anwar: Are we supposed to bring anything?

Sue: I don't think so. I was going to make some potato salad, but I didn't have time.

Anwar: Well, I bought them a box of chocolates. Do you think that'll be OK?

Sue: I don't know. Isn't Brad on a diet? He's not supposed to eat stuff like that. But Gayle will like them.

Patty: Jen and Martin are late. They were supposed to pick me up at 7:00.

Junko: Gosh, it's 7:30 already. Maybe they forgot. Do you want me to come and get you? I can take you home, too.

Patty: That'd be great. But I'm supposed to be at work early tomorrow, so I can't stay late.

Junko: That's OK. I think the party's supposed to end at 11:00, but we can leave a bit earlier.

1 Getting started

A What do you do to get ready for a party? Tell the class.

B 2.01 Listen. Brad and Gayle are having a party tonight, and their friends are getting ready. What do you find out about the party?

Figure it out **C** How might Brad and Gayle's friends say the things below? Replace the underlined words with an expression each person has already used above.

1. Phil   They say it's going to be really warm.
2. Sue   Brad shouldn't eat chocolate.
3. Patty   I have to get up early tomorrow.
4. Anna   I should be working on a paper.
5. Patty   Jen and Martin agreed to be here by 7:00.
6. Sue   I intended to make a dessert, but I didn't.

2 Grammar *be supposed to; was / were going to* 🔊 2.02

Extra practice p. 143

***Be supposed to* can mean "They say . . . ."**	It**'s supposed to** be a barbecue. It**'s supposed to** rain later.
It can also mean "have to" or "should."	I**'m supposed to** work tomorrow. He**'s not supposed to** eat chocolate.
It can contrast what should happen with what does or will happen.	I**'m supposed to** be studying for an exam (but I'm not). I**'m not supposed to** stay out late (but maybe I will).
***Was / Were supposed to* can mean what was expected didn't or won't happen.**	They **were supposed to** come at 7:00 (but they didn't). I **wasn't supposed to** go by myself (but I'll have to).
***Was / Were going to* has a similar meaning and can also mean "intended to."**	He **was going to** give us directions (but he didn't). I **wasn't going to** go to the party (but I guess I will).

Complete the conversations with the correct form of *be supposed to* or *was / were going to* and the verb. Sometimes more than one answer is possible. Then practice in pairs.

In conversation

Over 60% of uses of *be supposed to* are in the present tense. About 10% are negative.

1. A It _____ (rain) tonight. Do you want to go see a movie?

   B Yeah. I want to see that new Stephen King movie.
   It _____ (be) good. I _____ (see)
   it last weekend, but I ended up going to a party instead.

   ✗ Common errors

   Be sure to use the correct form of *be supposed to*.

   ***I'm supposed* to work tomorrow.**
   (NOT ~~I suppose to~~ work tomorrow.)

2. A Do you have plans for the weekend? I heard the
   weather _____ (not / be) very good.

   B Yeah. I _____ (go) to a family reunion, but I'm not really looking forward to it.

   A Why not? Reunions _____ (be) fun.

   B Well, I _____ (make) 80 cupcakes. I _____ (buy) them, but my
   husband said that's cheating!

3. A What did you do last night? Did you go out?

   B No. I _____ (cook) dinner for a friend. I mean, I _____ (not / make)
   anything special, but then he called, and it turned out he _____ (go) to soccer
   practice or something, so he didn't come. So I had a TV dinner! How about you?

   A Actually, I _____ (go) to a movie, but then I decided to stay home.

3 Talk about it Weekend fun

Group work Discuss the questions about this weekend.

▸ What's the weather supposed to be like?

▸ Are there any events that are supposed to be fun?

▸ Are you supposed to go anywhere or see anyone in particular?

▸ Are you supposed to do anything that you're not looking forward to?

▸ Is there anything you were going to do last weekend that you're going to do this weekend instead?

A What's the weather supposed to be like this weekend?

B I heard it's supposed to be nice.

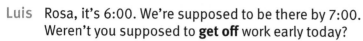

Lesson B / We have to get going.

1 Building vocabulary and grammar

A 🔊 2.03 **Listen. Where are Luis and Rosa going? Do they want to go? Practice the conversation.**

Luis Rosa, it's 6:00. We're supposed to be there by 7:00. Weren't you supposed to **get off** work early today?

Rosa Well, my boss called a meeting, and I couldn't **get out of** it. I had to go. Anyway, I don't **get it** – why is your cousin getting married on a Friday and not a Saturday, like everyone else?

Luis I don't know. All I know is that my mother will never **get over** it if we walk in late. So we have to **get going**.

Rosa OK. Uh, do you think I can **get away with** wearing pants?

Luis No way! It's supposed to be a formal wedding. Look, I got your silk dress ready for you.

Rosa Oh, I'll never **get used to** dressing up for these fancy weddings. Can we try to **get home** early?

Luis Rosa, I **get the feeling** that you don't really want to go.

Rosa Well, I just hope I can **get through** the reception.

Luis Oh, come on. Let's just go and enjoy it. It's a chance for you to **get to know** my family better. By the way, did you **get around to** buying a gift?

Rosa Weren't *you* supposed to do that?

Word sort **B** **Find a *get* expression from the conversation above to complete each sentence below. Are the sentences true for you? Compare with a partner.**

get around to	1. I was so busy last week that I didn't *get around to* doing my homework.
	2. Sometimes I _____ that people are annoyed with me for being late.
	3. It's hard for me to finish long novels. I just can't _____ them.
	4. Why don't some people dress up for weddings? I don't _____ .
	5. I'll never _____ wearing formal clothes. They don't feel right.
	6. I wish I could _____ wearing jeans to work. They're so comfortable.

C **Find six more *get* expressions in the conversation above. Write a sentence with each expression. Compare your sentences with a partner.**

📙 **Vocabulary notebook** p. 42

get off - My sister gets off work early all the time.

Figure it out **D** **Circle the correct choice to complete the questions. Use the conversation to help you.**

1. Will Luis's mother **get over it / get it over** if they're late?

2. Rosa had to attend a meeting at work. Why couldn't she **get out of it / get it out of**?

3. Can Rosa get away with **wear / wearing** pants?

36

2 Grammar Inseparable phrasal verbs ◀)) 2.04

Extra practice p. 143

With these verbs, the object always comes after the particle or preposition.

Verb + particle + object	**Verb + particle + preposition + object**
Weren't you supposed to **get off** work early?	Can **I get away with** wearing pants?
She'll never **get over** feeling embarrassed.	No. You can't **get away with** it.
I'm sure she'll **get over** it.	Couldn't you **get out of** the meeting?
I hope I can **get through** the reception.	No, I couldn't **get out of** it.
I know you can **get through** it.	Did you **get around to** buying a gift?
	No, I never **got around to** it.

About you Complete the questions. Put the words in order, and use the correct form of the verbs. Then ask and answer the questions with a partner.

1. If you weren't ready for a test, would you try to __*get out of it*__ (of / out / it / get)?

2. Do you find it hard to _____ (the day / through / get) without texting your friends?

3. Do you know anyone who tries to _____ (of / get / go / out) to parties because they are shy? Is it possible to _____ (get / feel / over) shy?

4. Have you ever told a "white lie" to _____ (of / get / an invitation / out)? Did you _____ (get / it / away / with)?

5. How do you feel about buying gifts? Does it take you a long time to _____ (to / get / choose / around) something?

6. Do you often argue with your friends? How long does it take you to _____ (over / get / an argument)?

7. Does it take you a long time to _____ (start / to / get / around) your homework assignments because you're on social networking sites?

3 Speaking and listening Going out

About you **A Pair work** Discuss the sentences below. Which choice is most like you?

1. **I'm one of those people who . . .**
   a. gets ready at the last minute.
   b. spends ages getting ready.

2. **If I'm late for something, I usually . . .**
   a. hurry to try to be on time.
   b. take my time and arrive late.

3. **When I go out, I always . . .**
   a. make an effort to dress up.
   b. try to get away with wearing jeans.

4. **If a friend cancels plans we made, . . .**
   a. I stay home and feel disappointed.
   b. I get over it and do something else instead.

B ◀)) 2.05 Listen to Paula and Roberto talk about their plans for tonight. What happens?

C ◀)) 2.05 Listen again. How would Roberto complete the sentences above? Circle his choices.

About you **D Pair work** What other habits do you have when you get ready or go out?

"I always say yes to invitations and then regret it and try to get out of them."

((· Sounds right p. 137

You're going this time, right?

1 Conversation strategy Checking your understanding

A Check (✓) which statements are true for you. Tell the class.

☐ I love going to big parties where I don't know many people.

☐ I prefer going to small parties with a few friends I know well.

☐ I like going to parties with my co-workers or classmates.

B 🔊 2.06 Listen. How does Greg feel about parties?

Hugo	So, there's another work party on Friday. You're going this time, right?
Greg	I don't know. To be honest, I hate those things.
Hugo	Really? Why's that?
Greg	Well, I know it's supposed to be fun, but I'm just not very good at all that small talk.
Hugo	So parties aren't your thing, huh?
Greg	Not really. I just don't like big groups of people. I'd rather talk one on one, so . . .
Hugo	So you're not going to go?
Greg	No. I'll probably try and get out of it somehow. So, yeah. I'll just say I have other plans.

C **Notice** how Hugo checks his understanding. He asks questions in the form of statements. People often add *huh*, *right*, or *then* at the end of questions like these. Find more examples.

"So parties aren't your thing, huh?"

D 🔊 2.07 Read more of Hugo and Greg's conversation. Change the questions to "statement questions." Then listen and notice what they say.

Hugo So, aren't you going to show up at all? _So you aren't going to show up at all, huh?_

Greg No. Those work parties aren't my thing. Do you like them? _____

Hugo Yeah. But don't you want to network? You may get a promotion. _____

Greg Yeah. But I'm happy in my job right now. I'm not looking for a promotion or anything.

Hugo Oh. Don't you want to work your way up in the organization? _____

Greg Actually, um, no. Not really. So are you pretty ambitious? _____

Hugo I guess I am. But, the parties are fun anyway, and the people are interesting.

Greg So, do you know a lot of people in the company? _____

2 Strategy plus *so*

You can use *SO* in many ways, including:

To start a topic, often with a question
So, there's another work party on Friday.

To check your understanding
So parties aren't your thing, huh?

To pause or let the other person draw a conclusion
I'd rather talk one on one, so . . .

To close a topic
So, yeah. I'll just say I have other plans.

So parties aren't your thing, huh?

In conversation

So is one of the top 20 words.

A Find three places where you can use *so* in each conversation. Change the capital letters and add commas where necessary. Then practice with a partner.

1. A _____So,_____ ^w̶hat do you think of surprise parties?

   B _____ I don't know. _____ I've never had one or been to one, _____ . . . .

   A _____ No one has ever given you one? Do you think your friends would ever do that _____ ?

   B _____ No. My friends don't do that kind of thing.

2. A _____ Have you thrown any parties in the past year?

   B _____ Actually, yes. I had one last month. _____ A lot of people came.

   A _____ All your friends came?

   B _____ Yeah, they did. _____ It was great.

About you **B** **Pair work** Ask and answer the first question in each conversation above. Give your own answers.

3 Speaking naturally Being sure or checking

If you are sure: *So your birthday's on Friday.* **If you are checking:** *So your birthday's on Friday?*

               So all your friends came.   *So all your friends came?*

A ◀)) 2.08 Listen and repeat the sentences. Notice how the intonation falls when you say something you are sure about and rises when you're checking information.

B ◀)) 2.09 Listen to four conversations. Are the speakers sure (S), or are they checking (C)? Add a period or a question mark, and write *S* or *C*.

1. So you go out a lot ____

2. So you're a real people person ____

3. So you don't like parties very much ____

4. So you never celebrate your birthday ____

About you **C** **Pair work** Ask and answer the questions. Check your understanding and use *so* where you can.

1. How often do you go to parties?

2. Do you like to go out in large groups?

3. What do you do on Saturday nights?

4. What do you usually do on your birthday?

1 Reading

A What kinds of behaviors are typical of extroverts and introverts? Make two lists. Scan the article for more ideas.

B Read the article. What does Susan Cain think our society can learn from introverts? Why?

Reading tip

Writers often use these words and expressions to say what people think or say: *argue, believe, contend, explain, according to (someone).*

EXAMINING the "EXTROVERT IDEAL"

"Solitude matters. And for some people, it is the air they breathe." Susan Cain, author of *Quiet: The Power of Introverts in a World That Can't Stop Talking*, firmly believes this to be true. She also believes that introverts struggle in our society because of the deep bias against them. She says that "our most important institutions, our schools and our workplaces, they are designed mostly for extroverts, and for extroverts' need for lots of stimulation."

According to Cain, introverts are sensitive to overstimulation and tend to enjoy quiet, contemplative environments. They think before they speak and are usually good listeners. In contrast, extroverts tend to be socially confident and quick on their feet.

Unfortunately for introverts, modern professional and academic settings are not planned with them in mind. People are expected to behave like extroverts – chatty, confident, and charismatic. Cain emphasizes that this proves difficult for those who identify as introverts – nearly half of all

Americans – and they regularly face discrimination when they fail to act like their more outgoing counterparts.

In the competitive world we live in, Cain explains, there is pressure to stand out in a crowd. There is an expectation that being dominant will lead to success. As a result of this "Extrovert Ideal," workplaces and classrooms nowadays are often uncomfortable for introverts, who are frequently left feeling overlooked or disrespected. Collaborative brainstorming sessions are the norm. Talkers are considered smarter. Workers with strong "people skills" are praised, and "open plan" offices are common. While the assumptions that extroverts have better ideas or make better leaders are simply not true, introverts' valuable contributions are nevertheless likely to go unnoticed.

Furthermore, Cain contends that workplace innovation and productivity suffer when extroverts are valued more than introverts. In fact, research indicates that brainstorming in groups results in lower quality ideas, whereas there is a strong link between solitude and creativity. In general, open office plans reduce concentration, lower productivity, and make it difficult to retain good employees. "Our most important institutions are designed for extroverts. We have a waste of talent," says Cain.

Ultimately, Cain believes our society can learn a great deal from introverts. "It's a very powerful thing to be quiet and collect your thoughts."

C Can you find words or expressions in the article that mean these things? Underline them.

1. too much activity
2. thoughtful
3. on the other hand
4. charming and attractive
5. prejudice
6. look or be different
7. bossy or pushy
8. says or argues
9. keep (staff)

D Read the article again. Complete the sentences below with the correct information. Choose *a* or *b*.

1. Companies encourage their workers to be ___*b*___ .
   a. introverts   b. extroverts

2. Cain believes extroverts are _____ .
   a. not valued enough   b. valued too highly

3. Self-assured people are more likely to be _____ .
   a. introverts   b. extroverts

4. The "Extrovert Ideal" means that introverts _____ .
   a. get fired   b. feel ignored

5. In open office plans, employees are more likely to _____ .
   a. leave the company   b. work harder

6. Cain believes that extrovert behavior leads to _____ performance in the workplace.
   a. better   b. worse

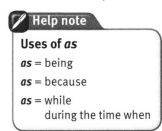

 Listening and writing Extrovert or introvert?

About you **A Pair work** Take the magazine quiz. Then discuss your answers with a partner. Are you the same?

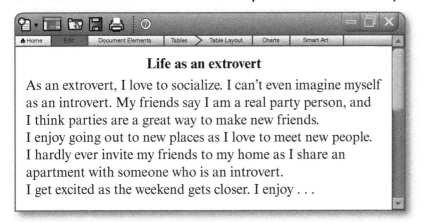

WHAT'S YOUR SOCIAL *STYLE?*		ANSWERS	
		Me	Jessica
Do you prefer to . . .			
① ⊢ a. go out and socialize?	⊢ b. see friends at home?	① a b	a b
② a. have lots of friends?	b. have just a few close friends?	② a b	a b
③ a. go out in a big group?	b. go out with one or two friends?	③ a b	a b
④ a. be the center of attention?	b. keep a low profile?	④ a b	a b
⑤ a. tell jokes and stories?	b. listen as other people tell jokes?	⑤ a b	a b
⑥ a. engage in chitchat?	b. have more serious conversations?	⑥ a b	a b
⑦ a. do tasks with others?	b. figure things out alone?	⑦ a b	a b
⑧ a. think of yourself as a "social animal"?	b. think of yourself as an individual?	⑧ a b	a b

(EXTROVERT / INTROVERT)

B ◀» 2.10 Listen to Jessica talk about her social life. How would she answer the quiz? Circle her answers.

C Read the extract below and the Help note. Circle the examples of *as*. What do they mean?

Life as an extrovert

As an extrovert, I love to socialize. I can't even imagine myself
as an introvert. My friends say I am a real party person, and
I think parties are a great way to make new friends.
I enjoy going out to new places as I love to meet new people.
I hardly ever invite my friends to my home as I share an
apartment with someone who is an introvert.
I get excited as the weekend gets closer. I enjoy . . .

> **Help note**
>
> **Uses of *as***
> ***as*** = being
> ***as*** = because
> ***as*** = while
>   during the time when

About you **D** Write a short article about your social style. Are you an introvert, an extrovert, or a little of both? Use *as* in your article.

E Read your classmates' articles. How many introverts are in your class? How many extroverts?

Free talk p. 131

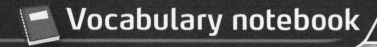

Learning tip *Expressions in context*

When you learn a new expression, write an example sentence that uses it in context. Think of something you might want to say, and add ideas that set the scene or help you remember its meaning.

In conversation

Get into it!

These are the top 10 particles and prepositions after *get*:

1. out   6. up
2. into   7. on
3. in   8. away
4. to   9. off
5. back   10. down

1 Complete the sentences using a *get* expression from the box.

get away with it	get it	get out of it	get to know
get going	get off	get over it	get used to

1. I'm late. I'd better _____ .

2. I love meeting new people. I think it's a lot of fun to _____ people.

3. Weekends seem so short. I wish I could _____ work early every Friday.

4. You're not supposed to go into clubs under the age of 18, but I know some kids manage to _____ .

5. I'll never _____ wearing a suit to work.

6. I don't understand why some people stay home all the time. I just don't _____ .

7. I was going to go to my class reunion. But I've decided to try and _____ .

8. When I failed the exam, I thought I would never _____ , but actually, I'm enjoying taking this class again.

2 **Word builder** Find out the meaning of the *get* expressions in the sentences below. Then write another sentence before each one that provides a context for the expression.

1. _____ She **gets on my nerves**.

2. _____ I just need to **get away from it all** so I can relax.

3. _____ Maybe there's a way to **get around** that problem.

4. _____ I don't want to **get behind** on my payments.

On your own

Get a flip pad. Make different sections for common verbs like *get, go, do,* and *have*. Write as many expressions as you can for each verb.

Can Do! Now I can . . .

✓ I can . . .	? I need to review how to . . .

- ☐ talk about going out and socializing.
- ☐ talk about things I am *supposed to* do.
- ☐ talk about things I think will happen or plans that changed.
- ☐ check my understanding with "statement questions."

- ☐ use *so* in different ways.
- ☐ understand people discussing their evening plans.
- ☐ understand someone talk about her social style.
- ☐ read an article about introverts and extroverts.
- ☐ write an article about my social style.

Law and order

☑ **Can Do!** In this unit, you learn how to . . .

Lesson A
- Talk about the legal age for activities using the passive of modal verbs

Lesson B
- Talk about crime and punishment using the *get* passive

Lesson C
- Organize your views with *First of all*, etc.
- Show someone has a valid argument with expressions like *That's a good point*.

Lesson D
- Read an article about privacy issues with smartphones
- Write a comment responding to a web article

1

2

3

Before you begin . . .

Do you have laws about these things in your country? What are they?

- Getting rid of trash and recycling
- At what age you can ride a motorcycle and what you have to wear
- Wearing seat belts and using a cell phone in a car

The Age of MAJORITY

In many countries, the law permits you to engage in new activities at the age of 18. We asked people what they think about 18 as the "age of majority."

When you turn 18, you can go see an "R-rated" movie – a movie that's restricted to adults. What do you think about that?

"What do I think? Well, I think the law ought to be changed – 18 is too young. Actually, I think R-rated movies should be banned altogether. They're far too violent."

– Bill Hughes

Do you think you should be able to get married before you're 18?

"No way. In fact, you shouldn't be allowed to get married until you're at least 21 or even older. Then there might be fewer divorces. Actually, I think a law should be passed that says if you want to get married, you have to take marriage classes first!"

– Maya Diaz

You can get your own credit card at the age of 18. Is this too young?

"I don't think so. I mean, young people have to be given their freedom at some point. You know, they ought to be encouraged to manage their own finances and things. They can always learn from their mistakes."

– Jared Blake

Do you think you should be allowed to vote at 18?

"I guess. I mean, you can do everything else at 18. Why not vote? It's too bad more young people don't vote, though. I think everyone should be made to vote."

– Aiko Nakano

The legal age for most things is 18, but in many places you can drive at 16. Is that a good idea, do you think?

"I must say I've always thought 16 is too young. Too many teenagers get involved in traffic accidents, and something really must be done about it. The legal age for driving could easily be changed to 18 or 21 or something like that."

– Pat Johnson

1 Getting started

A At what age can you do the following things in your country?

drive a car	get a part-time job	see a violent movie
get a credit card	get married	vote in an election

B 🔊 2.11 Listen to the interviews above. What five things do the people talk about? Do they think 18 is the right age to start doing these things?

Figure it out **C** How do the people above say these things? Find the sentences in the article, and underline them. Do you agree with these views? Discuss with a partner.

1. They should ban R-rated movies.
2. They shouldn't allow you to get married until you're 21.
3. You have to give young people their freedom at some point.
4. They could easily change the legal age for driving to 18.
5. They ought to encourage young people to manage their own finances.

2 Grammar The passive of modal verbs ◀)) 2.12

Extra practice p. 144

The passive of modal verbs for the present is modal verb + *be* + past participle.

R-rated movies **should be banned**.
You **shouldn't be allowed** to marry at 18.
They **have to be given** their freedom.

The legal age **could** easily **be changed**.
Something **must be done** about it.
The law **ought to be changed**.

A Rewrite these comments about different laws. Start with the words given.

1. They should ban plastic shopping bags.
   Plastic shopping bags should be banned.
2. They ought to stop employers from reading employees' personal email. *Employers . . .*
3. They have to do something about all the litter on the buses and in subways. *Something . . .*
4. They shouldn't allow people to eat food on public transportation. *People . . .*
5. They ought to fine people for making noise after midnight. *People . . .*
6. They really must do something about speeding on freeways. *Something . . .*
7. They shouldn't make movies with violent scenes. *Movies with . . .*
8. They could encourage people to stop smoking if there were more anti-smoking laws. *People . . .*
9. They have to do something about people who download music illegally. *Something . . .*
10. They shouldn't allow children to quit school until they are 18. *Children . . .*

> **In conversation**
>
> *Must* means "have to" in 10% of its uses. In this meaning, it is often used in expressions like *I must admit* and *I must say*.
>
> 90% of the uses of *must* are for speculation:
>
> ***Things must be hard for couples who marry young.***

About you **B** Pair work Discuss the sentences above. Which do you agree with?

> A *Well, I agree that plastic bags should be banned – especially in supermarkets.*
> B *Yeah. They could easily be replaced with paper bags or something like that.*

3 Speaking naturally Saying conversational expressions

I mean, you can do everything else at 18. Why not vote? **You know what I mean?**
You know, *they ought to be encouraged to manage their own finances* **and things**.
The legal age for driving could easily be changed to 18 or 21 **or something like that**.

A ◀)) 2.13 Listen and repeat the sentences above. Notice how the expressions in bold are said more quickly, even when the speaker is speaking slowly.

About you **B** Group work Discuss the questions in the interviews on page 44. Use the conversational expressions above. Then decide on . . .

- three laws that should be passed.
- three things that people should be encouraged to do.
- three things people ought to be allowed to do.

> *"You know, something should be done about movie ratings. They ought to be made stricter. You know what I mean?"*

1 Building vocabulary and grammar

A 🔊 **2.14** Read the questions and answers on the website below. What questions are the people answering? Number the questions 1 to 8. Then listen and check.

http://www.questions... 🔍

Ask What punishment best fits the crime? OK

QUESTIONS:

8 Q: What's the right **penalty** for **jaywalking**?

☐ Q: Should they **arrest** drivers who get caught **speeding**?

☐ Q: What should happen to someone who is **convicted of burglary**?

☐ Q: How should **vandals** be **punished**?

☐ Q: What punishment should you get for **robbing** someone?

☐ Q: Should all **murderers** be sentenced to **life in prison**?

☐ Q: What kind of **sentence** should you get for **kidnapping**?

☐ Q: What should happen if you get caught **shoplifting** from a store?

BEST ANSWERS:

1 I think **shoplifters** should be **fined** at first, but if they **get caught stealing** again and again, they should **go to jail**.

2 That depends. If you **commit armed robbery**, you know, use **a gun** or **a knife**, you should be sent to prison.

3 Well, **vandalism** can be serious, so they should pay for any damage. And **vandals** should be made to clean up any **graffiti** they paint.

4 You don't usually **get arrested** for speeding unless you cause an accident, and that seems fair. But if you get stopped a lot, you should **lose your license**.

5 I don't know. Some people **get sentenced** to only 10 or 15 years for **murder**. **Killing** another person is the worst crime, but it's a complex issue.

6 **Kidnappers** should go to prison for a long time. I mean, **taking someone captive** is a very serious offense.

7 **Breaking into** someone's home is serious. But first-time **burglars** should just be **put on probation**.

8 A **fine**, maybe? I know it's **against the law** to just cross the street anywhere, but it's a relatively minor **offense**. And the law doesn't **get enforced** much.

Word sort **B** Make word webs like these. Add other words you know, and compare with a partner. Then discuss the crimes and say what punishments are appropriate.

murder

(Crimes)

having a gun without a license

(Criminals)

shoplifter

(Punishments)

get fined

enforce a law

(Other)

"Having a gun without a license is a crime."

📔 **Vocabulary notebook** p. 52

Figure it out **C** Circle the correct words to complete the sentences. Use the article to help you. Are the sentences true in your country? Discuss with a partner.

1. Murderers usually get **sentenced / sentencing** to life in prison.
2. Burglars who get **catch / caught** are never sent to prison.
3. If you are caught **shoplift / shoplifting**, you usually get **arrest / arrested**.

2 Grammar *get* passive vs. *be* passive ◀)) 2.15

Extra practice p. 144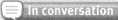

The passive is usually formed with *be*, but sometimes you can use *get*.

People who speed **don't** usually **get arrested**.
Some murderers **get sentenced** to only 10 years.

After *should*, the *be* passive is more common.
People who speed should **be arrested** if they cause an accident.
Some murderers should **be sentenced** to life in prison.

Notice: Use *catch* (+ person) + verb + *-ing*.
What happens if they **catch** you **shoplifting**?
What happens if you get **caught shoplifting**?

In conversation

People use the ***get*** passive much more frequently in speaking than in writing.

A Complete the comments about law enforcement. Use the *get* passive or *be* passive with the verb given, and use the correct form of the verb after *catch*.

1. People who hack into computers should _*be punished*_ (punish) more severely. I mean, cyber crime is really serious.

2. Careless drivers hardly ever _____ (stop) by the police. The laws against speeding and other driving offenses should _____ (enforce) more strictly.

3. Lots of executives _____ (catch / steal) from their companies, and they often _____ (send) to prison for a long time. White-collar crime is a big problem.

4. When vandals _____ (arrest), they shouldn't _____ (punish) so severely. I mean, they should just _____ (sentence) to a month of community service.

5. More people _____ (catch / shoplift) these days because of all the cameras they have in stores. But most shoppers are honest, and they really shouldn't _____ (record).

6. A big problem is that most criminals never _____ (catch), and the ones that _____ (arrest) often _____ (not convict).

About you **B** **Pair work** Discuss the opinions above. Do you agree?

Common errors

Remember to include *get* in *get* passives.

*Shoplifters often **get** fined.*
(NOT ~~Shoplifters often fined.~~)

3 Listening We got robbed!

A ◀)) 2.16 Listen to Jenny talk about a burglary. Answer the questions.

1. When did the burglary happen?
2. Who discovered it and how?
3. What was stolen?
4. Did the burglars get caught?

B ◀)) 2.16 Listen again. How does Jenny feel about the burglary? Check (✓) the sentences that are true.

- [ ] She never expected it to happen.
- [ ] She thinks it was inconvenient.
- [ ] She was scared.
- [ ] She thinks it was funny.
- [ ] She was upset.
- [ ] She felt disappointed with the burglars' punishment.

C **Pair work** Discuss the burglars' punishment in Jenny's case and the questions in Exercise 1A on page 46. What punishments are appropriate?

"Well, in Jenny's case, I don't think the punishment was severe enough. I mean, if burglars get caught, then they should be sentenced to at least two years in prison."

1 Conversation strategy Organizing your views

A Where do you often see security cameras? Make a list. Do you think they're a deterrent? If so, what against? Or are they intrusive and an invasion of privacy?

B 🔊 **2.17** Listen. What do Adam and Selina think about security cameras on buses?

Adam	Did you hear they have cameras on all the buses now?
Selina	Yeah. They should be put in all public places.
Adam	So, you're in favor of them?
Selina	Oh yeah. For a couple of reasons. I mean, first of all, they're a good deterrent – people know they'll get caught if they cause trouble or whatever. And second, they make sure people pay.
Adam	Yeah . . . that's true.
Selina	And another thing is, for the drivers – especially late at night. I mean, basically, it's safer for them.
Adam	Well, you've got a point there. But on the other hand, don't you think all these cameras are a little intrusive? The thing is, it's like an invasion of privacy – someone watching you all the time.
Selina	I must admit, I never really thought of it that way.

C Notice how Selina and Adam organize what they say by using expressions like these. Find the ones they use.

Giving main ideas:	*(Well,) basically . . . The point / thing is . . .*
Adding ideas:	*Another thing is . . .*
Introducing a list:	*There are two problems . . .*
	. . . for a couple of reasons.
Ordinal numbers:	*First (of all), . . . Second (of all), / Secondly, . . .*
Numbers or letters:	*(Number) One, . . . Two, . . . or A, . . . B, . . .*

D Pair work Have a conversation about security cameras. Use these ideas or your own, and organize what you say. Take turns arguing for and against.

For security cameras
They help the police solve crimes.
They make people feel safer.
They're a deterrent.

Against security cameras
They're intrusive, and an invasion of privacy.
They're expensive. They're a waste of money.
They give people a false sense of security.

A *Do you think there should be security cameras everywhere?*
B *Well, basically I think it's a good idea to have them. I mean, for a couple of reasons. First, . . .*

2 Strategy plus *That's a good point.*

You can use *That's a good point* and other expressions like these to show someone has a valid argument – even if you don't completely agree:

That's true.
You've got a point (there).
I never (really) thought of it that way.

They're a good deterrent.

Yeah, that's true.

In conversation

That's true is the second most common expression with *That's*, after *That's right*.

A Respond to each comment. Use an expression above and add a different view.

1. I think metal detectors should be used in all public buildings. It'd be safer.
   You've got a point, but we shouldn't be made to go through one in every building.
2. If kids get caught skipping school without permission, then their parents should be fined.
3. More police should be put on the streets. That would help reduce crime.
4. Cameras should be installed in cars that teenagers drive. It could prevent accidents.
5. I think kids as young as 12 or 13 should be held responsible for their crimes.

B Pair work Take turns presenting the views above. Continue your arguments.

3 Listening and strategies Different points of view

A 🔊 2.18 Listen to the class debate. Answer the questions.

1. Which of these topics is the class discussing? Check (✓) the topic.

☐ Raising the age limit to get married   ☐ Banning cars from city areas
☐ Sending dangerous drivers to prison   ☐ Raising the legal age for driving

2. What two arguments are given *in favor of* changing the law and *against* it? Take notes.

About you **B** 🔊 2.19 Listen to five opinions from the debate again. Prepare a response to each point of view. Use an expression from the box, and add your own opinion.

1. _____
2. _____
3. _____
4. _____
5. _____

Useful expressions

That's a good point, but . . .
Absolutely! I agree with that.
Maybe, but on the other hand, . . .
That's a good idea.
I'm not sure about that for two reasons.

About you **C** Group work Discuss the topics in part A above. Organize your views, and remember to show that your classmates have valid arguments. Do you share the same views?

"I think the age limit to get married should be raised for two reasons. First of all, . . . "

((• **Sounds right** p. 138

1 Reading

A What kind of privacy issues do people worry about? Make a list. Do you worry about them, too?

B Read the article. What types of information does it mention? Which of the ideas you discussed above does it include?

Reading tip

Articles sometimes describe the background to a problem and then list a set of problems and possible solutions.

http://www.smartphoneprivacy...

Is your smartphone too smart for your own good?

Gone are the days when a cell phone just made calls. We use our smartphones to text, take and post photos online, access email and social networks, get directions, check prices in stores, find nearby restaurants, and even find nearby friends. However, the risks smartphones pose can be underestimated. The truth is that smartphones are a bit too smart when it comes to gathering and sharing our personal information, such as location, contacts, messages, photos, and even financial data. Obviously, laws can be passed to protect us against invasions of privacy, but lawmakers simply haven't kept up with changes in technology. Why should anyone be concerned?

First of all, smartphone service providers typically save information about who you call, what messages you send, where you are, and much more. They often share this information with third parties, such as marketers who want to know your location, friends, and personal tastes. Ask your provider how to "opt out" of this part of your contract. Also, if you don't want your phone to keep track of your location, turn off this feature.

Second, your smartphone apps may be quietly collecting your private data. Perhaps this shouldn't be allowed, but it is. So before you download a new app, read the privacy statement. If it collects information that it doesn't really need, you probably shouldn't download it.

Third, think twice before you use the Wi-Fi in a coffeehouse as there's always a chance that someone will use illegal "malware" to spy on your private data, such as your bank account details. To avoid getting hacked, don't use public Wi-Fi to access sensitive personal information.

Finally, think about what would happen if your phone got stolen. Unless you have good password protection, your personal and financial data could be accessed immediately. Choose a password that can't easily be guessed. Also, don't let your smartphone remember your other passwords. Have every website request your password each time you access it. In addition, you can use programs that allow you to erase all the data from your phone if it's lost or stolen. Ask your service provider for information.

Laws may need to be passed to ensure smartphone privacy, but in the meantime, it's up to you to "outsmart" your smartphone.

C Find expressions in the article to complete these sentences.

1. You usually need to type in a password in order to _____access_____ your email.

2. The risks of smartphones are often _____ . People think they're safer than they actually are.

3. It's worrisome that apps collect private information without your permission.
   You should be _____ .

4. The company that you pay for your phone service is called your _____ .

5. Sometimes you can _____ of certain parts of your phone contract — you can choose not to accept them.

6. Many apps know where you are as you move from place to place — they _____ of your location.

7. Criminals sometimes use _____ , or malicious software, to access your financial data.

8. If you use Wi-Fi in a coffeehouse, your computer could get _____ by a criminal.

9. You need to _____ your smartphone — and be smarter than your phone is.

D Read the article again and answer these questions.

1. Why are there so few laws against the invasion of privacy through smartphones?
2. What should you do in order to keep your location private?
3. Why do you think third parties want to know your location and personal tastes?
4. What should you do before you download a new app?
5. What two pieces of advice does the article give about passwords?
6. What else do you know about protecting your privacy?

2 Speaking and writing Posting a comment on a web article

About you **A** Pair work Answer the questions about the article on page 50. Take notes on your answers. Then discuss the questions with a partner.

1. What did you think of the article? Did you find the information relevant and helpful?
2. Are you concerned about all the personal information that is collected by smartphones?
3. Have you ever had a problem because personal information was shared by a service provider or app?
4. Do you know anyone who has gotten hacked by a criminal with malware?
5. What should be done about the invasion of privacy through smartphones?

B Read the comment below and the Help note. Underline the clauses that give reasons.

posted 2 hours ago

Worried about smartphone privacy

I found this article very relevant because it gives helpful suggestions for protecting personal information. I also found it worrisome as it seems there aren't enough laws against the invasion of privacy.

I haven't had any problems with my smartphone because I am very careful about how I use it. A friend of mine, however, received a lot of annoying spam because she downloaded an app for shopping discounts. Another friend got hacked when he used the Wi-Fi in a coffeehouse to check his bank account.

We need more laws to protect our privacy since everyone now has a smartphone. A commission of experts should be created to propose new laws, and the laws should be passed quickly. Also, service providers should be required to give users clear instructions on how to protect their personal information as it's difficult to know how to do this.

Olivia95

> **Help note**
>
> **Giving reasons**
>
> You can use *because*, *since*, and *as* to give reasons.
>
> You can use *because* in all cases.
>
> *I found this article very relevant **because** it gives . . .*
>
> Use *since* only to give reasons the reader already knows or can guess.
>
> *We need more laws to protect our privacy **since** everyone now has a smartphone.*
>
> *As* is more formal.
>
> *I also found it worrisome **as** it seems there aren't enough laws . . .*

C Use the notes you took in Exercise A to write a comment on the article on page 50. Give reasons for your comments.

D Group work Read your classmates' comments. Which do you agree with? Are there any ideas that you don't agree with? Discuss.

Free talk, p. 130

Learning tip *Word charts*

One way to write down new words is to use word charts. You can group related ideas together, which will help you learn and remember them.

1 Complete the word chart about crime using the words and expressions in the box.

burglar	murderer	steals from stores	paints on public buildings
murder	shoplifting	vandalism	breaks into a building to steal

Crime	Criminal	Activity
burglary		
	vandal	
		kills or murders people
	shoplifter	

2 **Word builder** Find out the meaning of the words below. Then make and complete a chart like the one above, adding more words and definitions.

arson	blackmail	hijacking	joyriding	mugging

 On your own

Look through an English-language newspaper, and highlight all the words that are connected with crime and law. How many of them do you already know?

 Can Do! Now I can . . .

✓ I can . . .	? I need to review how to . . .

- ☐ talk about what the legal age should be for different activities.
- ☐ discuss rules and regulations.
- ☐ talk about crimes and what punishments should apply.
- ☐ use expressions like *Basically, . . .* to organize what I say.

- ☐ use expressions like *That's a good point* to show someone has a valid argument.
- ☐ understand a conversation about a crime.
- ☐ understand a class debate about changing the law.
- ☐ read an article about privacy issues with smartphones.
- ☐ write a comment responding to a web article.

Strange events

☑ **Can Do!** In this unit, you learn how to . . .

Lesson A
- Talk about coincidences using the past perfect

Lesson B
- Talk about superstitions
- Show things in common in responses with *So* and *Neither*

Lesson C
- Repeat ideas to make your meaning clear
- Use *just* to make what you say stronger or softer

Lesson D
- Read an article about identical twins
- Write about a family story

1

When you see an unexplained object in the sky, you might be seeing _____.

2

When you have the strange feeling that you have been somewhere or experienced something before, you are having _____.

3

4

When you unexpectedly run into someone you know – for example, in another city – you call it _____.

When you can tell what someone else is thinking, you are experiencing _____.

Before you begin . . .

Complete the sentences with the words below.

- telepathy
- déjà vu
- a coincidence
- a UFO (unidentified flying object)

Have you ever had experiences like these?

Do you know anyone else who has?

Have you ever experienced an
AMAZING COINCIDENCE?

"Oh, yeah, I think life is full of coincidences. I remember one time – I had just met my husband-to-be, and we hadn't known each other long. Well, he was showing me photos of an old friend that he hadn't seen or spoken to in years, a college friend who'd moved to Spain, Gerry. Anyway, there we were, looking at these photos, when the phone rang, and – you'll never believe it – it was his friend Gerry! He just called out of the blue."

—Emma Rivers

"Actually, yeah. One thing that sticks in my mind is . . . years ago, I was out in the Australian outback, driving through the desert. One night, I had set up camp and was cooking, and this van appeared out of nowhere with two guys in it. It was nice to have company because I hadn't spoken to anyone in days – I'd gone on this trip by myself, you see. Well, it turned out one of them had graduated from the same college I did. Small world, huh?"

—Glen Hutt

1 Getting started

A What kinds of coincidences happen to people? Make a list.

You meet a stranger, and you realize you both know the same person.

B 🔊 **2.20** **Listen. What coincidences did Emma and Glen experience? Were they on your list?**

Figure it out **C** Complete the answers. Use the anecdotes above to help you.

1. What did Emma find out about Gerry?   He _____ to Spain years ago.
2. Were Emma's husband and Gerry close?   Yes, but they _____ to each other in years.
3. Why was Glen alone?   Because he _____ on the trip by himself.
4. Why was Glen happy to have company?   Because he _____ to anyone in days.

2 Grammar The past perfect 🔊 2.21

Extra practice p. 145

Use the past perfect to talk about things that happened before an event in the past.

I **had set up** camp and was cooking, and this van appeared out of nowhere.
I **had** just **met** my husband-to-be, and he was showing me photos . . . when the phone rang.

The past perfect is often used to give explanations or reasons why things happened.

It was nice to have company because I **hadn't spoken** to anyone in days.
Gerry was a college friend that he **hadn't seen** in years. He**'d moved** to Spain.

Questions and short answers in the past perfect

Had you **gone** by yourself?	**Had** they **been** in touch?	Where **had** he **moved** to?
Yes, I **had**.	No, they **hadn't**.	To Spain.

A Complete the stories with either the simple past or past perfect. Sometimes both are possible. Then practice with a partner.

1. A Have you ever been talking about someone and then they got in touch with you?

    B Yeah. In fact, last week I was talking about a friend who I _____ (not speak) to in a long time. I think he _____ (change) his cell phone and he _____ (not give) me the number. Anyway, he _____ (text) me out of the blue because he _____ (run into) my brother at a restaurant, and they were talking about me. So he _____ (decide) to get in touch. It _____ (be) great to hear from him.

2. A Have you ever been thinking about someone and then you've run into them?

    B Not really, but I experienced another coincidence recently. I _____ (go) to the post office because we _____ (get) someone else's mail. It _____ (happen) before, three or four times. So anyway, I was waiting in line, and I _____ (start) talking to this guy who _____ (come) in right after me. He was there because he _____ (not / receive) some of his mail. So I _____ (ask), "You don't know a Mr. Ling, do you?" And he said, "Yeah, that's me." I couldn't believe it! I _____ (have) his mail!

3. A Have you ever met anyone with the same birthday as you?

    B Actually, on my last birthday, my girlfriend _____ (decide) to take me to this restaurant that she _____ (go) to with some friends. I _____ (hear) about it, but _____ (not / have) a chance to go there. Anyway, we _____ (show) up at the restaurant, and my co-worker was there, celebrating her birthday, too.

About you **B** Pair work Ask and answer the questions above. Tell your own stories.

3 Listening It's a small world!

A 🔊 2.22 Listen to Elena tell a friend about a coincidence. Answer the questions.

1. Why had Elena joined an online chess forum?
2. What does she think about her online chess partner?
3. How had Elena and Derek met?
4. What did Elena discover about Derek? How did she find out?
5. What does Elena say about coincidences?

B Pair work Take turns retelling Elena's story. How many details can you remember?

Lesson B / Superstitions

1 Building vocabulary

A Read the superstitions. How many do you know? Do you have similar ones in your country?

SUPERSTITIONS FROM AROUND THE WORLD

TAIWAN If you see a crow in the morning, you will have a bad day.

JAPAN It's lucky to find a tea leaf floating upright in a cup of green tea.

THAILAND Dream of a snake holding you tightly, and you will soon meet your soul mate.

BRAZIL If you leave your purse on the floor, your money will disappear.

VENEZUELA If someone sweeps over an unmarried woman's feet with a broom, she'll never get married.

SOUTH KOREA If you give a boyfriend or girlfriend a pair of shoes, he or she will leave you.

ARGENTINA Pick up any coins you find, and you'll soon come into money.

PERU If you put clothes on inside out, you will get a nice surprise.

MEXICO If a bride wears pearls, she will cry all her married life.

TURKEY Your wish will come true if you stand between two people with the same name.

Word sort B Complete the chart with the superstitions above. Add ideas. Then compare with a partner.

It's good luck to . . .	It's bad luck to . . .
find a green tea leaf floating upright.	*leave your purse on the floor.*

2 Speaking and listening Lucky or not?

Vocabulary notebook p. 62

A Do you know any superstitions about the things below? Tell the class.

 □ ___    □ ___    □ ___    □ ___

B 🔊 2.23 Listen to four people talk about superstitions. Number the pictures above 1 to 4. Is each superstition lucky (L) or unlucky (U)? Write *L* or *U*.

C 🔊 2.23 Listen again. Write down each superstition. Then compare with a partner.

❸ Building language

A 🔊 **2.24 Listen. Is Angie superstitious? How about Terry? Practice the conversation.**

Angie	Gosh, this looks good. I'm so hungry.
Terry	So am I. Could you pass the salt?
Angie	Sure. . . . Whoops! You know, it's supposed to be unlucky to spill salt.
Terry	It is? I didn't know that.
Angie	No, neither did I, until I read it on the Internet.
Terry	Actually, I don't believe in all that superstitious stuff.
Angie	Oh, I do. Now I always throw a pinch of salt over my shoulder if I spill it. And I never put shoes on the table.
Terry	Well, neither do I. But that's because they're dirty.
Angie	And I always walk around a ladder – never under it.
Terry	Oh, so do I. But that's so nothing falls on my head!

 B **Find responses with *so* and *neither*. What do they mean? What do you notice about them?**

❹ Grammar Responses with *So* and *Neither* 🔊 2.25

Extra practice p. 145

Present of *be*	**Simple present**	**Simple past**
I'm hungry.	I walk around ladders.	I knew that.
So am I. (I am too.)	**So do I.** (I do too.)	**So did I.** (I did too.)
I'm not superstitious.	I don't believe in superstitions.	I didn't know that.
Neither am I. (I'm not either.)	**Neither do I.** (I don't either.)	**Neither did I.** (I didn't either.)

In conversation

Responses in the present tense are the most common.

▮▮▮▮▮▮▮▮▮ So / Neither do I.
▮▮▮▮▮▮▮ So / Neither am I.
▮▮▮▮ So / Neither did I.
▮ So / Neither have I.
▮ So / Neither was I.

A **Respond to each of these statements with *So* or *Neither*. Then practice with a partner.**

1. I'm not at all superstitious.   *Neither am I.*
2. I always pick up coins when I see them on the sidewalk.
3. I don't know many superstitions.
4. I didn't know the superstition about putting shoes on a table.
5. I'm usually a very lucky person.
6. I've never found a four-leaf clover.
7. I've always avoided walking under ladders.
8. I was superstitious when I was a kid.

About you **B** **Pair work Take turns making the sentences true for you and giving true responses.**

A Actually, I'm a little superstitious.

B So am I. But I think it's habit.   **OR**   *Really? I'm not superstitious at all.*

About you **C** **Group work Do you believe in any superstitions? Tell the group. Are there any that you all have in common?**

"I always make a wish when there's a full moon."   *"So do I, if I remember."*

1 Conversation strategy Making your meaning clear

A Do you ever remember your dreams?
What do you dream about? Tell the class.

B 🔊 2.26 Listen. What kinds of dreams does
Olivia usually have? What about Hugo?

Hugo	Do you ever remember your dreams?
Olivia	Yeah, sometimes. I mean, occasionally, not every time, and I often have the same dream, too – you know, a recurring dream. Like I dream I'm sitting in a garden, waiting for someone.
Hugo	Yeah? Who?
Olivia	I don't know. I always wake up before they get there.
Hugo	Yeah? Is it upsetting?
Olivia	No, it's a nice dream, a happy dream. It's just a little strange. I always have pleasant dreams. They're never bad or scary or . . .
Hugo	So, you never have nightmares or anything?
Olivia	Not really.
Hugo	That's good. I often have weird dreams, really weird, I mean, just off the wall. Like I dream I'm falling or flying. Then I wake up and I'm like, "Whoa! Where am I?"

C Notice how Olivia and Hugo repeat their ideas to make their meaning clear. Sometimes they repeat the same words, and sometimes they use different words. Find examples in the conversation.

"I often have weird dreams, really weird, I mean, just off the wall."

About you **D** Complete each sentence by using a word from the list to repeat the main idea. Then discuss the statements with a partner. Do you agree with them?

fascinating	frightening	scared	terrible	unusual	worried

1. It's interesting to find out what dreams mean. It's _____ , actually.
2. Dreams about your childhood can mean you're anxious. You know, _____ .
3. You know, nightmares can be very scary. They can be really _____ .
4. Insomnia must be just awful. I mean, not being able to sleep is _____ .
5. It's silly to be afraid of the dark. I mean, there's no point being _____ .
6. Talking in your sleep is pretty common. It's nothing _____ . A lot of people do it.

2 Strategy plus *just*

You can use *just* to make what you say stronger. It can mean "very" or "really."

> I often have weird dreams, just off the wall.

You can also use *just* to make what you say softer. It can mean "only."

> It's just a little strange.

In conversation

Just is one of the top 30 words. Over half of its uses are to make ideas stronger or softer.

A 🔊 **2.27 Listen. Are these people using *just* to make what they say stronger or softer? Check (✓) the boxes.**

	Stronger	Softer
1. I often think about people and then they call me. It's just amazing.	☐	☐
2. I just love all those TV shows about telepathy. They're fascinating.	☐	☐
3. I don't believe people can read minds. They just make good guesses.	☐	☐
4. I believe you can make wishes come true. You just have to try, that's all.	☐	☐
5. I think people who believe in UFOs are just crazy.	☐	☐
6. I just don't believe in coincidences.	☐	☐
7. I don't really believe in luck. I just think people make their own good luck.	☐	☐
8. Coincidences are just events that you notice more than others.	☐	☐

About you

B **Pair work** Are any of the sentences above true for you? Tell a partner.

"I often think about people and then I see them or they call. But I think it's just a coincidence."

3 Speaking naturally Stressing new information

*I have some strange **dreams** . . . some **weird** dreams. **Really** weird dreams. And they're **scary**. They're **always** scary.*

A 🔊 **2.28 Listen and repeat what the woman says about her dreams. Notice how the new information in each sentence gets the strongest stress.**

B 🔊 **2.29 Can you predict which words have the strongest stress in the conversation below? Underline one word in each sentence. Then listen and check.**

A Do you ever have bad <u>dreams</u>?

B You mean scary dreams? Like nightmares?

A Yeah. Dreams that make you all upset.

B No. I usually have nice dreams. Fun dreams. What about you?

A Oh, I never dream. At least, I never remember my dreams. So, do you ever have recurring dreams?

B Not really. My dreams are always different. But they're always happy dreams.

About you

C **Practice the conversation above with a partner. Use your own information.**

🔊 **Sounds right** p. 138

1 Reading

A **What do you know about twins? Make a class list.**

"They can be identical."   *"They're often very close."*

Reading tip

The title of a news article is often a summary of the story.

B **Read the article. Why did it take so long for these identical twins to meet?**

http://www.twinstories...

SEPARATED at birth, then happily REUNITED

Elaine Logan and Mary Holmes the year they met for the first time

Like many identical twins, Mary Holmes and Elaine Logan are extremely close. They talk on the phone several times a week, and they spend holidays and vacations together. They're so close, in fact, that it's amazing to think that they didn't even meet until they were 30 years old.

Mary and Elaine were born in England after World War II. Their mother, who was renting a small room in a house, was unable to look after the girls. Another renter in the house, a soldier named Patrick Logan, adored the little girls, and with his wife, decided to adopt one of them – Elaine. The second twin, Mary, was adopted by another family from the Logans' hometown, the Blacks, on the condition that the two girls would never meet.

Nevertheless, the twins became aware of each other early on. When Mary Black was five, she saw a poster of some local school children. One of the children looked exactly like her. Mary thought it was a photo of herself. In fact, it was her twin sister, but her mother offered no explanation. Then, some years later during a doctor's visit, a little girl in the waiting room insisted on calling her "Elaine." Mary's parents decided it was time to tell Mary that she was adopted and that she had a twin sister in the same town. However, Mary's mother was still determined that Mary would never meet her twin.

Around the same time, Elaine Logan's mother pointed out a girl across the street one day. She explained that it was Elaine's sister, but that Elaine couldn't talk to her because the girl's mother wouldn't allow it. Elaine already knew she was adopted, but she was dumbfounded to find out she had a sister!

Mary decided not to contact her sister until she was 21 years old to avoid hurting her mother. However, at age 21, Mary got married and moved to Singapore. She still hadn't contacted her sister. Coincidentally, just three months later, Mary got word from a friend that her sister had tried to find her. Elaine had gone to the office where Mary had worked, but after learning that Mary was now in Singapore, she had left discouraged, and didn't even ask for Mary's address.

Several years later, after moving back to the UK, Mary figured out a way to contact Elaine. The two sisters spoke on the phone soon after and hit it off immediately. When they finally met, it was as if they had known each other all their lives.

By now, well over 30 years have passed, and it seems unimaginable that Mary and Elaine spent their first 30 years in totally separate worlds.

C **Read the article again and answer these questions.**

1. What condition did the Blacks set before they would adopt Mary?
2. How did Mary learn about Elaine? How did Elaine learn about Mary?
3. What happened the first time Elaine tried to contact Mary?
4. How did the twins feel when they first met in person?
5. In your opinion, why are identical twins often so close to each other?

D Find the expressions below in the article. Can you guess what they mean from the context? Match them with the meanings given.

1. look after _____
2. become aware of _____
3. insist on _____
4. dumbfounded _____
5. get word _____
6. hit it off _____

a. shocked and surprised
b. receive news
c. learn that something or someone exists
d. become friends quickly
e. take care of
f. continue to do something, though others disagree

2 **Speaking and writing** Amazing family stories

^{About you} **A** Pair work Discuss the questions below. Do you have any family stories to tell? Write notes about a family story you have.

1. What's your family's background or history? Does your family have an interesting story?
2. How did your parents meet? How about your grandparents? What stories do they tell?
3. Does anyone in your family have an interesting profession? How did he or she get into it?
4. Are there any "colorful" characters in your family? Do you have any anecdotes about them?
5. Are you close to one particular member of your family? How did you become close?

B Read the article below and the Help note. Underline the four examples of prepositional time clauses.

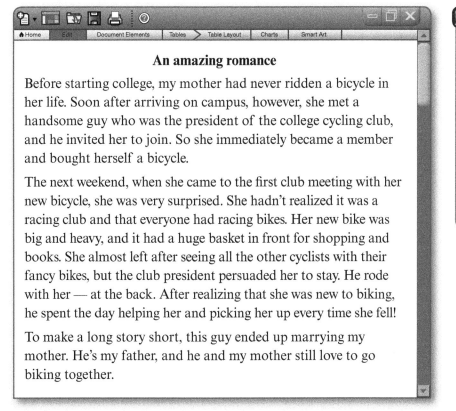

An amazing romance

Before starting college, my mother had never ridden a bicycle in her life. Soon after arriving on campus, however, she met a handsome guy who was the president of the college cycling club, and he invited her to join. So she immediately became a member and bought herself a bicycle.

The next weekend, when she came to the first club meeting with her new bicycle, she was very surprised. She hadn't realized it was a racing club and that everyone had racing bikes. Her new bike was big and heavy, and it had a huge basket in front for shopping and books. She almost left after seeing all the other cyclists with their fancy bikes, but the club president persuaded her to stay. He rode with her — at the back. After realizing that she was new to biking, he spent the day helping her and picking her up every time she fell!

To make a long story short, this guy ended up marrying my mother. He's my father, and he and my mother still love to go biking together.

 Help note

Prepositional time clauses

Before starting college, she had never ridden a bicycle. = "Before she started college, she had never ridden a bicycle."

Soon after arriving on campus, she met a guy. = "Soon after she arrived on campus, she met a guy."

She almost left *after seeing* all the other cyclists. = "She almost left after she saw the other cyclists."

^{About you} **C** Use your notes, and write a story about your family. Use at least three time clauses. Then read your classmates' stories. Which story interests you most? Tell the class.

Free talk p. 132

Vocabulary notebook / Keep your fingers crossed.

Learning tip *Grouping vocabulary*

A good way to learn sayings, like proverbs or superstitions, is to group them according to topics, using word webs.

> **In conversation**
>
> **Good luck!**
> More than 50% of the uses of the word *luck* are when people talk about or wish others ***Good luck!***
> Less than 5% of its uses are to talk about ***dumb, bad, poor, tough,*** or ***rotten luck.***

1 **For each topic below, find and write superstitions from this unit.**

Dream of a snake, and you'll find your soul mate.

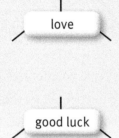 love

money

good luck

bad luck

2 **Word builder** **Can you complete these superstitions? If you don't know them, you can look them up in quotation marks (" ") on the Internet. Then add them to the word webs above.**

Bringing a new broom into a new house . . . If you open an umbrella indoors, . . .
Cut your nails on Friday, . . . Leave a house by the same door . . .
Finding a ladybug . . . Putting clothes on with your left arm first . . .

 On your own

Ask five people if they are superstitious about anything. Translate their superstitions into English.

ENGLISH TEST 9 a.m.

✓ **Can Do!** **Now I can . . .**

✓ I can . . .   ? I need to review how to . . .

- ☐ talk about coincidences and superstitions.
- ☐ talk about the order of events in the past.
- ☐ give reasons for why things happened.
- ☐ show things I have in common.
- ☐ repeat ideas in other words to be clear.

- ☐ use *just* to make what I say softer or stronger.
- ☐ understand someone talking about a coincidence.
- ☐ understand conversations about superstitions.
- ☐ read an article about identical twins.
- ☐ write about a family story.

1 What are you supposed to do?

What do these signs mean? Write an affirmative and a negative sentence for each sign using *be supposed to*. Compare with a partner. Where might you see these signs?

A This one means you're not supposed to use your cell phone. You're supposed to turn it off.

B Yeah. You're supposed to turn cell phones off in hospitals, I think. And on planes.

2 You can say that again!

A Can you complete the second sentence so that it repeats the main idea of the first sentence? Add *just* to make the meaning stronger or softer. Compare with a partner.

1. I really enjoy going to parties. I _just love going to parties_ .
2. I sometimes get a bit nervous when I meet new people. I _____ .
3. I don't go out every night because it's too expensive. It _____ .
4. I'm never on time when I have to meet friends. I _____ .

B Make the sentences true for you. Tell a partner your sentences. Use statement questions to check that you understand your partner's sentences.

A I really don't enjoy going to parties. I just hate being with a lot of people.

B Really? So you prefer to stay home?

3 Crime doesn't pay.

A How many ways can you complete the sentences below? Make true sentences.

	Crime		Punishment		Criminals		Punishment
People who are convicted of	_shoplifting_	usually get	_fined._	I think	_shoplifters_	should be	_fined._
	_____		_____		_____		_____
	_____		_____		_____		_____
	_____		_____		_____		_____

B Pair work Organize and explain your views. Say when your partner makes a good point.

A People who are convicted of shoplifting usually get fined. I think shoplifters should be fined. First, because it's not a really serious crime, and second, . . .

B That's a good point. But I think sometimes shoplifters should be sent to jail for repeat offenses or when they steal something really expensive.

4 A weird week

A Read the story and answer the questions below. Use the past perfect in your answers.

Last week, Eric had some bad luck and some good luck. Monday was a bad day. First, he saw a crow on his car when he left for work. After work, he went shopping with his girlfriend. She spent all her money on an expensive sweater, so he had to buy them both dinner. In the restaurant, Eric yelled at her for spending so much money, and she got very angry. On Tuesday, Eric bought her a gift to apologize – some sneakers – but she was still mad, and on Wednesday, she broke up with him.

On Thursday, Eric had a strange dream about a snake winding itself tightly around his leg. He didn't sleep well and overslept on Friday morning. He got dressed in a hurry and accidentally put his sweater on inside out. Later, while he was waiting in line at the bank, a woman behind him said, "Excuse me. Your sweater is inside out." He turned around and realized she was his old college friend, Sarah. He hadn't seen her since their graduation six years ago. What a nice surprise! Eric remembered his dream and suddenly thought, "This is the woman I'm going to marry."

1. Why did Eric pay for his girlfriend's dinner?
2. Why did Eric want to apologize?
3. Why did he oversleep on Friday morning?
4. Why was his sweater inside out?
5. Why was it a surprise to see Sarah?
6. Why did Eric have that last thought?

"Eric had to pay for his girlfriend's dinner because she had spent all her money on a sweater."

B **Pair work** Look at the superstitions on page 56. How might a superstitious person explain the events in the story? How many superstitions can you use? Discuss your ideas.

"Maybe Eric had a bad day on Monday because he'd seen a crow in the morning."

5 Get this!

Fill in the blanks with the correct forms of the *get* expressions in the box. Then practice the conversation.

get around to	get over	get through	✓get it	get the feeling	get used to

Ann My sister and her boyfriend just broke up. She's so upset.
Bill I don't ___*get it*___ . They were the perfect couple.
Ann I _____ that she was expecting it. She'll _____ it soon.
Bill Did they ever get engaged? Or didn't they _____ it?
Ann They did, but she'll soon _____ being single again.
Bill It's a tough time, but she'll _____ it.

6 Things in common?

Complete the sentences and compare with a partner. Say if you are the same or different. If you are the same, use *So* or *Neither*.

I believe in . . .	I don't believe in . . .	I was going to . . .
Once I tried . . .	I'm not a fan of . . .	I'm not supposed to . . .

"I believe in UFOs."   *"So do I. I think I saw one once."*

Problem solving

 Can Do! In this unit, you learn how to . . .

Lesson A
- Talk about things others do for you using *get* and *have*

Lesson B
- Describe household problems using *need* + passive infinitive or *need* + verb + *-ing*

Lesson C
- Speak informally in "shorter sentences"
- Use expressions like *Uh-oh* and *Ouch* when things go wrong

Lesson D
- Read an article about problem solving
- Write a proposal on how to solve a problem

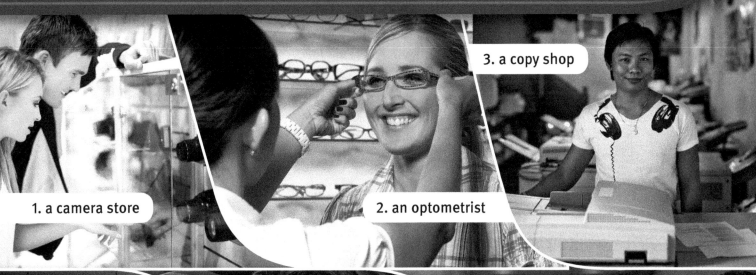

1. a camera store

2. an optometrist

3. a copy shop

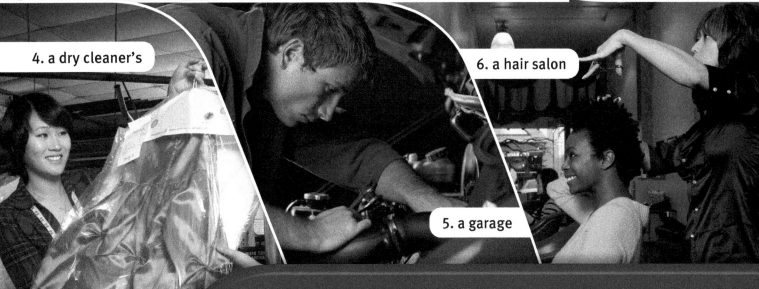

4. a dry cleaner's

5. a garage

6. a hair salon

Before you begin . . .

Where do you go when . . .

- you need a haircut?
- you need new glasses?
- you need some photocopies?
- there's a big stain on your jacket?
- you need a memory card for your camera?
- your car or motorcycle breaks down?

Do it yourself!

We asked people what jobs they do themselves in order to save money. Here's what they said:

Have you ever cut your own hair to save money?

"I have, actually. But it looked so bad that I went to the most expensive place in town and had a hairdresser cut it again. I'll never try that again! Now I always get it cut professionally at a good hair salon, though I get a friend to cut my bangs occasionally. That saves me some money."

—*Min-sook Kim, Seoul, South Korea*

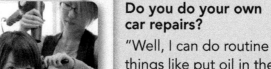

Do you do your own car repairs?

"Well, I can do routine things like put oil in the car. But, to be honest, I get my brother to fix most things. And if there's something seriously wrong with my car, I have my uncle take a look at it at his garage. I can get it fixed there pretty cheaply. I also have it serviced there once a year."

—*Marcus Aldóvar, Bogotá, Colombia*

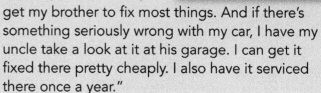

Do you do your own home decorating?

"My wife and I are having a new house built right now, but we're going to do all the painting and decorating ourselves. We've done it before. My sister's an interior designer, so we'll have her choose the colors and get her to pick out curtains, too. She's got great taste."

—*Martin and Jill Snow Calgary, Canada*

Do you ever do your own repairs around the house?

"Not anymore! Once I tried fixing the dishwasher myself because I didn't want to pay to have someone come and repair it. But I didn't realize I had to turn off the water first. So I fixed the problem, but I flooded the entire apartment! And it cost a fortune to have the water damage repaired."

—*Bella Clark, Miami, U.S.A.*

 Getting started

A Which of these things do you do yourself? What other jobs do you do? Make a class list.

cut your own hair	do your own repairs around the house	put oil in your car
decorate your home	fix your computer	

B 🔊 3.01 Listen. What jobs have the people above done themselves? Were they successful?

Figure it out **C** Complete *b* so it has a similar meaning to *a*. Use the interviews to help you.

1. a. I ask my brother to fix things.
   b. I _____ my brother _____ things.
2. a. We'll ask my sister to choose the colors.
   b. We'll _____ my sister _____ the colors.
3. a. Someone in a salon cuts my hair.
   b. I _____ my hair _____ at a good salon.
4. a. I had to pay someone to repair the damage.
   b. I had to _____ the damage _____ .

2 Grammar Causative *get* and *have* ◀)) 3.02

Extra practice p. 146

You can use *get* and *have* to talk about asking other people to do things for you.

When you want to show who you ask, you can use
get + *someone* + *to* + verb or *have* + *someone* + verb.

I **get my brother to fix** my car.
We'll **get my sister to choose** colors for our house.
My hair looked bad, so I **had a hairdresser cut** it again.
I didn't pay to **have someone repair** my dishwasher.

When who you ask is not important, use
get or *have* + *something* + past participle.

I **get my car fixed** at my uncle's garage.
I always **get my hair cut** professionally.
We're **having a new house built** now.
It cost a lot to **have the water damage repaired**.

About you **A** Circle the correct options, and write your own answers to the questions. Then ask and answer the questions with a partner.

1. Do you usually get your hair **cut** / **to cut** professionally? How often do you get it cut?
   I always get my hair cut professionally. I usually . . .
2. Have you ever **had** / **gotten** a friend cut your hair? How did it turn out?
3. Do you have a bicycle, motorcycle, or car? Where do you get it **fixed** / **fix**?
4. If you had a flat tire, would you get someone **to change** / **change** it for you or do it yourself?
5. Do you ever take clothes to the dry cleaner's? Is it expensive to get things **to clean** / **cleaned**?
6. Do you iron your own clothes? Do you ever get someone **iron** / **to iron** things for you?
7. Do you ever fix things around the house, or do you have small jobs **done** / **do** by a professional?

B **Pair work** What things do people often have done professionally? Make a list. Then discuss each item on your list. Where do you get them done? Is it expensive?

"Well, people often get their cars cleaned professionally. We get a local company to clean ours."

3 Listening Wedding on a budget

A ◀)) 3.03 Listen to Molly and Mark talk about things they need to do to get ready for their wedding. What topics do they agree on? Check (✓) the boxes.

B ◀)) 3.03 Listen again. Which things are Molly and Mark going to have done professionally? Which things are they or their families going to do themselves? Make two lists.

About you **C** **Pair work** Imagine you are organizing a wedding or a family event. What things would you do? What would you have someone else do?

"If I had to organize a wedding, I'd get my friends to take the photos."

1 Building language

A 🔊 3.04 Listen. What is Isaac good at fixing? Practice the conversation.

Anna   Isaac, something's wrong with the shower. It won't turn off completely. It keeps dripping.

Isaac   Yeah? Maybe the showerhead needs replacing.

Anna   Oh, it's probably just a washer or something that needs to be replaced. Can you take a look at it?

Isaac   Me? I'm not a plumber. I don't even know what's wrong with it.

Anna   I know. But you're always so good when the TV needs to be fixed. You know, when the screen needs adjusting.

Isaac   Yeah, well, that's an emergency!

Figure it out **B** Find two different ways to say *We need to replace the showerhead* in the conversation. Complete the sentences below.

The showerhead needs _____ . **OR** The showerhead needs _____ .

2 Grammar   *need* + passive infinitive and *need* + verb + *-ing* 🔊 3.05

Extra practice p. 146

You can use *need* to talk about things that should be done.

***need* + passive infinitive**
The TV needs **to be fixed**.
The screen needs **to be adjusted**.

need* + verb + *-ing
The TV needs **fixing**.
The screen needs **adjusting**.

The structure ***need* + verb + *-ing*** is mainly used for everyday chores like fixing, changing, cleaning, adjusting, replacing, recharging, etc.

✗ Common errors

Don't use *I need* + verb + *-ing* to say what you are going to do.

*I **need to change** my tire.*
(NOT *I need ~~changing~~ my tire.*)

A Complete the sentences below in two ways. Use *need* + passive infinitive and *need* + verb + *-ing*. Compare with a partner.

1. My computer's very slow. Maybe the memory *needs to be upgraded / needs upgrading* (upgrade).
2. There's a problem with our car. The brakes _____ (adjust).
3. I can't make any calls right now because my cell phone _____ (recharge).
4. My camera is always going dead. The batteries _____ (replace) constantly.
5. The closet light won't turn on. The bulb _____ (change or tighten).
6. Our air conditioner isn't working very well. Maybe the filter _____ (clean).
7. One of our bookshelves is falling apart. It _____ (fix).
8. There are bills and papers all over the house. They _____ (file).
9. Our piano is out of tune. It really _____ (tune).

About you **B** **Pair work** Are any of the sentences above true for you? Do you have any similar problems?

A I don't have any problems with my computer, but some software needs to be upgraded.

B Yeah? My keyboard needs replacing. Some of the keys aren't working properly.

3 Building vocabulary

A Anna is pointing out more problems to Isaac. Can you guess the things she's talking about? Complete the sentences below. Then compare answers with a partner.

1. "The ___microwave___ **isn't working**. Nothing's happening. It **won't turn on**."
2. "The _____ **is leaking**. And there's **a dent** in the door."
3. "The _____ **keeps flickering** on and off. And I **got a shock** from it."
4. "The _____ is **loose**. If it **falls off**, we won't be able to open the door."
5. "The ceiling _____ **is making a funny noise**."
6. "The _____ has **a** big **scratch** on it."
7. "That _____ is **torn**. And look – there's **a** big **hole** in the other one."
8. "There's **a coffee stain** on the _____ ."
9. "The _____ is a half hour **slow**. Actually, it **stopped**. The battery must be **dead**."

Word sort **B** Can you think of two items for each of the problems below? Do you have any things like these that need to be fixed? Tell a partner.

Things that often . . .	Things that are often . . .	Things that often have . . .
leak: *refrigerator, pen*	scratched:	a dent in them:
fall off:	torn:	a stain on them:
make a funny noise:	loose:	a hole in them:
won't turn on:	slow:	dead batteries:

Vocabulary notebook p. 74

C Pair work Make a "to do" list for Anna and Isaac, and prioritize each task. How can they get the problems fixed? Which things need to be done right away?

A *They need to get their microwave fixed. They should get someone to look at it.*

B *Actually, I think it probably needs to be replaced.*

1 Conversation strategy Speaking in "shorter sentences"

A What kinds of jobs do you get your friends to help you with? Make a class list.

B 🔊 3.06 Listen. What are Kayla and Hector trying to do? Do they succeed?

Kayla	Hi, there. . . . Ooh! Want some help?
Hector	Sure. Just take that end. Got it?
Kayla	Yeah. Think so. Oops! Wait a second.
Hector	OK. . . . Ready? One, two, three, lift.
Kayla	Ooh, it's heavy! . . . Ow! Just broke a nail.
Hector	Ouch! You OK?
Kayla	Yeah. But hurry up!
Hector	There. Shoot! It's not straight.
Kayla	Want me to fix it? . . . Better?
Hector	Yeah, . . . up a bit on the left.
Kayla	There you go. Done.
Hector	Thanks. Like it?
Kayla	Love it. It looks good. Really good.
Hector	Want some coffee?
Kayla	No, thanks. Can't drink it. Got any soda?
Hector	Sure. . . . Uh-oh! Don't have any. Sorry.

C Notice how Kayla and Hector speak in "shorter sentences." They leave out words like *I* or *you* and verbs like *do*, *be*, and *have*. People often do this in informal conversations, especially when it's clear who or what they're talking about. Find more examples.

"(Do you) Want some help?"

"(I) Just broke a nail."

"(Are) You OK?"

D Rewrite the conversation with shorter sentences. Compare with a partner and practice.

A Do you need this screwdriver? Here it is.
B Thanks. I can't get this shelf off the wall.
A Do you want me to try getting it off for you?
B Yes, thanks. Are you sure you've got time?
A Yes. . . . OK. That's done. Do you need help with anything else?
B Thank you. No, there's nothing else. Would you like a drink?
A I'd love one. Have you got any green tea?

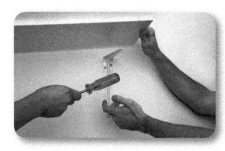

2 Strategy plus *Uh-oh!*

Ow!

You can use words like *Uh-oh!* and *Oops!* when something goes wrong.

Ooh!	=	when you see a problem
Uh-oh!	=	when you suddenly discover a problem
Oops! / Whoops!	=	when you make a small mistake
Ow! / Ouch!	=	"That hurt." / "It sounds like that hurt."
Shoot!	=	"Oh, no!" (a general reaction)
Ugh! / Yuck!	=	"It's disgusting."

In conversation

 Ooh!
Uh-oh!
Ow!
Oops! / Whoops!
Ugh! / Yuck!
Shoot!
Ouch!

Write an expression you can use in each situation. Can you think of more expressions you can use? Compare with a partner.

1. You drop a hammer on your toe. ___Ow!___
2. You miss an important phone call. _____
3. You spill coffee on the table. _____
4. A friend tells you how she broke her arm. _____
5. You realized you just missed a class. _____
6. You put too much sugar in your coffee. _____

3 Speaking naturally Short question and statement intonation

Questions:	*Ready?*	*OK?*	**Statements:**	*Ready.*	*OK.*

A 3.07 **Listen and repeat the words above. Notice the rising intonation for short questions and falling intonation for short statements.**

B ◀)) 3.08 **Listen. Is each sentence a question or a statement? Add a question mark (?) or a period (.).**

1. Better __?__
2. Got it ____
3. Broke a nail ____
4. Left a bit ____
5. Done ____
6. You need help ____
7. Got a drink ____
8. Ready ____

4 Listening and strategies Fix it!

A ◀)) 3.09 **Listen to four people talk about things they are trying to fix. Number the pictures 1 to 4. There is one extra picture.**

☐ ____ ☐ ____ ☐ ____ ☐ ____ ☐ ____

B ◀)) 3.09 **Listen again. Do they solve the problems? Write *Yes* or *No* on the lines.**

C Pair work **Choose one of the pictures, and write a conversation using shorter sentences. Perform it to another pair. Can they guess what activity you are doing?**

A You OK? Need some help?
B Yeah. This just fell off. Can't get it back on.

 Sounds right p. 138

71

1 Reading

A **What's the best way to solve problems? Do you do any of these things? Tell the class.**

- [ ] Ignore the problem and do something else.
- [ ] Brainstorm or make a mind map.
- [ ] Watch your favorite comedy before you start.
- [ ] Try different solutions until one works.
- [ ] Concentrate on the problem in a quiet place.
- [ ] Take enough time to think of ideas.

B **Read the article. Which of the ideas above are recommended?**

 Reading tip

> As you read, highlight two or three useful collocations you can use in your daily life, such as *tackle an assignment*, *solve a problem*.

DEVELOPING YOUR PROBLEM-SOLVING SKILLS

Can you solve these two classic puzzles?

1. You have a candle and a box of thumbtacks. How can you attach the candle to the wall?
2. Two ropes hang from the ceiling. They're too far apart for you to hold both ropes at the same time. They need to be tied together. How can you tie them?

Daily life presents us with a huge variety of problems, many of which seem to have no ready or easy solutions. From deciding which apartment to rent to figuring out how to tackle an assignment at school or work, or even handling relationships, day in and day out we have to find ways of solving our problems. Techniques like brainstorming, mind mapping, or listing the pros and cons of different options take an analytical approach and involve "left-brain" thinking. While these techniques can be successful and lead to solutions, good problem solvers tend to switch between this analytical (left-brain) thinking and a more creative and emotional (right-brain) approach.

However, recent research into the brain's behavior while problem solving suggests that traditional techniques for solving problems — concentrating on a task and focusing on finding a solution — may not be the most effective after all. What might be more significant is simply inspiration — that sudden "aha" moment when the solution to a problem appears.

Neuroscientist Mark Beeman's studies into brain activity show that inspiration happens in the brain's right temporal lobe — an area that *isn't* associated with concentration at all. It's an area of the brain that's responsible for facial recognition, connecting memories, and understanding language. Brain imaging scans show

a constant low frequency activity in this area, indicating that it's always quietly working in the background of our minds. Beeman suggests that when you're *not* focused on a particular task, for example when you're relaxing before bed or taking a walk, the constant brain "chatter" quiets and the temporal lobe can make connections between distant, unrelated memories. Less than two seconds before inspiration hits, there's a burst of high frequency activity, and eureka! You have a solution.

Now that scientists know *where* problem solving happens, they're beginning to understand *how* to improve it. In tests, people solved more puzzles after watching funny videos than after watching boring or scary movies. This is probably because the people who were watching the funny videos were more relaxed, thus allowing the temporal lobe to perform more effectively.

People were also more likely to solve the puzzles in an "aha!" moment than by analysis. Beeman suggests this is because when people are happy, their brains notice a wider range of information.

The conclusion seems to be that if you want to solve a problem, don't focus on it. Let your brain be quiet and the answer might arrive in a sudden flash of inspiration. Now try solving the problems in the box again. Aha – did it work?

ANSWERS:
1. Tack the box to the wall and stand the candle on top.
2. Attach something heavy to one of the ropes and swing it toward the other.

C Are the statements below true or false according to the article? Check (✓) the boxes.

		True	False
1.	Good problem solvers use the right side of their brain more than the left.	☐	☐
2.	The right temporal lobe is active all the time.	☐	☐
3.	When the brain is busy, it makes faster connections between memories.	☐	☐
4.	Watching videos makes it more difficult for people to solve problems.	☐	☐
5.	When people are in a good mood, they are more able to solve problems.	☐	☐

D Read the article again. Answer the questions. Then discuss with a partner.

1. What does the latest research say about the traditional techniques for problem solving?
2. What are three things that happen in the brain's right temporal lobe?
3. How does brain activity change in the moments before you find a solution to a problem?
4. What kind of videos should you watch to improve your problem-solving ability?
5. What *shouldn't* you do if you want to make inspiration more likely to arrive?

2 Speaking and writing A good solution

A Group work Read the problem below. Discuss your ideas and agree on a solution.

The events management company that you work for is holding a Movie Awards Ceremony in your city five days from now. Famous actors and directors are attending as well as the international media. However, you have just received very bad news. A serious fire has completely destroyed the concert hall where the event is supposed to be. The Awards Committee wants to cancel the event, but you will lose millions of dollars, and the city is depending on the awards to boost its tourism industry. What can you do to save your event?

B Read the proposal below. Then write your own proposal persuading the Awards Committee to agree to your ideas. Describe the problem and how you plan to solve it.

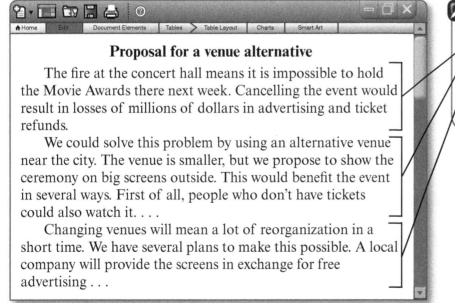

Proposal for a venue alternative

The fire at the concert hall means it is impossible to hold the Movie Awards there next week. Cancelling the event would result in losses of millions of dollars in advertising and ticket refunds.

We could solve this problem by using an alternative venue near the city. The venue is smaller, but we propose to show the ceremony on big screens outside. This would benefit the event in several ways. First of all, people who don't have tickets could also watch it. . . .

Changing venues will mean a lot of reorganization in a short time. We have several plans to make this possible. A local company will provide the screens in exchange for free advertising . . .

Help note

Presenting a solution
• Present and explain the problem.
• Offer a solution and explain its benefits.
• Explain how the solution will be implemented.

C Read your classmates' proposals. What are the best ideas?

Free talk p. 132

Vocabulary notebook / Damaged goods

Learning tip *Different forms of the same word*

When you learn a new word, find out what type of word it is – a verb, a noun, an adjective, etc. – and whether it has a different form that can express the same idea.

> There's a <u>leak</u> in the bathroom. (noun)
> The pipe is <u>leaking</u>. (verb)
>
> There's a <u>scratch</u> on this DVD. (noun)
> This DVD <u>is scratched</u>. (adjective)

1 What's wrong with Mark's things? Complete the two sentences for each problem. Use the words in the box.

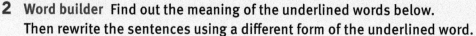

dent / dented   leak / leaking   scratch / scratched   stain / stained   tear / torn

1. There's a big _____ in the wheel of Mark's mountain bike. It's _____ .
2. There's a dark _____ on his T-shirt. It's _____ .
3. His shorts are _____ . There's a _____ in them.
4. His sunglasses are _____ . They have a _____ on them.
5. There's a _____ in his water bottle. It's _____ .

2 **Word builder** Find out the meaning of the underlined words below. Then rewrite the sentences using a different form of the underlined word.

1. My coffee mug is <u>chipped</u>.
2. The mirror is <u>cracked</u>.
3. There's a lot of <u>rust</u> on my car.
4. There's a lot of <u>mold</u> in my shower.

 On your own

Look around your home. What problems are there? Label each one. Remove the label when the problem is fixed!

 Can Do! **Now I can . . .**

✓ I can . . .   ❓ I need to review how to . . .

- [ ] talk about things you have other people do for you.
- [ ] talk about things that need to be fixed.
- [ ] use short sentences in informal conversations.
- [ ] use expressions like *Uh-oh* when something goes wrong.

- [ ] understand a conversation about planning an event.
- [ ] understand people talking about things they need to fix.
- [ ] read an article about problem-solving skills.
- [ ] write a proposal presenting a solution to a problem.

Can Do! In this unit, you learn how to . . .

Lesson A
- Talk hypothetically about the past using *would have*, *should have*, and *could have*

Lesson B
- Describe emotions and personal qualities
- Speculate about the past using *must have*, *may have*, *might have*, and *could have*

Lesson C
- Share experiences using expressions like *That reminds me (of)*
- Use *like* in conversation

Lesson D
- Read an article on making apologies
- Write a note of apology

Before you begin . . .

Can you think of any situations that would make you . . .

- hug someone?
- laugh out loud?
- sulk? mope?
- lose your temper?
- hang up on someone?
- get mad and yell at someone?

Last night this guy called, trying to sell me something. Normally, I would have been more polite – you know, I would have just said no and then hung up. But he was the fourth caller in three hours, and it was after 10:00. So I just lost it. I yelled at him for several minutes, and I finally hung up on him. At that point, I couldn't have done much else, I don't think, because I was too mad. I know I shouldn't have lost my temper – he was just doing his job – but, I mean, what would you have done? Would you have gotten mad? I suppose I could have apologized. Or I could have asked him to put me on their "do not call" list. Actually, that's what I should have done. I'll do that next time!

1 Getting started

A What kinds of unwanted calls do people get? If you get unwanted calls, what do you say?

"Well, I get calls from people who are trying to sell things. I usually say . . . "

B 🔊 3.10 Listen to Amelia tell her friends about a phone call she got last night. What made Amelia lose her temper? How did she behave toward the caller?

Figure
it out **C** What does Amelia say about her behavior? What do you think? Complete the sentences. Then compare with a partner.

Amelia says . . .

1. I shouldn't _____ .
2. I could _____ .
3. What would you _____ ?

I think . . .

4. Amelia shouldn't _____ .
5. I would _____ .
6. I wouldn't _____ .

2 Speaking naturally Reduction of *have* in past modals

> *Amelia should **have** been more polite. (should've)*
> *She shouldn't **have** lost her temper. (shouldn't've)*
> *She could **have** apologized. (could've)*
>
> *She couldn't **have** done much else. (couldn't've)*
> *I would **have** said no and hung up. (would've)*
> *I wouldn't **have** yelled at him. (wouldn't've)*

A 🔊 3.11 Listen and repeat the sentences. Notice the reduction of *have*.

About
you **B** **Pair work** Which sentences do you agree with? Tell a partner.

A *Amelia really should have been more polite.*
B *I agree. She shouldn't have lost her temper.*

3 Grammar Past modals 🔊 3.12

Extra practice p. 147

> You can use *would / should / could* + *have* + past participle to talk hypothetically about the past.
>
> **Imagine your behavior in a situation:**
> What **would** you **have done**?
> I **would have said** no politely.
> I **wouldn't have lost** my temper.
>
> **Would** you **have gotten** mad?
> Yes, I probably **would have**.
>
> **Say what was the right thing to do:**
> What **should** she **have done**?
> She **should have said** no politely.
> She **shouldn't have yelled** at him.
>
> **Should** she **have yelled** at him?
> No, she really **shouldn't have**.
>
> **Say what other possibilities there were:**
> What else **could** she **have done**?
> She **could have told** him not to call again.
> She **couldn't have done** much else.
>
> **Could** she **have been** more polite?
> I feel she **could have**.

📧 **In conversation**

I would is 20 times more common than *I'd* with past modals.

About you

A Read the situations and complete the questions. Then write your own answers. How many ideas can you think of?

1. Josh saw someone in a parked car throw litter out of the window. He picked it up and threw it right back into the car. Should he *have thrown* (throw) it back in? What else could he _____ (do)?
   He shouldn't have thrown it back in the car. He could have . . .

2. Sofia was late for a meeting because she slept late. She called the office and told them she'd gotten tied up in traffic. What other excuses could she _____ (make)? Should she _____ (tell) the truth?

3. Dan was in a parking lot. He saw a driver accidentally hit another car. The driver left thinking that no one had seen him. What could Dan _____ (say)? What should the driver _____ (do)?

4. Katy saw her boyfriend talking to another girl. She called him, told him she didn't want to see him again, and then hung up. Should she _____ (hang) up? How else could she _____ (react)?

5. Andrea's friends were making too much noise late one night. Her father yelled at them and asked them to leave. Should he _____ (lose) his temper? How else could he _____ (respond)?

6. Jun was in a café. A girl pushed past him and spilled his coffee on him. She just walked away. Could she _____ (offer) to clean it up? Should she _____ (apologize)?

B Pair work Compare your ideas and discuss the situations above. What would you have done?

"Actually, I don't think I would have done anything. I would have been annoyed, but . . ."

4 Talk about it True stories

Group work Take turns telling true stories about the situations below. Listen to your classmates and make suggestions. How should they have reacted? What could they have done differently?

Think about the last time you . . .

▶ weren't very polite.
▶ had an argument.

▶ hung up on someone.
▶ lost your temper.

▶ sulked or moped.
▶ made a complaint.

1 Building vocabulary

A Read the article. Do you agree or disagree with the statements? Check (✓) the boxes.

EMOTIONAL INTELLIGENCE

*Emotional **intelligence*** is the ability to manage your own and other people's emotions. Emotionally **intelligent** people can express their feelings clearly and appropriately, and they are generally optimistic and positive, with high self-esteem. Take the quiz and find out if you have high EQ. (Answer below.)

SELF-AWARENESS

		AGREE	DISAGREE
1.	I'm **decisive**. I know what I want.	☐	☐
2.	I'm not **impulsive**. I think before I act.	☐	☐
3.	**Jealousy** is not part of my life. I am not a **jealous** person.	☐	☐

MANAGING EMOTIONS

		AGREE	DISAGREE
4.	I don't feel **guilty** or **ashamed** about things I've done in the past.	☐	☐
5.	**Aggressive** people don't **upset** me. I can cope with their **aggression**.	☐	☐
6.	I don't get **angry** and **upset** if people disagree with me.	☐	☐

MOTIVATION

		AGREE	DISAGREE
7.	I'm very **motivated**, and I set **realistic** goals for myself.	☐	☐
8.	I have the **confidence**, **determination**, and **self-discipline** to achieve my goals.	☐	☐
9.	My main **motivation** in life is to make others **happy**.	☐	☐

EMPATHY

		AGREE	DISAGREE
10.	I know when my friends feel **sad** or **depressed**.	☐	☐
11.	I'm very **sympathetic** when a friend has a problem.	☐	☐
12.	I think it's important to be **sensitive** to how other people are feeling.	☐	☐

SOCIAL SKILLS

		AGREE	DISAGREE
13.	If friends want to do things I don't want to do, I try to be **flexible**.	☐	☐
14.	I think it's good to express emotions like **grief**, **hate**, and **anger**, but in private.	☐	☐
15.	**Honesty** is important to me. I'm **honest** with people unless it will upset them.	☐	☐

People with good EQ would agree with the statements above. The more Agree answers you gave, the higher your EQ score.

About you **B** **Pair work** Compare your answers. Are you alike? Give more information.

"I'm usually pretty decisive. It doesn't take me long to make decisions."

Word sort **C** Complete the chart with nouns and adjectives from the article. Then choose five words from the chart, and make true sentences about people you know to tell a partner.

noun	adjective	noun	adjective	noun	adjective
aggression	*aggressive*	guilt		realism	
	angry	happiness		sadness	
	confident	honesty			self-disciplined
depression			intelligent	sensitivity	
	determined	jealousy		shame	
flexibility			motivated	sympathy	

 Vocabulary notebook p. 84

2 Building language

A 🔊 **3.13 Listen. What guesses do Paul and Ella make about why their friends are late?**

Paul So, where are Alexis and Sam? Do you think they might have forgotten?

Ella They couldn't have forgotten. I talked to Alexis just yesterday. They must have gotten tied up in traffic.

Paul Or they might have had another one of their fights. Maybe Sam is off somewhere sulking, like the last time.

Ella Either way, Alexis would have called us on her cell phone.

Paul Well, she may not have remembered to take it with her. She forgets things when she's stressed out.

Ella That's true. . . . Oh, guess what? My phone's dead! So she could have tried to call and not gotten through.

Paul Oh, my gosh! The movie's about to start. We'd better go in.

Figure it out **B Can you think of some reasons why Alexis and Sam are late? Complete the sentences below. Use the conversation to help you.**

1. They must _____.   2. They could _____.   3. They may _____.

3 Grammar Past modals for speculation 🔊 **3.14**

Extra practice p. 147

> **You can use *must / could / may / might* + *have* + past participle to speculate about the past.**
>
> They **must have gotten** tied up in traffic.   = *I'm sure they got tied up in traffic.*
> She **could have tried** to call.   = *It's possible she tried to call.*
> They **may / might have had** a fight.   = *Maybe they had a fight.*
> She **may not / might not have remembered**.   = *It's possible she didn't remember.*
>
> **Use *could not* + *have* + past participle to say what is not possible.**
>
> They **couldn't have forgotten**.   = *It's not possible they forgot.*

💬 **In conversation**

Affirmative statements with past modals are much more common than negative statements.

A Imagine these situations. Complete the two possible explanations for each one.

❌ **Common errors**

Use the past participle, not the base form of the verb.

*They could have **tried** to call.* (NOT *They could have try to call.*)

1. One of your co-workers hasn't shown up for a meeting.
   She may _____ (forget), or she could _____ (get) tied up in another meeting.

2. You've sent your friend several text messages. She hasn't replied.
   She must _____ (not / receive) my messages. Her phone might _____ (die).

3. A friend promised to return a book he borrowed. He hasn't. He's normally very reliable.
   He could _____ (lose) it. On the other hand, he might _____ (not / finish) it yet.

4. A friend walked past you in the street and didn't stop to talk. She looked upset.
   She could _____ (not / see) you. She must _____ (have) something on her mind.

5. Your brother is supposed to drive you to the airport. He's already 20 minutes late.
   His car must _____ (break) down. Or he may _____ (not / remember).

B Pair work Think of two other explanations for each situation above. Discuss the possibilities.

🔊 **Sounds right** p. 138

I had that happen to me.

1 Conversation strategy Sharing experiences

A Think of different ways to complete this sentence. Tell the class.

I get upset when people _____ on the subway.

B 🔊 3.15 Listen. What annoys Mara and Hal?

Mara	Hey! That guy almost knocked you over getting off the elevator.
Hal	Yeah. He acted like we were in his way.
Mara	I get so annoyed with people like that.
Hal	Me too. Like, I get upset when people push on the subway. It's so rude.
Mara	Yeah, and speaking of rude people, how about the people who stand right in front of the subway doors and won't let you get off?
Hal	Oh, I had that happen to me just last night. These guys were like totally blocking the doors. And when I tried to get past them, they were like, "What's your problem?"
Mara	That reminds me of the time I got on the subway with my grandfather, and all these people pushed ahead of him to get seats.
Hal	Isn't he like 80 years old?
Mara	Yeah. I probably should have said something, but I didn't.

C **Notice** how Mara and Hal use expressions like these to share their experiences. Find examples in the conversation.

I had that happen to me.	*That reminds me (of) . . .*
That happened to me.	*That's like . . .*
I had a similar experience.	*Speaking of . . . ,*

D Match the comments and responses. Then practice with a partner.

1. I hate it when you're going to park your car and someone takes your parking spot. _____

2. We went to this restaurant once. The waiter got our orders all wrong. He was terrible. _____

3. Don't you hate it when people start texting in the middle of a movie at the theater? _____

4. I was in line at an ATM last week, and this guy cut in line – he walked right in front of me. It was so rude. _____

a. Yeah. That's like when people are talking, and you miss something. It's so annoying.

b. I had that happen to me. This woman almost hit my car. I should have said something to her.

c. Speaking of rude people, I had a similar experience in the bank today. Someone pushed ahead of me.

d. That happened to me, so I complained. The manager just said sorry. We should have gotten a free dessert, at least!

About you **E** **Pair work** Do you agree with the people above? Have you had similar experiences? Discuss.

"I had that happen to me. Someone took my parking spot. They nearly hit my car."

2 Strategy plus *like*

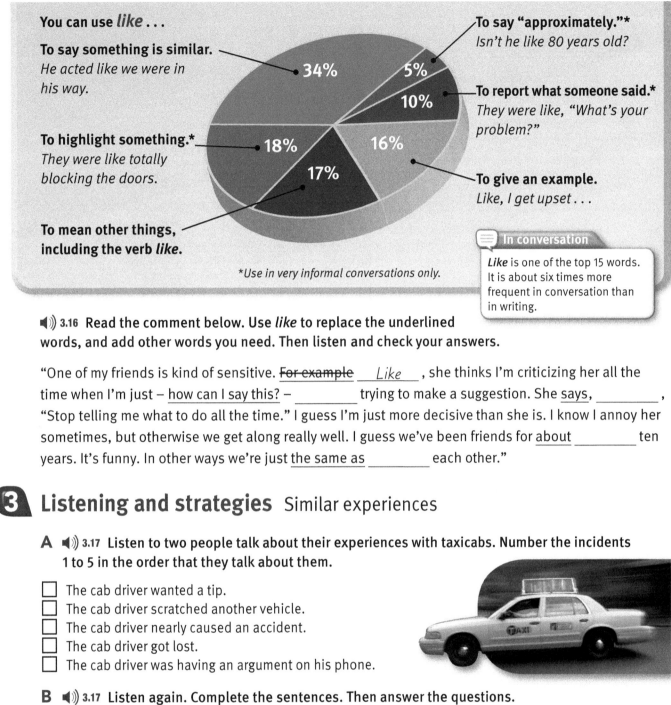

You can use *like* ...

To say something is similar.
He acted like we were in his way.

34%

5%

To say "approximately."*
Isn't he like 80 years old?

10%

To report what someone said.*
They were like, "What's your problem?"

To highlight something.*
They were like totally blocking the doors.

18%

16%

17%

To give an example.
Like, I get upset ...

To mean other things, including the verb *like*.

*Use in very informal conversations only.

> **In conversation**
>
> *Like* is one of the top 15 words. It is about six times more frequent in conversation than in writing.

🔊 **3.16 Read the comment below. Use *like* to replace the underlined words, and add other words you need. Then listen and check your answers.**

"One of my friends is kind of sensitive. ~~For example~~ ___*Like*___ , she thinks I'm criticizing her all the time when I'm just – how can I say this? – _____ trying to make a suggestion. She <u>says</u>, _____ , "Stop telling me what to do all the time." I guess I'm just more decisive than she is. I know I annoy her sometimes, but otherwise we get along really well. I guess we've been friends for <u>about</u> _____ ten years. It's funny. In other ways we're just <u>the same as</u> _____ each other."

3 Listening and strategies Similar experiences

A 🔊 **3.17 Listen to two people talk about their experiences with taxicabs. Number the incidents 1 to 5 in the order that they talk about them.**

☐ The cab driver wanted a tip.
☐ The cab driver scratched another vehicle.
☐ The cab driver nearly caused an accident.
☐ The cab driver got lost.
☐ The cab driver was having an argument on his phone.

B 🔊 **3.17 Listen again. Complete the sentences. Then answer the questions.**

1. The woman says, "I had a similar experience _____." What happened?

2. The man says, "That reminds me of the time I was taking a cab home _____." Why did the cab driver make rude comments?

3. The man says, "That's like when they _____." What example does he give?

4. The woman says, "I had that happen to me. The taxicab _____." What happened?

About you **C** **Pair work Have you had any similar experiences with taxicabs? Discuss with a partner.**

Free talk p. 133

1 Reading

A Think of a time when you apologized to someone. How did you do it? What advice do you have for someone making an apology? Make a list of "dos and don'ts."

"Don't wait too long."　　　*"Make sure your apology is sincere."*

B Read the article. Does the writer have any of the same advice?

APOLOGIES: THE KEY TO MAINTAINING FRIENDSHIPS

It's not always convenient or easy to say you're sorry. Sometimes we're too preoccupied to notice when we've hurt someone, or if we do, too busy to make a proper apology. In other cases, personal pride keeps us from admitting we've done something wrong. There are probably times when deep down we feel that we weren't entirely at fault, that the other person owes us an apology! Nevertheless, if we want to maintain good relationships with friends and colleagues, it's essential to know when and how to apologize:

1. _____ Even if it feels awkward to say you're sorry, do it as soon as possible. If you wait for the perfect moment, you may end up not apologizing at all. At the same time, if you've waited a bit too long, remember that it's never too late to say you're sorry and set things right.

2. _____ Don't let your personal pride get in the way of apologizing. Accept fully that you might have said or done something hurtful. Don't say, "I'm sorry if I offended anyone" or "I'm sorry you feel that way." This implies that you didn't really do anything wrong, that the other person is just overly sensitive. None of us is perfect, and there's no reason to feel embarrassed about needing to apologize.

3. _____ Our mistakes often have unpleasant consequences. An apology isn't complete unless you take responsibility both for hurting someone's feelings and for the specific problems you may have caused in that person's life.

4. _____ To show you're sincerely sorry, offer to repair any damage you've done. If you've broken something, offer to replace it. If you forgot a birthday, offer to take your friend out to dinner. Or if you're not sure what to do, say, "How can I make this up to you?"

5. _____ After admitting that you made a mistake, promise not to do it again, and keep to your commitment! If you have to apologize over and over for the same offenses, you'll soon lose the confidence of your friends.

Finally, sometimes we hesitate to say we're sorry because we feel the other person is more at fault and should apologize first! In these cases, remember that there are rights and wrongs on both sides of any conflict. Even if what happened wasn't 100 percent your fault, be the first to come forward and offer an apology. This act of kindness will make it clear just how much you value the other person's friendship. And it will make you feel better, too.

C Write the missing subheadings in the article.

a. Offer to make things right.

b. Apologize right away.

c. Promise to act differently in the future.

d. Acknowledge any damage caused.

e. Admit you did something wrong.

> **📖 Reading tip**
>
> Read the subheadings in an article first to see what it covers.

D Find expressions in the article that are similar to the underlined expressions in the questions. Then ask and answer the questions with a partner.

1. Do you ever get so <u>busy thinking about something</u> that you forget to do things?
2. Have you ever said you were sorry, but <u>secretly in your mind</u> didn't mean it?
3. Can you think of any situations where it feels really <u>uncomfortable</u> to apologize?
4. What kinds of things <u>keep people from</u> apologizing?
5. Have you ever said to anyone, "How can I <u>compensate for this</u>?" What had you done?

2 Speaking and listening Good and bad apologies

A 🔊 3.18 Listen to four conversations. Why is each person apologizing? Match the person to the reason. Write the letter. There is one extra reason.

1. Alex _____
2. Nora _____
3. Gregory _____
4. Adriana _____

a. forgot to meet a friend.
b. handed in an assignment late.
c. forgot someone's birthday.
d. offended a friend.
e. got into an argument.

B 🔊 3.18 Listen again. Were the apologies effective? Give reasons. Complete the chart.

	Was it effective?	Why or why not?
1. Alex	Yes / No	_____
2. Nora	Yes / No	_____
3. Gregory	Yes / No	_____
4. Adriana	Yes / No	_____

About you **C** Pair work How would you apologize in the situations above? Discuss your ideas.

3 Writing A note of apology

A Read the email and the Help note. Underline the expressions Jason uses to apologize. Does his email follow the advice from the article on page 82?

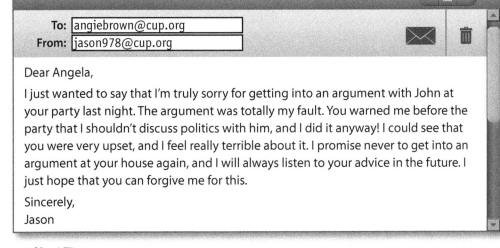

To: angiebrown@cup.org
From: jason978@cup.org

Dear Angela,

I just wanted to say that I'm truly sorry for getting into an argument with John at your party last night. The argument was totally my fault. You warned me before the party that I shouldn't discuss politics with him, and I did it anyway! I could see that you were very upset, and I feel really terrible about it. I promise never to get into an argument at your house again, and I will always listen to your advice in the future. I just hope that you can forgive me for this.

Sincerely,
Jason

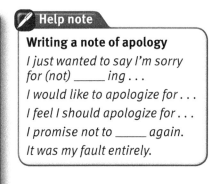

Help note

Writing a note of apology
I just wanted to say I'm sorry for (not) _____ ing . . .
I would like to apologize for . . .
I feel I should apologize for . . .
I promise not to _____ again.
It was my fault entirely.

About you **B** Think of a time when you apologized or should have apologized to someone. Write an email to apologize. Then read your classmates' emails. Are the apologies effective?

83

Vocabulary notebook / People watching

Learning tip *Making connections*

When you learn new vocabulary, make a connection with something or someone you know. Think of how or when you would use the word or expression to talk about your life.

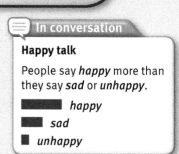 **In conversation**

Happy talk

People say *happy* more than they say *sad* or *unhappy*.

▬▬▬▬ *happy*
▬▬ *sad*
▪ *unhappy*

1 Think of a person you know for each of the qualities below.

1. _____ has a lot of self-confidence.
2. _____ is very good at controlling his or her anger.
3. _____ has no sympathy for people who complain a lot.
4. _____ has the motivation and determination to do well at work.

2 Write a sentence for each adjective. Make a connection with a person or an experience.

| aggressive | flexible | impulsive | sensitive |
| depressed | guilty | jealous | |

My sister says she feels guilty when she eats too much chocolate.

3 Word builder Find and write the meaning of these expressions. Use words in Unit 8 to help you.

1. be / feel down in the dumps _____
2. be full of yourself _____
3. be / turn green with envy _____
4. be heartless _____
5. be set on doing something _____
6. go nuts / bananas _____

 On your own

Do some people watching! The next time you are out and about, watch the people around you. Write notes when you get home.

He's getting really upset.

✔ Can Do! Now I can . . .

✔ I can . . .   ? I need to review how to . . .

- [ ] talk about reactions and behavior.
- [ ] talk hypothetically about the past.
- [ ] describe emotions and personal qualities.
- [ ] speculate about the past.
- [ ] use expressions like *That reminds me (of)* to share experiences.
- [ ] use *like* in informal conversations.
- [ ] understand people sharing taxi experiences.
- [ ] understand a conversation about rude behavior.
- [ ] read an article on making apologies.
- [ ] write a note of apology.

Material world

☑ **Can Do!** In this unit, you learn how to . . .

Lesson A
- Talk about possessions and being materialistic
- Report things that people said

Lesson B
- Discuss money management
- Report questions that people asked

Lesson C
- Report the content of conversations
- Quote other people or sources of information

Lesson D
- Read a blog about decluttering
- Write a survey article about your classmates' possessions

Before you begin . . .

- What are your most important possessions?
- Is having a lot of possessions a good thing or bad thing?
- Do you think you are materialistic?

BUT IS IT ART?
British artist destroys his possessions.

"My goal is to destroy all my possessions. I have been making an inventory of everything I own, and it comes to 7,006 items, from televisions to reading material to records to old love letters to my Saab 900. These are the things I have accumulated in the 37 years of my life. Some of them are hard to part with, like my father's sheepskin coat, which he gave to me many years ago. But I have made a conceptual decision as an artist to shred and granulate everything."

". . . I am also destroying artwork – my own as well as some by my friends. They said it was OK. They understand my project. At the end of this week, after my possessions are turned into granules, I want to bury them underground in a shopping center. I haven't found the right shopping center yet."

A conveyor belt takes Michael Landy's possessions to a shredding machine.

1 Getting started

A What kind of art do you see around your town or city? Make a list. Do you like it?

"You see a lot of sculptures in the park. Some are interesting."

B Read what artist Michael Landy says about one of his projects. What is the project? Could you do the same thing with all your possessions?

C ◀))) **3.19** Listen to Ginny talk about the article. Which facts didn't she get right? Do you agree with her opinion?

"I read about this British artist who came up with a really unusual art project. He said his goal was to destroy all his possessions and that he wanted to bury them in a parking lot! Can you believe it? He explained that he had been making a list of everything he owned and that it came to 17,000 items! And that he had made an artistic decision to shred and granulate everything. You can actually watch him destroying all his things. Someone explained to me that this is 'performance art.' I guess this guy really hates materialism. So do I, but I can't throw anything away. Just the same, maybe I'll stop buying so much stuff. . . . You know, I wonder why he didn't just give his stuff away. But I think it's a really interesting idea. I'd like to know more about this type of art."

Figure it out **D** Complete these sentences to report what Michael Landy said. Use Ginny's interview to help you.

1. Landy said his goal _____ to destroy all his possessions.
2. He explained some things _____ hard to part with.
3. He said his inventory _____ to 7,006 items.
4. He said he _____ a decision to bury them, but he _____ the right place yet.

2 Grammar Reported speech 🔊 3.20

Extra practice p. 148

When you report the things people said, the verb tense often "shifts back."

Direct speech	Reported speech
Michael Landy:	He said (that) . . .
"My goal **is** to destroy all my possessions."	his goal **was** to destroy all his possessions.
"I **want** to bury them underground."	he **wanted** to bury them underground.
"My father **gave** me a sheepskin coat."	his father **had given** him a sheepskin coat.
"I **haven't found** the right shopping center."	he **hadn't found** the right shopping center.
"I **have been making** an inventory."	he **had been making** an inventory.
Ginny:	She said (that) . . .
"I **can't** throw anything away."	she **couldn't** throw anything away.
"Maybe I'**ll** stop buying so much stuff."	maybe she **would** stop buying so much stuff.

When you report information that is still true, the verb tense often remains the same.
Someone explained to me that this **is** what you call "performance art."

Here are some things people said about their possessions. Complete the sentences to report what they said. Compare with a partner. Do you know any people like these?

1. "I'm not at all materialistic – I have very few possessions."
   A friend of mine said that he ___*wasn't materialistic*___ and that he _____*had very few possessions*_____ .

2. "My closets are all full, but I can't stop buying new clothes."
   Someone at work told me that her closets _____ , but she _____ .

3. "I'm always throwing things away. Once I threw out an antique vase by mistake."
   My aunt said that she _____ and that once she _____ .

4. "We're in debt because we've spent too much money on stuff for our apartment."
   My brother told his wife that they _____ because they _____ .

5. "I have a huge collection of comic books that I just don't have room for."
   One of my teachers told me that he _____ .

6. "We'll have to have a yard sale to get rid of all the junk we've been buying at yard sales."
   My neighbors said they _____ .

7. "I never throw things away. I just leave things in the garage."
   Years ago, my cousin told me he _____ .

3 Speaking and listening Who's materialistic?

About you **A** Pair work Discuss the questions. How materialistic are you?

1. Do you like to have all the latest gadgets?
2. How thrifty are you? Are you careful with money?
3. Are you very attached to your possessions?
4. Have you ever gotten upset because you lost or broke something valuable?
5. Do you often buy things you don't need?

B 🔊 3.21 Listen to Howard answer the questions above. Take notes on one thing he says in answer to each question. Then compare with a partner. How much detail can you remember?

"Howard said that he wasn't really interested in gadgets at all."

1 Building vocabulary

A 🔊 **3.22** Listen and read the questionnaire from a money magazine. What kind of money manager are you?

What kind of money manager are you?

Go through our checklist to find out. Tally your answers and read your profile.

	Yes	No
1. Do you have a **monthly budget** and **stick to** it?	☐	☐
2. Do you **keep track of** how much you spend each week?	☐	☐
3. Do you give yourself an **allowance** for special "treats"?	☐	☐
4. Do you **pay** all your **bills** on time?	☐	☐
5. Do you **set aside money** each month in a **savings account**?	☐	☐
6. Do you have a bank account that **pays** good **interest**?	☐	☐
7. Do you **invest money in** reliable **stocks** and **bonds**?	☐	☐
8. Have you **put** enough **money away** for "a rainy day"?	☐	☐
9. Do you **pay in cash** or **by check** to avoid **charging** too much to a **credit card**?	☐	☐
10. When you borrow money from friends or family, do you **pay** it **back** right away?	☐	☐
11. If you **took out** a **loan**, would you **pay** it **off** as soon as you could?	☐	☐
12. If you **got into debt**, would you know how to **get out of debt**?	☐	☐

0-6 Yes answers: You're relaxed about managing your money. You're not worried about how much money you have, but you might need to do something to get things under control.

7-12 Yes answers: You're very systematic and careful with your money. Managing your money is important to you. You might need to make sure it doesn't make you feel stressed.

Word sort **B** **Pair work** What are your money habits? Complete the chart with sentences. Use ideas from the questionnaire, and add your own. Compare with a partner.

I...	I don't...
have a monthly budget.	*invest money in stocks.*

"I have a monthly budget, but I don't always stick to it."

Vocabulary notebook p. 94

2 Building language

A 🔊 3.23 **Listen. What did the market researcher ask John? Practice the conversation.**

John I was stopped by one of those market researchers today. She was doing a survey on money.

Mother Really? What kind of things was she asking?

John She wanted to know whether I was a spender or a saver and how I usually paid for things.

Mother Hmm. Did you tell her I pay for everything?

John Uh, no. . . . Anyway, then she asked me how many times I'd used a credit card in the past month. I told her I didn't have one, and the next thing I knew, she asked if I wanted to apply for one!

Mother But you're only 18!

John Well, I filled out the application anyway. The only thing is, . . . she asked if a parent could sign it, so . . .

Figure it out B **How would John report these questions? Write sentences starting with *She asked me* . . .**

1. Are you a regular saver?
2. Do you want a credit card?
3. How many times have you spent too much?
4. Can you sign this form?

3 Grammar Reported questions 🔊 3.24

Extra practice p. 148

Direct questions	Reported questions
The market researcher:	She asked (me) . . . / She wanted to know . . .
"**Are** you a spender or a saver?"	if / whether I **was** a spender or a saver.
"How **do** you usually **pay** for things?"	how I usually **paid** for things.
"How many times **have** you **used** a credit card?"	how many times I'**d used** a credit card.
"**Can** one of your parents **sign** the application?"	if / whether one of my parents **could sign** it.

A Imagine the market researcher asked you these questions. Write reported questions.

❌ Common errors

Use statement word order in reported questions.

*She asked how **I usually paid** for things.*
(NOT *She asked how ~~did I usually pay~~ for things.*)

1. "What is your main source of income?"

    She asked me what my main source of income was.

2. "Are you relaxed about spending money?"
3. "Do you usually pay in cash, or do you often charge things to a credit card?"
4. "Can you stick to a monthly budget?"
5. "Have you taken anything back to a store recently?"
6. "How many times have you borrowed money from friends or family?"
7. "How much money can you spend on treats each month?"
8. "Do you have any loans? Are you paying them off as soon as you can?"

About you B **Pair work** Take turns reporting the questions and giving your answers.

"She asked me what my main source of income was, and I told her it was my parents!"

(((**Sounds right** p. 139

1 Conversation strategy Reporting the content of a conversation

A Do you agree with the saying, "Money can't buy happiness"? Tell the class.

B ◀)) 3.25 Listen. What does Lucy know about Jeff and Lee?

Lucy	I ran into Max last week. He was telling me that Jeff and Lee aren't getting along that well. They've only been married six months. Apparently, they're having money problems.
Omar	But I heard they're pretty wealthy. Or so someone was telling me.
Lucy	Yeah, well, evidently the honeymoon and the diamond ring and everything were all paid for on credit cards. Max was telling me that Lee had no idea they were in debt.
Omar	Really? How could she *not* know? There's got to be something wrong, you know, if she had no idea what was going on.
Lucy	Yeah, that's what Max was saying. He went to see them, and he was saying how much stuff they have in their house. But as he said, "Money can't buy happiness."
Omar	Obviously not.

C Notice how Lucy talks about her conversation with Max. She uses past continuous reporting verbs to focus on the content rather than the actual words she heard. Also, she generally doesn't "shift" tenses. Find examples.

> *"Max was telling me that Jeff and Lee aren't getting along that well."*

D Imagine people you know said the things below. Rewrite the sentences to report what they said. Use past continuous reporting verbs.

1. A friend of yours: "I'm saving up to buy a car. I want a little two-seater sports car."
   A friend of mine was telling me she's saving up to buy a car. She was saying . . .
2. Your classmate: "My fiancée and I are going to have a small wedding. We decided big weddings are a waste of money. We'd rather have a nice honeymoon, so we've set aside some money for a trip to Sydney."
3. Your neighbors: "We want to put in a new kitchen, but we're going to have to take out a loan to pay for it. It's expensive."
4. Your co-worker: "I'm thinking of leaving my job and going back to school. I want to become a teacher. I think I'll be happier in that kind of a job than I am now."

About you **E Pair work** What have people told you recently? Tell a partner.

2 Strategy plus Quoting information

When you quote information you've heard, use these expressions to identify the source:
Max was telling me / was saying / told me . . .
(As) he said, " . . . " According to Max, . . .

Use these when you don't identify the source:
Apparently, . . . Evidently, . . .
I was told . . . I('ve) heard . . .
They say . . . I('ve) read . . .

> Apparently, they're having money problems.

> As he said, "Money can't buy happiness."

Pair work Discuss the questions. Use the expressions above in your answers to talk about what you've heard or read.

1. Who's the richest person in the world?
2. What's a good way to invest money?
3. What's the best way to set money aside for college?
4. What's the quickest way to make a million dollars?
5. Which businesses have been successful in your city?
6. What's the most expensive thing you think you'll ever buy?
7. What's the best way to keep track of your spending?
8. Which jobs pay the best salaries? the worst?
9. Where's a good place to get a part-time job?

A Isn't it Carlos Slim Helú? I've heard he's worth billions.

B Yeah. My friend was telling me there are a lot of billionaires in Mexico now.

3 Speaking naturally Finished and unfinished ideas

	Finished idea:	**Unfinished idea:**
Sue was telling me about her job.	*It pays really well.*	*It pays really well . . .*

A 🔊 **3.26** Listen and repeat the sentences above. Notice how the intonation falls to show the speaker has finished an idea and rises to show there's more to say.

B 🔊 **3.27** Listen. Which of these sentences are finished ideas (F)? Which sound unfinished (U)? Write *F* or *U*.

1. Dan was telling me about his new career ____
2. Evidently he's quit his job ____
3. He has no other source of income ____
4. He's trying to sell his art online ____
5. It all seems a little risky to me ____
6. I hope it pays off for him in the end ____

C 🔊 **3.28** Now listen to the full extract, and check your answers. Do you think Dan's situation is risky?

About you **D Group work** What are some good ways to make money? Which jobs pay well? Which don't? Tell your group about things you've heard and read.

"My sister was telling me her boyfriend is a stockbroker. Apparently, he makes a fortune."

1 Reading

A Have you ever bought things that you don't use? What are they? Tell the class.

B Read the article. What was Leda's problem? What did she do about it?

> 📖 **Reading tip**
>
> Journalistic feature articles and blogs sometimes pretend to "speak" to the reader, e.g., *You know what?* Don't do this in academic writing.

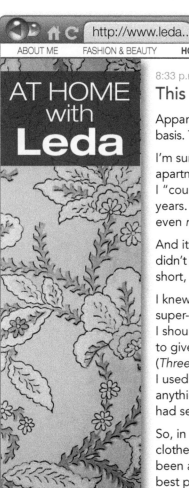

http://www.leda... +

ABOUT ME   FASHION & BEAUTY   **HOME & DESIGN**   FOOD & DRINK   TRAVEL   CONTACT ME   FAQS   PHOTO GALLERY   OLDER POSTS

AT HOME with Leda

8:33 p.m. September 26

This Stuff's Gotta Go!

Apparently, we only use 20 percent of the stuff we own on a regular basis. The rest just sits in our drawers and closets, cluttering up our lives.

I'm sure that's true in my case. As of last month, every corner of my apartment was crammed with cardboard boxes, full of junk that I "could never live without." Most of those boxes I hadn't opened in years. And you know what? I hadn't missed any of it. Actually, I didn't even *remember* what was in those boxes.

And it wasn't just the boxes. I had closets overflowing with clothes I didn't wear, books I was attached to but never read, old electronics that no longer worked – in short, my home was full of clutter, and I didn't have room for it all.

I knew I had to get things under control, so I called up my friend Willow. You know, that super-organized, less-is-more kind of friend that many of us have? Yeah, her. She said that I should go through all of my belongings and make an inventory. She then told me I needed to give away or sell anything I had more than one of . . . like the *three* coffee pots I had. (*Three* coffee pots? How did I even *get* three coffee pots?) Finally, Willow asked me how often I used my things. She explained that she keeps her home clutter-free by getting rid of anything that she hasn't worn or used in the last year. She added that I could keep things that had sentimental value, as long as they were *really* important and special.

So, in the past month, I've gotten rid of more than TWENTY boxes of junk and bags of clothes. Some of it I donated, recycled, or trashed, but most of it I sold. Decluttering has been an enormous task, but it has felt great to reclaim the space in my home again. And the best part? The cash I earned helped me pay off my credit card debt – something I had, no doubt, because I had bought too much stuff in the first place. ☺

C Read the article again. Are these sentences true or false? Check (✓) the boxes. Find the sentences in the article that support your answers.

	True	False
1. The writer says people use most of their things on a regular basis.	☐	☐
2. She used to think she needed most of the things in her boxes.	☐	☐
3. She had plenty of space in her closet for her clothes.	☐	☐
4. The writer's friend, Willow, told her to make a list of her belongings.	☐	☐
5. Willow told her to keep one thing out of each box.	☐	☐
6. Willow believes you should only keep things you use and need.	☐	☐
7. The writer found decluttering difficult but is happy that she has done it.	☐	☐
8. The writer solved another problem with the money she made from selling her stuff.	☐	☐

^{About}you **D** Find expressions in the article to replace the underlined expressions below. Then ask and answer the questions with a partner.

1. Do you think you use only 20 percent of your things <u>regularly</u>?
2. Do you have closets that are <u>full of</u> things you don't need?
3. Which of your possessions are you <u>especially fond of</u>?
4. Could you get rid of anything that has <u>a deep, emotional meaning</u> for you?
5. Have you ever tried to <u>get rid of things you don't want in</u> your home? Was it a big <u>job</u>?

2 **Listening and writing** I couldn't live without . . .

A 🔊 **3.29** Listen to four people talk about things they couldn't live without. What do they talk about? Why couldn't they live without these things? Complete the chart.

	He / She couldn't live without . . .	because . . .
1. Bruno		
2. Diana		
3. Midori		
4. Max		

^{About}you **B** 🔊 **3.30** Listen again to the opinions. Do you agree? Write a response to each person.

1. _____
2. _____
3. _____
4. _____

C Class activity Ask your classmates, "What's one thing you couldn't live without? Why?" Take notes on three interesting ideas.

D Read the Help note and the article below. Underline the verbs used for reporting speech. Then write an article about your classmates. Use both direct speech and reported speech.

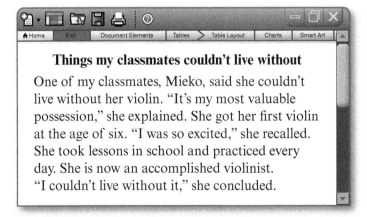

Things my classmates couldn't live without

One of my classmates, Mieko, said she couldn't live without her violin. "It's my most valuable possession," she explained. She got her first violin at the age of six. "I was so excited," she recalled. She took lessons in school and practiced every day. She is now an accomplished violinist. "I couldn't live without it," she concluded.

 Help note

Reporting verbs for direct and reported speech

- Saying and explaining:
  "It's valuable," she **said / told me / explained**.
  She **said / told me / explained** that it was valuable.
- Remembering:
  "I lost it once," she **remembered / recalled**.
  She **remembered / recalled** that she had lost it once.
- Adding and finishing:
  "I love my violin," she **added / concluded**.
  She **added / concluded** that she loved her violin.

E Read a classmate's article. Then tell the class about something one of your classmates couldn't live without. Which thing is the most interesting or unusual?

Free talk p. 134

Learning tip *Collocations*

When you learn a new word, notice its *collocations* – the words that are used with it. In this example, *open* and *close a bank account* are collocations.

> *bank account: You can open and close a bank account.*

1 Cross out the words that are *not* collocations of the verbs below.

make	a credit card / a budget / a living
apply for	a job / a credit card / a bill
open	a savings account / a restaurant / a debt
pay off	a debt / a budget / a loan
invest in	loans / bonds / stocks

💬 In conversation

Talk about money

The top 10 verbs that collocate with ***money*** are *spend, save, earn, make, have, invest, get, pay, borrow,* and *owe.*

2 Write collocations for these words and expressions. How many ideas can you think of?

Find verbs for these nouns

an allowance	cash
a bank account	a discount
a bill	money
a budget	

Find adjectives for these nouns

allowance	expense
account	job
a budget	

earn / make / spend money

3 **Word builder** Find the meanings of the words and expressions below. Use them in a sentence.

credit limit   due date   interest rate   nest egg   overdrawn account

 On your own

Make a wish list of your financial goals. What would you like to accomplish in the next 5 years? 10 years? 20 years?

 **Now I can . . .**

✓ I can . . .   ？ I need to review how to . . .

- [ ] talk about possessions and materialism.
- [ ] discuss money management.
- [ ] report things that people said.
- [ ] report questions that people asked.
- [ ] report the content of conversations I've had.
- [ ] quote other people or sources of information.

- [ ] understand an interview about possessions.
- [ ] understand people talking about what they couldn't live without.
- [ ] read a blog about decluttering.
- [ ] write a survey article about my classmates' possessions.

1 What would you have done?

A Complete the story using the correct forms of the verbs and expressions in the box.

apply for a credit card	get out of debt	invest money in	pay good interest	set aside money
✓ get an allowance	have a budget	keep track of	pay in cash	take out a loan

When Andrew was growing up, he was careful with his money. He _got an allowance_ every week from his parents, and because he wanted to go to college, he _____ every month. He opened a savings account that _____ , so his savings grew. When he started college, he didn't have much money, but he _____ and stuck to it. He _____ the money he spent, and when he bought things, he always _____ .

But then, Andrew won $1 million in a lottery, and everything changed. He didn't _____ stocks and bonds. Instead, he went on a spending spree. He bought a house, a car, designer clothes, and a laptop, and he spent a lot on travel and entertainment. Soon he had nothing left, so he _____ and started charging his everyday expenses. To pay his college tuition fees, he _____ , which he is still paying off. Andrew graduated from college and has a good job now, but he still hasn't _____ .

B Answer the questions using past modals *would have*, *should have*, *could have*, *must have*, *might have*, or *may have*. Discuss your answers with a partner.

1. What should Andrew have done with the money he won?
2. Is there anything he shouldn't have done?
3. What would you have done differently? What wouldn't you have done?
4. How do you think he must have felt after he'd spent all the money?
5. Why do you think Andrew went on a spending spree?

C Pair work Take turns retelling Andrew's story. Use the expressions *Apparently*, *Evidently*, and *I heard that*. Does it remind you of similar stories? Share them using *That reminds me* or *That's like*.

2 How many words can you remember?

Complete the charts. How many words can you think of to describe personal qualities or emotions? Compare with a partner. Then ask and answer questions using words from your charts.

Nouns		
honesty		

Adjectives		
happy		

"Is honesty important to you?"   *"Are you generally a happy person?"*

3 So what were they saying?

A Complete these quotations with a problem and then add a solution, using the appropriate form of the verb given.

1. John: "I went rock climbing, and I got this really big _hole / tear_ in my backpack. It needs _to be sewn / sewing_ (sew). Are you good at sewing?"

2. Alice: "My kitchen faucet keeps _____ , and I can't turn it off. It needs _____ (fix), but I can't afford to get a plumber _____ (do) it right now. Can you take a look at it?"

3. Robert: "I have this big oil _____ on my good jacket. I have to have it _____ (clean) before my job interview next week. Which dry cleaner's has the fastest service?"

4. Maria: "My watch has been running _____ . I've never had the battery _____ (change), so it probably needs _____ (replace). How much will a new battery cost?"

5. Hilary: "I had a car accident, and one of my doors got a big _____ in it. I've been looking for a place to get it _____ (fix). Who fixed your car after your accident?"

B Report the general content of each person's problem, using *was saying (that)* or *was telling me (that)*. Then report exactly what the person said and asked about the solution, shifting the tenses back.

"John was saying that he got a hole in his backpack when he went rock climbing. He said that it needed to be sewn, and then he asked if I was good at sewing!"

4 Want some help?

A Complete the conversations with words like *Yuck, Ow, Ouch, Oops, Ooh, Ugh, Uh-oh,* and *Shoot.* Sometimes more than one answer is possible. Then practice with a partner.

1. A ___Ow!___ I just got an electric shock. I should get that iron fixed.

   B _____ I bet that hurt. Are you OK?

2. A _____ My computer just crashed again. I can't understand it. It keeps happening.

   B _____ Maybe you have a virus. Do you want me to look at it?

3. A _____ I'm hungry. Do you want a snack?

   B Sure. Let's see. Do you want some scrambled eggs?

   A _____ I can't stand eggs.

   B _____ I just dropped them. Oh, well, never mind.

4. A _____ I forgot to hand in my homework today.

   B _____ Will your teacher be mad?

   A Probably. _____ look, it's all messed up. And oh _____ . There's chewing gum stuck to it.

B Pair work Make each sentence shorter if possible, and practice again. Can you continue the conversations?

A Ow! Just got a shock. I should get that fixed.

B Ouch! Bet that hurt. You OK?

A Yeah. Think so. Guess I ought to . . .

Fame

 Can Do! In this unit, you learn how to . . .

Lesson A
- Talk about celebrities' rise to fame
- Use *if* clauses to say how things might have been different

Lesson B
- Talk about achieving and losing fame
- Use tag questions to give opinions or check information

Lesson C
- Use tag questions to soften advice and give encouragement
- Answer difficult questions with expressions like *It's hard to say*

Lesson D
- Read an article about child stars
- Write a profile of a successful person

3 Ang Lee
Film director

1 Duke and Duchess of Cambridge

5 Javier Bardem
Actor

2 Usain Bolt
Olympic gold medalist

4 J.K. Rowling
Author

Before you begin . . .
- What are some ways that people become famous?
- What do you think is the best thing about being famous?
- What is the worst thing about being famous?

97

http://www.watsoninfo...

A lucky break

Russell Watson's rise to fame was remarkable and unexpected. The English-born tenor had no formal music training, was an average student, and quit school at 16 to work in a factory. To make extra money, he sang in pubs in his spare time. Several years later, he sang in a radio talent contest and won, and his life took an amazing turn. He quit his job, got a manager, and started singing in clubs full-time. One night he ended a set of pop songs with an aria from an opera and got a standing ovation. He realized he was on to something. That's how he became a famous singer. By the age of 28, he had released his first album, *The Voice*, and had become an international star.

Comments

Dennis
I think it's a good thing he entered that contest. If he hadn't won, he might not have had the confidence to become a singer. And what would have happened if he had stayed in school? Maybe he would have done something entirely different.

Stephanie
Well, it's hard to know for certain, but I think he would have found a way to be a singer anyway. In fact, if he had continued his education, he could have had formal training and gotten an earlier start as a singer.

Anne
You might be right, Stephanie, but it was pretty brave of him to quit his job. If he hadn't quit and gotten a manager, he might not have had a singing career at all. What amazes me, though, is that he had enough nerve to sing something from an opera in a club! If he had only sung pop songs, he wouldn't have realized how much people loved his opera voice.

1 Getting started

A What kinds of talent contests can you enter? Would you enter one?

B Read the article "A lucky break" above. How did Russell Watson get his start as a professional singer?

C ◀)) 4.01 Listen to the comments that people posted on the website about Russell Watson's career. Which comments do you agree with?

Figure it out **D** Can you complete the sentences below? Compare with a partner.

1. If Russell Watson had stayed in school, maybe he _____ had a very different career.

2. If he _____ won that talent contest, he might not have become a singer.

3. If he had only sung pop songs, he _____ known people loved his opera voice.

4. What _____ happened if he had only sung pop songs?

2 Grammar Talking hypothetically about the past 🔊 4.02

Extra practice p. 149

You can use sentences with *if* to talk hypothetically about the past.
Use the past perfect form in the *if* clause and a past modal in the main clause.

If + past perfect	Past modal *would have, could have, might have,* etc.
If Watson **had stayed** in school,	maybe he **would have done** something entirely different.
If he **hadn't won** the talent contest,	he **might not have had** the confidence to become a singer.
If he **had continued** his education,	he **could have gotten** formal music training.

Hypothetical questions about the past
What **would have happened** if he **had stayed** in school?
What **would** he **have done** if he **hadn't won** the talent contest?
Would he **have become** a singer?

💬 In conversation

People often say *If I would have* instead of *If I had*, but this is not considered correct in writing.

❌ Common errors

Use *if* + past perfect, not simple past.

If he **hadn't quit** his job, he wouldn't have become a singer.
(NOT *If he ~~didn't quit~~ his job . . .*)

A Read the extract about a woman who became famous through the Internet.
Then complete the sentences using the verbs given.

Rebecca Black became an online sensation when her mother paid a record company to produce a music video of her daughter singing a song called "Friday." The video was uploaded onto a video-sharing website and watched by millions of people. Many music critics and viewers didn't like it, and some people called it "the worst song ever." Black appeared on several talk shows, and "Friday" soon became the most-watched video of the year. Black became a "viral star" and is now a successful artist.

1. If Rebecca's mother _hadn't paid_ (not pay) the record company, they _wouldn't have produced_ (not produce) the video, and they _____ (not upload) it.

2. If the record company _____ (not upload) the video, millions of people _____ (not watch) it, and Rebecca _____ (might not become) a viral star.

3. What _____ (happen) if the song _____ (got) good reviews? _____ Black _____ (become) famous if more people _____ (like) the song? It's hard to tell, but it _____ (might receive) less media attention.

4. If Black _____ (not have) all the bad publicity, her music career _____ (might not take) off. She _____ (miss) out if she _____ (listen) to all the critics.

About you **B** Write about two things that have happened to you. Use the ideas below or your own. How would your life have been different if these things hadn't happened?

a job you got	a person you met	something fun that happened to you	a trip you took

Getting my current job is one of the best things that has happened to me. If my friend hadn't told me about the job, I wouldn't have gotten it. If I had stayed in my old job, . . .

C **Pair work** Take turns talking about each situation. Ask your partner questions for more information.

1 Building vocabulary and grammar

A 🔊 **4.03 Listen. How did Lana become famous? Practice the conversation.**

Jon Look. Lana's at the Swan Club! You haven't seen her show yet, have you?

Kylie No, but I'd love to go. . . . She's a blues singer, isn't she?

Jon Actually, she's an **up-and-coming** rock star. She's been **in the headlines** a lot recently.

Kylie Really? I guess I'm a little out of touch, aren't I?

Jon She was on that talent show, and since then, her **career**'s really **taken off**.

Kylie Oh, I know who she is! She won the show this year, didn't she?

Jon Yeah, she did. Last year she was a student, and now she's **making headlines** as a rock singer. It's amazing, isn't it?

Kylie Huh. She must have **had connections**.

Jon I don't think so. She **got discovered** in a karaoke club by one of the show's producers. She was just **in the right place at the right time**.

Kylie I wonder what happened to the guy who won last year – Java Thomas. He's kind of **dropped out of sight**, hasn't he?

Jon Well, he **got** a lot of **bad press** when he got caught shoplifting.

Kylie Shoplifting? That wasn't too smart, was it?

Jon No, it wasn't, and his **career** has really **gone downhill**.

Word sort **B** Complete the chart using expressions in the conversation. Then tell a partner about someone famous. What do you know about him or her?

Ways to become famous	When you're becoming famous	When things don't work out
You get _discovered_ by someone. You're just in _____ . You have _____ .	Your career _____ . You make _____ . You're _____ a lot. You're an _____ star.	Your career _____ . You get bad _____ . You _____ of sight.

Vocabulary notebook p. 106

Figure it out **C** How would Jon and Kylie make these statements into questions?

1. Lana's a singer, _____ ?

2. She won a talent show, _____ ?

3. Java Thomas wasn't too smart, _____ ?

4. His career hasn't taken off, _____ ?

2 Speaking naturally Intonation of tag questions

You're not sure and want to check something:	You're sure and think someone will agree:
You haven't seen her show yet, have you?	*It's amazing, isn't it?*

🔊 **4.04 Listen and repeat the questions above. Notice how the intonation rises or falls depending on the purpose of the question. Then practice Jon and Kylie's conversation again.**

3 Grammar Tag questions 🔊 4.05

Extra practice p. 149

Tag questions are statements followed by short questions in the same tense, called "tags."

Affirmative statement + negative tag	Negative statement + affirmative tag
It's amazing, **isn't it?**	It's not easy to become famous, **is it?**
That was a dumb thing to do, **wasn't it?**	That wasn't too smart, **was it?**
She won the talent show, **didn't she?**	She didn't have connections, **did she?**
He's dropped out of sight, **hasn't he?**	His career hasn't taken off, **has it?**

Answer *yes* to agree.	**Answer *no* to agree.**
She won the talent show, **didn't she?**	That wasn't too smart, **was it?**
Yes, she did.	**No, it wasn't.**

💬 **In conversation**

Negative tags are much more frequent than affirmative tags.

A Complete the conversations with tag questions.

1.   A You've heard of Chris Martin, _____ ?

     B I think so. He sings with Coldplay, _____ ?

     A Yeah. He's their lead singer.

     B Right. They're not American, _____ ?

     A No, they're British. I love their music. They're a great band, _____ ?

     B Oh, yeah. They've raised a lot of money for charity, too, _____ ? I mean, they do a lot of charity concerts and stuff, _____ ?

     A Yeah. I went to one. It was amazing.

2.   A When was Marilyn Monroe famous? It was in the 1950s, _____ ?

     B Yeah, but she made a movie in the 1960s, too, _____ ?

     A I think you're right. She was mainly a movie star, _____ ? I mean, she wasn't a singer, _____ ?

     B Well, she sang in some of her movies, but she was basically an actress. You've seen her movies, _____ ?

     A No, but I'd like to. It's amazing, _____ ? She died years ago, but she's still famous.

B **Pair work** How would *you* say the tags above: with rising intonation (you're checking), or with falling intonation (you think your partner will agree)? Practice the conversations.

4 Talk about it Who's hot? Who's not?

Group work Discuss the questions. Who knows the most about people in the news?

▸ Where do you find out the latest celebrity news?

▸ Who's in the headlines these days? Why? Is anyone getting bad press?

▸ Who are the up-and-coming celebrities right now? Whose careers have taken off recently? Why?

▸ Can you think of any stars who have dropped out of sight? Why do you think their careers went downhill?

🔊 Sounds right p. 139

1 Conversation strategy Giving encouraging advice

A What advice would you give a friend who is not learning much from a class? Make a list of ideas.

B 🔊 4.06 Listen. What is Nela's problem, and what is Steve's advice?

Steve So, how's your acting class going?

Nela It's hard to say. It's fun, but I'm not learning much.

Steve Well, you could look for another class, couldn't you?

Nela Maybe. The thing is, I like the teacher, but she hardly notices me. She never gives me any feedback.

Steve Hmm. How can you get her attention?

Nela Good question. I wish I knew. Actually, I'm thinking of dropping out.

Steve Well, before you do that, it would be good to talk with her, wouldn't it?

Nela I'm not sure I want to know what she thinks! I mean, most of the other students have been acting since they were kids. Do you think that if I'd gotten an earlier start, I'd be a better actor by now?

Steve That's a tough one. I don't know. But you've only been in the class a few weeks. You should at least give it a chance, shouldn't you?

Nela You're right. I guess I should.

C Notice how Steve uses tag questions to soften his advice and give Nela encouragement. Find examples in the conversation.

> *"You could look for another class, couldn't you?"*

D Match the problems and advice. Then role-play the conversations, and take turns giving your own advice.

1. I'd really like to record my own podcast. But I'm not sure what topic to choose. _____

2. I really want to be a contestant on one of those TV game shows. But I'm not sure what kind of people they're looking for. _____

3. If I'd had formal training when I was young, I think I could have been a singer. _____

4. I'd like to act in a college play, but I get scared when I perform in front of people. _____

a. Well, it's never too late. You could still get voice lessons now, couldn't you?

b. It would help if you just practiced speaking out loud at home, wouldn't it? That might help with stage fright.

c. Well, you should pick something you know about, shouldn't you? Or something that interests you.

d. You could just look online, couldn't you? Though I bet they want confident people. Or people with a sense of humor.

2 Strategy plus *It's hard to say.*

You can use expressions like these when a question is difficult to answer.

It's hard to say.
(That's a) Good question.
That's a tough one.

How can you get her attention? | Good question. I wish I knew.

About you **Pair work** Ask and answer the questions. Use the expressions above if the question is difficult.

1. Would you like to be famous? Why or why not?
2. How would being famous change your lifestyle?
3. Do you think being famous would change you as a person? How?
4. If you became famous, would you keep all of your old friends?
5. They say everyone gets 15 minutes of fame. What would you like to be famous for?
6. What would you have done if you hadn't continued your education?

A *Would you like to be famous?*
B *Well, good question. I mean, it could be exciting. But I think I'd get tired of all the attention.*

3 Listening and strategies Great advice

A 🔊 4.07 Look at some advice for making a band successful. What else could you do? Then listen to Tom talk to George about his band. Check (✓) the things Tom needs to do.

☐ practice more
☐ write more new songs
☐ play more "gigs"
☐ contact the local radio station

☐ record music and put it online
☐ get a manager
☐ choose a catchy name for the band

B 🔊 4.07 Listen again. Answer the questions. Circle *a* or *b*.

1. What kinds of songs does the band play?
   a. their own original songs
   b. other bands' songs
2. Where have they played?
   a. at local colleges
   b. at one or two big clubs
3. What does George think about getting the band's name known?
   a. He says it's hard.
   b. He thinks it's easy.
4. What does Tom think of his band's name?
   a. It's a cool name.
   b. He doesn't really like it.

About you **C** Imagine you want to become famous. Choose an idea below or think of your own. What would you like to achieve? What problems would you face? Make a list.

become an athlete   start a band   go on a TV show   create a popular blog

D **Pair work** Discuss your ideas. Take turns giving advice.

A *Actually, I already write a blog, but I would like to get a wider audience. How do you do that?*
B *Well, that's a tough one. It would help if you added some useful links to your blog, wouldn't it?*

1 Reading

A Can you think of any child stars? How do you think their lives are different from other children's lives?

B Read the magazine article. What is "Child Star Syndrome"? How have some actors coped with it?

> **Reading tip**
> Writers often use words like *some*, *others*, and *many* to avoid repeating the same noun (e.g., child actors).

Three Child Stars Who Beat the Odds

"Child Star Syndrome"

So many former child actors reach their teens and end up in the headlines as they lose control of their lives. Some face pressure from parents and spend their early years working long hours, trying to achieve stardom. Others are unable to manage all the money, attention, and the glamorous lifestyle as they get older. Many simply find it difficult to grow up under the scrutiny of the media, and as they become adults, their careers often go downhill, or they eventually drop out of sight. However, not all child stars fail under the pressures of fame. Some have shown that it *is* possible to balance an acting career with a normal life.

Natalie Portman: In the Right Place at the Right Time

Actress Natalie Portman was 11 when she got discovered by an agent in a pizza shop. She became well known for her role in the *Star Wars* series beginning in 1999. The support of Portman's parents helped keep her life stable. They encouraged her to concentrate on her education even when she was traveling and filming. She even skipped the premiere of her first blockbuster movie to study for high school exams. In 2000, Portman took time off from acting to focus on her studies, and in 2003, she received a degree in psychology from Harvard University. After graduation, she starred in several movies, and in 2010, she won an Academy Award for her performance in the movie *Black Swan*. She admits that nothing is more important than her family life.

The Talented Young Stars of *Harry Potter*

English-born Daniel Radcliffe and Emma Watson were barely 11 years old when they began acting in the world-famous *Harry Potter* series in 2001. Fame and fortune certainly changed their lives, but with the support of their families (their parents were never impressed by fame) and the other actors on the set, they had healthy childhoods. Both Watson and Radcliffe earned excellent grades in school, and Watson was accepted into Brown University in Rhode Island and later Oxford University. As young adults, neither of them was interested in the glamorous lifestyle that their wealth would allow them to have. Their down-to-earth attitude hasn't stopped their ambitions, though. Both have secured leading roles in movies and the theater.

What's Their Secret?

If these actors hadn't had the support of parents and other adults, and if they hadn't had a high level of maturity, strength, and confidence, they might not have become the successful adult actors they are today. They've managed to cope extraordinarily well with the pressures of fame – a great achievement when you consider what could have gone wrong in their young lives.

C Find words and expressions in the article to replace the underlined words in the questions. Then ask and answer the questions with a partner.

1. What can happen to child actors who grow up <u>in the public eye</u>?
2. Is it possible to <u>combine</u> an acting career with an education?
3. What <u>very successful</u> movies has Natalie Portman starred in?
4. What did Portman decide to <u>concentrate</u> on in 2000?
5. How old were the *Harry Potter* stars when filming began – 10, or <u>only just</u> 11?
6. What types of <u>parts</u> have Daniel Radcliffe and Emma Watson <u>managed to get</u>?

D Which of these ideas does the article suggest? Check (✓) the boxes.

☐ All child actors have problems as they grow up.

☐ It is possible to be both a successful child and adult actor.

☐ Portman's career went downhill for a while.

☐ If Portman's parents hadn't made her study, she would have failed school.

☐ Radcliffe and Watson were both good students.

☐ As adults, all these former child actors are still successful.

☐ These actors became successful only due to the support of their parents.

2 Speaking and listening Success is . . .

A Pair work How do you define success? Discuss the ideas below and add your own.

being famous	having an important job	finding the right partner
enjoying life every day	doing fulfilling work	having lots of money

"I think you're successful if you become famous."

B 🔊 4.08 Listen to four people talk about success. What does success mean to them? Complete the sentences with ideas from above.

1. For Isabel, success is _____.

2. For Claire, success is _____.

3. For Carlo, success is _____.

4. For Vivian, success is _____.

C 🔊 4.08 Listen again. Do they think they have achieved success? Complete the chart.

	Are they successful?	Why do they think they are or aren't successful?
1. Isabel	Yes / No	_____
2. Claire	Yes / No	_____
3. Carlo	Yes / No	_____
4. Vivian	Yes / No	_____

3 Writing A success story

A Think of someone you know who has achieved success in some way. Make a list of reasons why he or she became successful. Then write a paragraph about him or her.

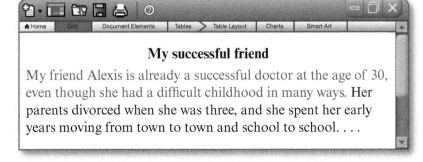

My successful friend

My friend Alexis is already a successful doctor at the age of 30, even though she had a difficult childhood in many ways. Her parents divorced when she was three, and she spent her early years moving from town to town and school to school. . . .

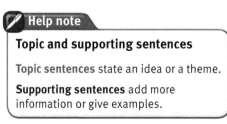

Help note

Topic and supporting sentences

Topic sentences state an idea or a theme.

Supporting sentences add more information or give examples.

B Read your classmates' paragraphs. Are any of the stories inspiring?

Free talk p. 133

Vocabulary notebook / Do your best!

Fame and fortune
The words most likely to be used with *fame* are:
1. fame *and fortune*
2. *gained* fame
3. *hall of* fame
4. *claim to* fame
5. *achieved* fame

Learning tip *Learning idioms*

Idioms are expressions in which the meaning isn't obvious from the individual words. When you learn a new idiom, it helps to write an example sentence that explains or clarifies its meaning.

1 **Match these sentences containing idioms with the explanations on the right.**

1. He's been <u>in the headlines</u> a lot lately. <u>c</u>
2. He's <u>getting</u> a lot of <u>bad press</u>. ____
3. He's an <u>up-and-coming</u> actor. ____
4. His <u>career</u> has really <u>taken off</u>. ____
5. He <u>got discovered</u> very young. ____
6. He <u>had connections</u> in the industry. ____
7. He's really <u>dropped out of sight</u>. ____
8. His acting <u>career</u> is <u>going downhill</u>. ____

a. His career is going really well.
b. People think he's going to be a great actor.
c. He's been in the news.
d. You don't hear about him anymore.
e. He knew people who helped his career.
f. He's getting fewer and fewer acting roles.
g. He started his career at a young age.
h. The news media are criticizing him.

2 **Word builder** **Now write explanation sentences for these idioms.
Find out the meaning of any expressions you don't know.**

1. A lot of young people really <u>look up to</u> pop stars. _____
2. My friend is a great singer. She's going to <u>go a long way</u>. _____
3. Some rock bands are still <u>going strong</u> after 20 or 30 years. _____
4. That young actor is going to <u>make a name for himself</u>. _____
5. She <u>knew the right people</u>, so she got the part. _____
6. He came to the city to try to <u>get into show business</u>. _____

 **On your own**

Make a list of 10 famous people you like. Can you use a different idiomatic expression about each person?

I really look up to him.

Basketball Heroes

1. Sun Ming Ming

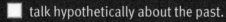 ## Can Do! Now I can . . .

✓ I can . . .   ? I need to review how to . . .

- ☐ talk hypothetically about the past.
- ☐ talk about celebrities and being famous.
- ☐ use tag questions to give opinions and check information.
- ☐ use tag questions to soften advice.

- ☐ answer difficult questions with expressions like *It's hard to say.*
- ☐ understand someone giving advice.
- ☐ understand people talking about success.
- ☐ read an article about child stars.
- ☐ write a profile of a successful person.

Trends

✓ **Can Do!** In this unit, you learn how to . . .

Lesson A
- Talk about social changes using the passive of the present continuous and present perfect

Lesson B
- Discuss the environment
- Use expressions like *although*, *because of*, *in order to*, and *instead*

Lesson C
- Use expressions like *As I said* to refer back in a conversation
- Use vague expressions like *and so forth*

Lesson D
- Read an article about success via the Internet
- Write a post for a website about technological trends

Before you begin . . .

Do any of these issues affect your city or country? Is the situation changing? What is the trend?

- traffic congestion
- work / life balance
- pollution
- an aging population
- urban development
- high unemployment

What social changes have you noticed recently?

1 "A lot of people are obsessed with losing weight and eating healthy foods. So the fast-food chains have been forced to change their menus. Now you can get salads and healthy stuff there as well as burgers and fries. And that's a good thing because obesity has become a big problem."

– Jake,
  New York City

2 "Well, people are talking about losing their jobs. In many places, unemployment is going up, and a lot of people have been laid off. And that's partly because their jobs are being outsourced to workers in other countries."

– Letitia,
  Detroit

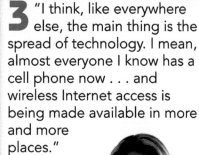

3 "I think, like everywhere else, the main thing is the spread of technology. I mean, almost everyone I know has a cell phone now . . . and wireless Internet access is being made available in more and more places."

– Daniela,
  Monterrey

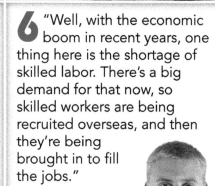

4 "We have a lot of problems with traffic congestion. Fortunately, a lot of new highways have been built, and there's a new monorail, but the problem hasn't been completely solved. So, commuting can still be a real problem."

– Somchai,
  Bangkok

5 "Well, young people are still being encouraged to go to college, which is good. It can be tough, though, because tuition fees have just been increased, and we're not being given enough financial support."

– Oliver,
  Manchester, UK

6 "Well, with the economic boom in recent years, one thing here is the shortage of skilled labor. There's a big demand for that now, so skilled workers are being recruited overseas, and then they're being brought in to fill the jobs."

– Ivan,
  Moscow

1 Getting started

A Have any of these issues been in the news recently? Why? Tell the class.

_____ college tuition fees	_____ obesity	_____ shortage of skilled workers
_____ new technology	_____ outsourcing jobs	_____ traffic congestion

B 🔊 4.09 Listen. Which of the issues above are the people talking about? Number the issues 1 to 6.

C How do the people express the ideas below? Rewrite the sentences.

1. They are encouraging young people to go to college.
2. They are not giving us enough financial support.
3. People have forced fast-food chains to change their menus.
4. They haven't completely solved the problem.

2 **Grammar** The passive 🔊 4.10

Extra practice p. 150

The passive of present continuous and present perfect

Use the active form of a verb to focus on the "doer" or cause of the action.	**Use the passive form to focus on the "receiver" of the action.**
Companies **are recruiting** workers overseas.	Workers **are being recruited** overseas.
They **are making** Internet access available.	Internet access **is being made** available.
Companies **have laid off** a lot of people.	A lot of people **have been laid off**.
They **haven't solved** the traffic problem.	The traffic problem **hasn't been solved**.

A Rewrite the comments, using the passive forms of the underlined verbs. Then compare with a partner.

That problem hasn't been solved yet. . . .

1. Teen car accidents are still a big concern for parents. They <u>haven't solved</u> that problem yet. However, they <u>are advertising</u> tracking devices. They<u>'ve developed</u> these devices to track speed. Some even turn the radio down. Apparently, they <u>have saved</u> a lot of lives.

2. They<u>'re providing</u> healthier lunches in high schools now. They <u>haven't taken</u> junk food <u>off</u> menus completely. But they<u>'re not using</u> processed food – well, not as much. Also, they<u>'re serving</u> more organic foods.

3. They<u>'re developing</u> the city center. They<u>'ve knocked down</u> a lot of older buildings, and they<u>'ve built</u> a lot of new hotels and offices. They<u>'re not solving</u> the housing shortage, though. They<u>'re building</u> too few homes.

About you **B** **Group work** Discuss the different trends in this lesson. Which are good? Which are not? Which are happening where you live? What other trends are there?

"Some roads in the city center are being closed to traffic. It's great. There are more outdoor cafés . . . "

3 **Speaking naturally** Reducing auxiliary verbs

*The education system **is** being reformed.*	*(system's being)*
*The education system **has** been reformed.*	*(system's been)*
*A lot of new schools **are** being built.*	*(schools're being)*
*A lot of new schools **have** been built.*	*(schools've been)*

A 🔊 4.11 Listen and repeat the sentences above. Notice the reduction of the auxiliary verbs.

About you **B** 🔊 4.12 Listen and complete the sentences. Are they true in your country? Are they good ideas? Discuss your views with a partner.

1. More women _____ encouraged to train as science and engineering teachers.
2. Bilingual programs _____ offered to elementary school students.
3. Students _____ required to do community service.
4. Education _____ given more funding.
5. Technology _____ introduced into more classrooms.
6. Courses _____ made available for more people in the community.

1 Building vocabulary and grammar

A Complete the article with words and expressions from the box. What do you learn?

air pollution	drought	environmentally friendly	a landfill	toxic chemicals
biodegradable	energy-saving	global warming	✓natural resources	water consumption

What can **YOU** do to protect the environment?

Although environmental problems can seem overwhelming, there is hope if everyone gets involved in protecting our <u> natural resources </u>. Here's what you can do:

CONSUME LESS ENERGY. Climates are changing and ocean levels are rising because of _____ . This growing problem is due to increased levels of carbon dioxide in the atmosphere as a result of the burning of oil, coal, and gas. In order to save electricity, use _____ lightbulbs, and turn the air-conditioning down or off when possible. To conserve gas or oil, turn down the heat by 2°F (1°C). You'll also cut 10 percent off your bill!

DON'T USE YOUR CAR IF YOU DON'T HAVE TO, because cars consume energy and also cause _____ . So instead of driving everywhere, use public transportation. Or ride a bicycle – you'll get good exercise and help improve your city's air quality.

AVOID TOXIC CLEANING PRODUCTS. Look for _____ brands, even if they're more expensive. This helps cut down on the _____ that contaminate our rivers and oceans and are generally harmful to the environment.

RECYCLE ALL OF YOUR GARBAGE. Recycle newspapers, magazines, batteries, and all packaging such as cartons, bottles, cans, and plastics so that they don't end up in _____ . Packaging that is not _____ can take years to decompose. And recycling paper, glass, plastic, and metal saves energy.

CONSERVE WATER. Even though 1.2 billion people in the world lack safe drinking water, people in developed countries use 15 bathtubfuls of water a day! You can cut your _____ in half by taking showers instead of baths. And water your lawn only once a week. Some people water lawns daily in spite of water shortages and _____ warnings.

Word sort **B** Which problems are you concerned about (or not)? What do you do, or not do? Make a chart like this with ideas from the article, and add your own. Compare with a partner.

I'm concerned about . . .	I'm not concerned about . . .
global warming. I don't use my car for short trips.	*conserving water. I take baths. I don't take showers.*

Figure it out **C** Can you choose the correct expression to complete each sentence? Compare with a partner. Are the sentences true for you?

1. I buy rechargeable batteries **in spite of / even though** the extra cost.
2. **Because / Because of** cars cause air pollution, I always take public transportation.
3. I turn down the air conditioning **in order to / so that** use less electricity.
4. I recycle cans **instead of / so** throwing them in the trash.

2 Grammar Linking ideas 🔊 4.13

Extra practice p. 150

Contrast	**Although / Even though** environmental problems are overwhelming, there is hope.
	Some people water their lawns daily **in spite of / despite** drought warnings.
Reason	Climates are changing **because of / as a result of / due to** global warming.
	Carbon dioxide levels are increasing **because** we are burning oil, coal, and gas.
Purpose	Turn down the air-conditioning **(in order) to** save electricity.
	Recycle garbage **so (that)** it doesn't end up in a landfill.
Alternative	Use public transportation **instead of** driving your car.
	Take showers **instead of** baths.

Notice:
in order to / to + verb
although / even though / because / so that / so + clause
in spite of / despite / because of / as a result of / due to / instead of + noun (or verb + -ing)

A Link the ideas in these sentences using expressions from the grammar chart. How many ways can you complete each sentence? Compare with a partner.

Common errors

Don't write *even though* or *in spite of* as one word.

Even though fuel is expensive, I drive my car a lot. (NOT ~~Eventhough~~ fuel is expensive, I drive my car a lot.)

1. *Even though / Although* there are a lot of environmental problems, the situation isn't hopeless.

2. It's better to use everyday items to clean your home _____ buying expensive cleaning products. For example, you can use vinegar to clean your mirrors _____ toxic chemicals.

3. _____ cut down on the paper you use, get all your bills delivered online.

4. A lot of vegetables from local areas are being sold in stores _____ consumer pressure. This is good _____ it supports local farmers and cuts down on transportation.

5. A lot of areas are being affected by air pollution _____ efforts to improve air quality. Ride a bicycle or walk _____ using the car. Or, if you buy a new car, get a hybrid vehicle _____ you can save on gas.

6. If you buy bottled water, make sure the bottle is biodegradable _____ you can prevent buildup in landfills.

7. There is more solar and wind power now _____ advances in technology. However, _____ recent advances, they're not being used as widely as they could be by consumers.

8. _____ we need to preserve our natural resources, we also need to use oil and gas for energy.

About you **B** Pair work Discuss the ideas above. Which ones do you agree with?

3 Talk about it Saving the planet

Group work Discuss the environmental problems below. What other problems are there? Which are the most serious? What is being done to solve the problems? What else could be done?

▶ air and water pollution   ▶ depletion of oil reserves   ▶ garbage in landfills
▶ global warming   ▶ nuclear waste disposal   ▶ endangered species

A *Even though air pollution is getting worse, not much is being done about it.*
B *Well, "no-drive" days are being introduced in order to cut down on traffic on the worst days.*

Sounds right p. 139

1 Conversation strategy Referring back in the conversation

A Read the comment below. What other workplace trends are making companies family-friendly?

> *Adam* *"I think there's a trend toward companies becoming family-friendly. For example, a lot of men are being offered paid leave when they become fathers."*

B 🔊 4.14 Listen. What other changes in the workplace do Adam, Celia, and Greg talk about?

Adam	As I was saying, companies are definitely more family-friendly these days. And like I said, there's more paternity leave, flexible hours, child-care centers, and so on.
Celia	Yeah. There are definitely more benefits and incentives for working parents. I think companies need to attract and keep good employees.
Greg	Right. And going back to what you were saying about benefits, a lot more people are being encouraged to telecommute instead of working at the office.
Celia	I think companies do it in order to save on costs. And with things like email, and web conferencing, and so forth, it's no problem.
Greg	I'm sure they get increased productivity, too. Fewer interruptions, fewer meetings, etc.
Adam	You mentioned earlier, Celia, about saving on costs. There seems to be a trend, too, toward offering internships to young people.
Celia	Right. I mean, it's a great way to get experience and contacts, and so forth . . .
Greg	Yeah, but basically it's just unpaid work.

C **Notice** how Adam, Celia, and Greg use expressions like these to refer back to things said earlier. Find examples.

You / I mentioned . . . earlier.	
As / Like	*I said / I was saying . . .*
Going back to what	*you said / you were saying . . .*

D 🔊 4.15 Listen to more of the conversation. Write the expressions you hear. Then discuss the ideas with a partner. Do you agree with any of them?

Greg I mean, _____, Celia, companies want to save on costs.

Celia But _____, it's good experience. And internships can lead to full-time jobs.

Adam True. And companies can see if someone is a good fit before they hire them. _____, Celia, they need good employees. It's _____, people want good benefits.

Celia Right. And _____, Greg, telecommuting is a kind of benefit.

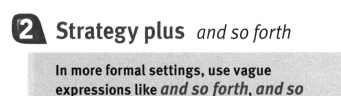

2 Strategy plus *and so forth*

In more formal settings, use vague expressions like *and so forth*, *and so on*, and *etc.*, instead of informal expressions like *and things like that*.

etc. = et cetera

And like I said, there's more paternity leave, flexible hours, child-care centers, and so on.

In conversation

Informal vague expressions like ***and things like that*** are more common than formal ones.

and things like that
and so forth
and so on
etc.

About you **Complete the sentences with the words in the box, and add a vague expression. Then discuss with a partner. Do you agree?**

equal pay	health insurance	improve their résumés	less time off	restaurants

1. Due to the state of the economy, people are being forced to work harder, with longer hours, ____________________________.
2. Companies should offer more benefits, like more vacation days, better ____________________________.
3. Men and women should be treated equally, with equal chances of promotion and ____________________________.
4. Young people do internships because of the opportunity they get to gain experience, ____________________________.
5. In order to survive, people are being forced to work into their 70s and 80s, in stores and ____________________________.

"People are being forced to work harder. Most people I know work late and work on the weekends, and so on."

3 Listening and strategies Trends in the workplace

A Look at the sentences below. Can you guess what else the people might say?

- ☐ As I was saying, working from home has some disadvantages, for example . . .
- ☐ Going back to what you were saying about desk sharing, it's good because . . .
- ☐ Going back to what you said about working flexible hours, it makes sense because . . .
- ☐ I mentioned earlier that calls and email are being monitored more. It's necessary . . .
- ☐ As I said, paternity leave isn't being offered in some companies, but . . .

B 4.16 Listen to extracts from four conversations. Which of the topics above are the people discussing? Number the sentences 1 to 4. There is one extra sentence.

C 4.16 Listen again. Write one advantage and one disadvantage of each trend.

About you **D Pair work Discuss each trend. What other advantages are there? What are other disadvantages? Which benefit would you most like to have?**

Free talk p. 135

1 Reading

A How do people use the Internet to promote themselves? List as many ways as possible.

"They post videos of their singing or acting."
"They create websites on a specific topic. They write interesting blogs."

> **Reading tip**
>
> As you read, ask yourself questions like, "Is this true?" "So, what does this mean?" "What examples can I think of?"

B Read the article. What are the three people mentioned in the article famous for?

http://www.internetsuccesses...

The Internet — The new pathway to success?

Years ago, the path to success in the world of entertainment seemed long and arduous. Aspiring artists often waited years before being noticed by the public. There were endless stories of actors waiting tables in Hollywood hoping to get discovered; of writers sending off hundreds of manuscripts to publishers only to accumulate a pile of rejection letters; of singers working for next to nothing in small clubs as they waited to get signed by a record company. Nowadays, however, instead of depending on big media companies to decide their future, more and more artists are following the trend of displaying their talents online – often with spectacular results.

Pop star Justin Bieber is perhaps the best-known Internet success story. This self-taught musician was a fifteen-year-old Canadian high school student whose only claim to fame was a second-place prize in a local talent show. When his mother began posting videos of Justin singing on the Internet, he became an "overnight sensation." Within months he was signing a contract with a major record label, and his first full-length album, *My World 2.0*, hit the charts around the world.

A growing number of novelists are gaining recognition on the Internet, too. That's where Darcie Chan self-published her first novel as an e-book even though it was rejected by ten publishers and more than a hundred literary agents. The novel, *The Mill River Recluse*, sold 400,000 copies in its first year. As a result of that success, Chan is now being courted by major publishers and even by movie studios.

A different sort of fame has been achieved by Michelle Phan, who got her start with online video tutorials on beauty and cosmetics. Within a few years, she had over 200 videos to her credit, and more than one *billion* Internet views. She has now been hired by a major cosmetics company to promote their products online.

Clearly, because of the Internet, talented people are increasingly less dependent on the power of the publishing, music, and movie industries. Of course, most stories of Internet success are much more modest. When a video of a cat playing the piano or a child singing opera goes viral, the fame doesn't last very long. As the artist Andy Warhol famously predicted in 1968: "In the future, everyone will be world-famous for 15 minutes." It's a prediction that certainly appears to be coming true. Who knows who or what trend will emerge in the next 15 minutes? Your guess is as a good as mine.

C Rewrite the questions below, replacing the underlined words with similar expressions from the article. Then read the article again, and ask and answer the questions with a partner.

1. When Justin Bieber was in high school, what was his <u>reason for being well known</u>?
2. Who helped Justin Bieber become <u>an instant success</u> on the Internet? How did it happen?
3. How did the Internet help Darcie Chan <u>become respected</u> as an author? What were the results?
4. How many video tutorials does Michelle Phan have <u>that she has made herself</u>? What evidence is there of her success?
5. What are some examples of Internet videos that <u>become extremely popular very quickly</u>?

D Pair work Discuss the questions with a partner.

1. What are some things aspiring artists used to do in order to get noticed? Name three things.

2. Do you know of other people who followed the same route to success as Justin Bieber, Darcie Chan, or Michelle Phan?

3. In what way is Andy Warhol's famous prediction coming true? Can you think of examples?

4. How will things change for publishers, record labels, and movie studios in the future?

2 Listening and writing Trends in technology

A 🔊 **4.17 Listen to four people talk about recent trends. What trends are they talking about? Write a to d. Then decide if the person feels positive (P) or negative (N) about the trend. Circle P or N.**

1. Adam _____ (P / N)
2. Emily _____ (P / N)
3. Tyler _____ (P / N)
4. Madison ____ (P / N)

a. home media systems
b. typing technology
c. phone use in social situations
d. online shopping

B 🔊 **4.17 Listen again. Why does each person like or dislike the new trend? Write at least one reason.**

1. Adam: _____

2. Emily: _____

3. Tyler: _____

4. Madison: _____

About you C Pair work Think of a trend in technology that has affected you. How has it changed your life? Do you feel positive or negative about it? Write down some notes. Then discuss it with your partner.

D Read the comment on a technology website and the Help note. Underline the expressions the writer uses to describe a trend. Then use your notes from Exercise C to write a similar post.

posted 3 hours ago

The trend away from laptops

Recently I've noticed that my friends and I are spending less time on our laptops and more and more time on our smartphones. Phones used to be used mainly for texting and for taking and sending photos, while laptops were used for everything else, like answering email, watching videos, getting directions, or searching the Internet. As people increasingly use their smartphones for these functions, the use of laptops is declining. For me, at least, this is a good change. I used to carry a heavy laptop from café to café in order to access the Internet. Now I can go online without paying for an expensive cup of coffee!

David128

Help note

Describing trends

*We're spending **more and more** time on our smartphones.*

*We're spending **less** time / **fewer** hours on our laptops.*

*People **increasingly** use their phones for a variety of functions.*

*The use of laptops is **decreasing** / **declining**.*

*The number of smartphones is **increasing** / **growing**.*

About you E Group work Read your group's posts. Have you all noticed the same trends? Discuss.

Vocabulary notebook / Try to explain it!

Learning tip *Writing definitions in your own words*

When you learn a new word or expression, you can write a definition or explanation in your own words to help you remember its meaning.

In conversation

It's in the air!
The type of pollution people talk about most is *air pollution*.

---

1 Match the expressions with their definitions or explanations.

1. The **atmosphere** refers to ___e___
2. **Carbon dioxide** is a gas in the atmosphere _____
3. If you **consume** something, _____
4. **Air quality** refers to _____
5. When there is a **water shortage**, _____
6. If something is **toxic** to the environment, _____
7. When you **recycle** something, _____
8. If something **decomposes**, _____

a. you use it up, and it can't be used again.
b. there isn't enough water for people.
c. you use it again instead of throwing it away.
d. it contaminates or pollutes the environment.
e. the air around the Earth.
f. that is produced when things burn or decay.
g. it decays, or breaks down into simple elements.
h. how much pollution is in the air.

2 Write sentences that define or explain these words.

air pollution   drought   global warming   toxic chemicals
biodegradable   environmentally friendly   a landfill   water consumption

3 **Word builder** Find out the meaning of these words and expressions. Then write a sentence to define or explain each one.

deforestation   fossil fuels   hybrid cars   pesticides
extinction   the greenhouse effect   the ozone layer renewable energy

 On your own

Post notes around your home in English reminding you to turn off the lights, recycle bottles, and so on.

 Can Do! Now I can . . .

☑ I can . . .   ❓ I need to review how to . . .

- [ ] talk about social changes.
- [ ] talk about environmental problems.
- [ ] link ideas with expressions like *although*, *because of*, *in order to*, and *instead*.
- [ ] refer back to points made earlier in the conversation.

- [ ] use formal vague expressions.
- [ ] understand a discussion about workplace trends.
- [ ] understand conversations about technology trends.
- [ ] read an article about success via the Internet.
- [ ] write a comment for a website about technological trends.

Careers

✓ **Can Do!** In this unit, you learn how to . . .

Lesson A
- Discuss career planning using *What* clauses and long noun phrases

Lesson B
- Discuss job prospects
- Talk about your career plans using the future continuous and future perfect

Lesson C
- Introduce what you say with expressions like *What I read was*
- Say *I don't know if . . .* to introduce ideas

Lesson D
- Read an article on how to answer tough interview questions
- Write a cover letter for a job application

1

2

4

3

Before you begin . . .

Which of these areas of work are hard to get into? Which are easier?
Which are the highest paid? Which are the most popular with your friends?

- the media
- travel and tourism
- medicine

- law
- finance
- entertainment

- social work
- teaching
- trades (carpentry, plumbing)

117

What's the best way to go about choosing a career?

Laura
I think the first thing to do is to decide on an area you're interested in. And then do some research to find out what jobs you can do in that area. I mean, what I'd do first is talk to people and find out what jobs they do. And maybe find out more on the Internet. The main thing you need is lots of information.

Jacob
Yeah, for sure. What you should do is think about what you really enjoy doing with your time. And then see if you can make a career out of it. The good thing about that is you end up with a job you love. I guess what I'm saying is that you need to choose a career you'll really like.

Jason
Right. And one thing I would do is see a career counselor and take one of those personality tests to find out what your strengths and weaknesses are. And then the career counselors . . . well, what they do is tell you what kinds of jobs you'd be good at.

Jenny
Another thing you can do is apply for an internship with a company. The advantage of that is that you get some work experience while you're still in school. What a friend of mine did was interesting. What she did was call up a bunch of companies and offer to work for free on her vacations. She got some great experience that way.

1 Getting started

A Which of these do you think are the best three ways to choose a career? Tell the class.

- ☐ do an internship
- ☐ talk to a career counselor
- ☐ do research online
- ☐ go to a job fair
- ☐ take a personality test
- ☐ ask a friend for advice

B ◀)) 4.18 Listen to four students talk about ways to choose a career. Which of the ideas above do they mention? Check (✓) the ideas. What other ideas do they suggest?

Figure it out
C How do the people above say these things? Underline what they say in the discussion.

1. Jenny   A friend of mine did something interesting. She called up a bunch of companies.
2. Jacob   I guess I'm saying that you need to choose a career you'll really like.
3. Laura   First you need to decide on an area you're interested in.
4. Jason   I would see a career counselor.

2 Grammar *What* clauses; long noun phrase subjects ◀》 4.19

Extra practice p. 151

What clauses and long noun phrases introduce important information. They are often the subject of the verb *be*, which can be followed by a word or a phrase (noun, adjective, or verb) or by a clause.

What clauses	Long noun phrases
What you need is lots of information.	**The main thing you need** is information.
What my friend did was interesting.	**Something my friend did** was interesting.
What I would do is talk to people.	**The best thing to do** is (to) talk to people.
What I'm saying is (that) you need to choose a career you'll really like.	**The good thing about that** is (that) you end up with a job you love.

A Choose the best expression on the right to complete each sentence.
Once you've chosen a career, how do you go about getting your dream job?

1. Well, _____the best thing to do_____ is to make contacts and network with people. _____ is ask all my friends and family if they know anyone who could help me. _____ is it could help you get an interview.

   - the good thing about that
   - ✓ the best thing to do
   - what I would do

2. _____ is get some work experience. _____ is it helps you find out if you'd really like a job in that area. _____ is try it out first.

   - what I'm saying
   - the advantage of that
   - what I would do first

3. _____ was get an internship. She said _____ is a good reference letter. Then _____ was interesting. She just walked into several different companies and introduced herself.

   - the main thing you need
   - something my friend did
   - what she did

4. _____ is a good résumé. _____ was good. She got hers done professionally. _____ is you make a really good first impression.

   - the best thing about that
   - what my classmate did
   - what you need

About you **B** Pair work How would you go about getting your dream job? Discuss ideas.

A *What I'd do first is update my social networking site and say I'm looking for a job.*
B *That's a good idea. The best thing to do is tell all your contacts.*

3 Speaking naturally Stressing *I* and *you*

Anne *What would you do if you found your dream job and then hated it?*
Matt *I don't know. What would **you** do if **you** hated your dream job, Cate?*
Cate *I have no idea what I'd do.*
Enzo *I know what **I** would do. I'd quit immediately. Life's too short. How about **you**?*

A ◀》 4.20 Listen and repeat the conversation. Notice how *I* and *you* are sometimes stressed to make clear who you are talking about. Then practice and continue the conversation with a partner.

B Group work Discuss the questions. Stress *I* and *you* if you need to.

- What's the best way to choose a career?
- What have some of your friends done to find work?
- What can you do if you can't decide on a career?

Building vocabulary and grammar

A 🔊 **4.21** Listen and read the interviews. What career plans do these students have?

Where do you think you'll be working five years from now?

Well, I'll have finished my degree in media studies by then, and what I really want to do is get a job in **communications.** You won't be seeing me on TV or anything – I'm not cut out for that – but I may be working in, like, **publishing** or **journalism** as an **editor** or writer or something. Or maybe I'll have gotten a job in **advertising** or **public relations.** That would be fun.
– Ashley

Well, in two years, I'll be graduating with a degree in **nursing** – so I'll be working in the field of **health care.** One thing I think I'd like to do is be a **psychiatric nurse,** but I'm not sure. Hopefully my wife will have graduated from medical school by then, too. She'd like to be a **pediatrician** . . . or else a **surgeon.**
– Albert

I won't be doing what I'm doing now – **telemarketing** – that's for sure! This fall, I'll be starting a degree in **business management,** so in five years, I'll have graduated and gotten a job in the **construction industry.** I probably won't have had much experience, but I'll be working with **civil engineers, contractors, construction workers,** and so on. – Jesse

I don't really know. I just hope I'll be using my languages. I might be working as an **interpreter** or a **translator** – or maybe I'll be working in the **travel industry.** – Cheryl

Hopefully I'll be working as a **financial analyst** in an investment bank. My dad's a **stockbroker,** and my mom's a **tax adviser,** so I guess I'm following them into the **financial sector.** – Simone

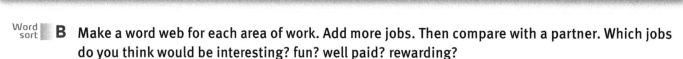

Word sort **B** Make a word web for each area of work. Add more jobs. Then compare with a partner. Which jobs do you think would be interesting? fun? well paid? rewarding?

Construction industry	Medicine and health care
Financial services	Travel industry
Media and communications	Sales and marketing

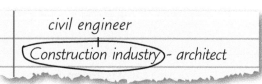

civil engineer

(*Construction industry*) - *architect*

Figure it out **C** Can you make these sentences true by changing the underlined words? Compare with a partner.

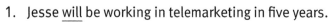
Vocabulary notebook p. 126

1. Jesse will be working in telemarketing in five years.
2. In two years, Albert won't be graduating with a degree in nursing.
3. Cheryl will be working as a translator five years from now.
4. Five years from now, Ashley will be studying for her degree in media studies.

2 **Grammar** The future continuous and future perfect ◄)) 4.22

Extra practice p. 151

Use the future continuous for ongoing activities in the future.
I'**ll be working** in health care.
I **won't be working** in this job.

Also use it for events you expect to happen.
I'**ll be graduating** in two years.
I'**ll be starting** a degree this fall.

You can use *might* and *may* instead of *will*.
I **may be working** in publishing.

Use the future perfect for events that are in the past when you "view" them from the future.
My wife **will have graduated** by then.
I probably **won't have had** much experience.

💬 **In conversation**

The future continuous is much more common than the future perfect.

A Complete the conversations using the future continuous or future perfect. Then practice with a partner.

1. A What do you think you'll _____ (do) five years from now?

    B I hope I'll _____ (work) as an architect. I'll _____ (finish) all the exams by then. How about you?

    A Well, by then I'll _____ (graduate), too – I hope to finish my nursing degree in two years. I might _____ (work) in a medical practice.

2. A Do you have any idea what your life will be like in ten years?

    B Well, I hope I'll _____ (enjoy) life. I think my boyfriend and I will _____ (get) married by then, and maybe we'll _____ (buy) our own home. I'm not sure if we'll _____ (start) a family, but if we have kids, I think I'll _____ (take) care of them, and I may _____ (work) part-time, too.

3. A What do you think you'll _____ (do) when you're 60?

    B Well, I probably won't _____ (stop) working, but I hope I won't _____ (work) long hours every day.

    A Me too. Maybe by then I'll _____ (retired), and I'll _____ (live) by the ocean.

4. A What kinds of jobs do you think people will _____ (do) 20 years from now?

    B I think more people will _____ (work) in health care because people will _____ (live) longer. Also the retirement age will _____ (rise), too, so people might still _____ (work) when they're 70.

^{About} **B** **Pair work** Ask and answer the questions. Give your own answers.
you Do you have similar hopes and dreams?

❌ **Common errors**

When you are making arrangements, use the future continuous to announce your intentions.

See you at 6. I'**ll be waiting** for *you in the lobby.* OR I'**ll wait** . . . (NOT ~~I'm waiting~~ . . .)

3 **Talk about it** Working lives

Group work Discuss the statements. Do you agree with them?

Ten years from now, . . .

▸ more people will be working from home.

▸ fewer people will have had a college education.

▸ people will be retiring at a younger age.

▸ people will still be learning English to help them with their careers.

▸ the working day will have become shorter.

 **Sounds right** p. 139

1 Conversation strategy Introducing what you say

A What kinds of summer jobs do students do? Make a list.

B 🔊 4.23 Listen to Jin-ho and Jenn. What does Jenn say about working at the theme park?

Jin-ho	Didn't you work in that theme park last summer?
Jenn	Yeah. In the ticket booth for the concert arena.
Jin-ho	Really? How was it? The reason I ask is I was wondering about applying for a job there myself.
Jenn	It was good. I mean, the best part was that I got to go on all the rides for free. I don't know if you know, but you get a free season pass.
Jin-ho	Cool.
Jenn	Yeah. And what I thought was really good was I got to see a lot of the concerts and meet some of the performers backstage.
Jin-ho	Great. Now, what I heard was that it's hard to get a job there.
Jenn	Well, yeah. What I was going to tell you was that they have a job fair in the spring. I don't know if you're familiar with one, but you go around the park and interview for different jobs.
Jin-ho	Yeah? Maybe I should go to that.

C Notice how Jin-ho and Jenn introduce what they say with expressions like these. Find the expressions they use.

What I thought was good was (that) . . .
The best part is / was (that) . . .
What I heard / read was (that) . . .
The reason I ask is (that) . . .
What I was going to tell you / say was (that) . . .

D 🔊 4.24 Listen. Write the expressions Jin-ho and Jenn use. Then practice.

1. **Jenn** Have you had any experience? _____ it helps when you have previous work experience.

   Jin-ho Actually, yeah. I worked in a restaurant one time. _____ I got good tips.

2. **Jin-ho** So what will you be doing during summer break?

   Jenn I'll be working as a camp counselor this year. My friend did it last year. She said it was great. _____ she got to go rafting and everything with the kids *and* she got paid for it.

3. **Jin-ho** How old were you when you got your first job? _____ my sister wants to work, but she's only 15.

   Jenn _____ you have to be 16 before you can get a job. But I'm not sure.

About you **E Pair work** Discuss the questions above. Give your own answers. Introduce what you say with expressions from the box.

2 Strategy plus *I don't know if...*

I don't know if...
can introduce a statement, often
to involve the other person in the topic.

> I don't know if you know, but you get a free season pass.

In conversation

Some of the most common expressions with *I don't know if* are:

I don't know if you've (ever) heard...
I don't know if you're familiar with...
I don't know if you've (ever) seen...

A Rewrite the sentences. Use *I don't know if* to introduce the topics.

1. Have you ever worked in a restaurant? It's really hard work.

   I don't know if you've ever worked in a restaurant, but it's really hard work.

2. Have you ever sent out your résumé? Often companies don't bother to reply.

3. Have you read about this? One of the most popular careers is engineering.

4. Do you know? The main thing employers want is reliable workers.

5. Have you heard? More and more people work while they're on vacation.

6. Are you familiar with all those jobs websites? You can post your résumé on them.

7. Did you read? 80% of people are not satisfied with their jobs.

8. Have you heard this? On average, people in the U.S. change jobs seven times before they turn 30.

B **Pair work** Take turns saying the sentences to start conversations.

3 Listening and strategies *An interesting job*

A ◄)) 4.25 Can you answer any of the questions below? Then listen to a personal trainer talk about her work. Which questions does she answer? Check (✓) the questions.

☐ What is a personal trainer's main role?
☐ Why do people hire personal trainers?
☐ How do you become a personal trainer?
☐ Is a personal trainer's job rewarding? Why?

☐ Are all trainers certified?
☐ What are the disadvantages of the job?
☐ How much do personal trainers earn?
☐ How do you find a good trainer?

B ◄)) 4.25 Listen again. How does the personal trainer answer the questions? Write two pieces of information for each question.

About you **C** **Group work** Discuss the questions.

• What's the most unusual or interesting job you've heard about?

• What jobs do people you know have? Which is the most challenging? Why?

• Are there any jobs that you really wouldn't want to do? Why not?

• What's the first job you ever did? Was it fun?

• What would be an exciting job? Why?

   "Well, I don't know if you've ever seen the work of an interior designer, but they seem to have a really interesting job. What I heard was..."

1 Reading

A What would you do to prepare for a job interview? Make a class list.

"One thing you need to do is research the company."

B Look at the three interview questions in the article. How would you answer them? Compare your ideas with a partner. Then read the article. How would you change your answers?

> **Reading tip**
>
> Try to predict the "great answers" to the questions before you read them.

---

http://www.jobhunting...

Ace that Interview! Tough Questions, Great Answers

Nothing can trip you up during an interview like an unexpected or difficult question. Whether you're applying for an internship, trying to get into college, or interviewing for a new job, here are a few questions that might stump you – along with the kinds of answers interviewers like to hear.

"Tell me about yourself."
Be ready to describe what makes you special as an individual. "What I *don't* want to hear is your life history," explains Dennis B., Director of Admissions at a major university. "I don't care how many siblings you have or where you were born. I want to know what makes you special. I want to see how well you project yourself, if you're articulate, and to hear your reasons for applying to do this course of study." The same applies at a job interview. Be concise and give concrete examples: "The main thing you should know about me is that while I was in college, I had a side job retrieving lost data from computers. I set up and marketed the business myself. I had 80 customers in the first year."

"What draws you to this line of work?"
Know what you're getting yourself into. "Publishing is a tough profession," says Tracy P., Editorial Director at a publishing house in New York City. "Unfortunately, some people want to get into it for the wrong reasons. Many candidates mention how much they love books and reading. However, that doesn't necessarily mean that editing or the business side of publishing is a good profession for you. You might be better suited to

teaching, for example. If someone doesn't understand the profession, the chances are they won't be a good fit for this type of work." In other words, show that you understand what the job involves in your response to the question and give an example of how you have acquired the relevant skills: "One skill you need to work in publishing is attention to detail. I worked on the college magazine and edited articles . . . "

"Tell me about a time you made a serious mistake. How did you handle it?"
"Many of our candidates get hired right after they graduate from college, before they've had a chance to get much work experience," notes Anita M., head of recruiting at a Fortune 500 financial company. "The reason I ask this question is that it's a tough question for everybody, and how a person answers is very revealing. It's important that people admit when they've made a mistake, rather than blame others. What I'm saying is that I expect candidates to be honest, and I look for signs that they've learned from the mistake." So, don't say you have never really made a mistake. Instead, try something along these lines: "One thing I did while I was working on a project in college was let down my team. I didn't complete my part of the project on time. I apologized. I also explained to the professor it was my fault and asked for an extension. Then I made it up to my teammates by working all weekend to finish the project. It taught me how to manage my time and not leave things until the last minute."

▶ **Remember:** Speak clearly and at a normal pace of conversation. Don't rush your words because you're nervous. Be calm and speak with confidence.

C Pair work Discuss your answers to the questions below.

1. What trips up some candidates during an interview, according to the article?
2. What mistake do some candidates make when they are asked to talk about themselves?
3. What two things do you need to tell an interviewer to show you're right for the job?
4. Why is it revealing when candidates talk about mistakes they have made?
5. Which question do you think is the most difficult one to answer? Why?

Listening and writing A fabulous opportunity!

A 🔊 **4.26** Read the online job advertisement. Can you guess the missing words? Then listen to Maria talk about the ad with her friend Alex. Were any of your guesses correct?

Job summary

Company
_____

Location
Montreal

Job type
- Part-time
- ○ Full-time

Tour Guide

A leading tour company is seeking someone who would enjoy meeting _____ from other countries. You must be fluent in _____ and _____ . You should be interested in the local area and its _____ . You'll be traveling around the region _____ days a week. Flexible, fun, and _____ applicants only.

Apply by email, and also send your _____ . Successful applicants will receive excellent pay and a generous benefits package.

[APPLY]

B 🔊 **4.26** Listen again. Why is Maria perfect for this job? Write four reasons.

C Imagine you want to apply for the job above. Read the Help note and write a cover letter like the one below.

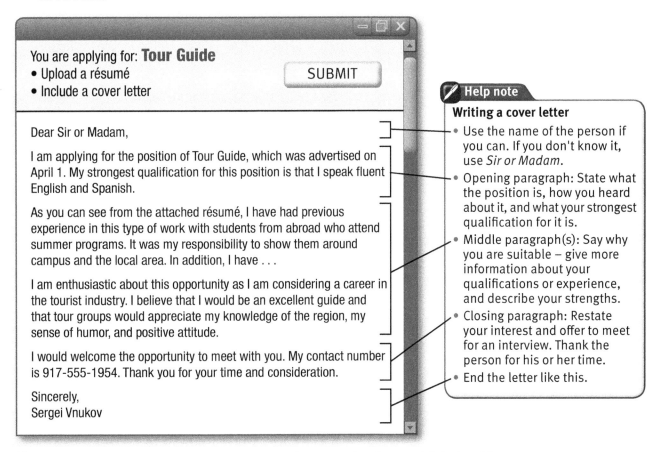

You are applying for: **Tour Guide**
- Upload a résumé
- Include a cover letter   [SUBMIT]

Dear Sir or Madam,

I am applying for the position of Tour Guide, which was advertised on April 1. My strongest qualification for this position is that I speak fluent English and Spanish.

As you can see from the attached résumé, I have had previous experience in this type of work with students from abroad who attend summer programs. It was my responsibility to show them around campus and the local area. In addition, I have . . .

I am enthusiastic about this opportunity as I am considering a career in the tourist industry. I believe that I would be an excellent guide and that tour groups would appreciate my knowledge of the region, my sense of humor, and positive attitude.

I would welcome the opportunity to meet with you. My contact number is 917-555-1954. Thank you for your time and consideration.

Sincerely,
Sergei Vnukov

Help note

Writing a cover letter
- Use the name of the person if you can. If you don't know it, use *Sir or Madam*.
- Opening paragraph: State what the position is, how you heard about it, and what your strongest qualification for it is.
- Middle paragraph(s): Say why you are suitable – give more information about your qualifications or experience, and describe your strengths.
- Closing paragraph: Restate your interest and offer to meet for an interview. Thank the person for his or her time.
- End the letter like this.

D **Group work** Read your classmates' cover letters. Who do you think should get the job?

Free talk p. 136

Vocabulary notebook / From accountant to zoologist

Learning tip *Word building with roots and collocations*

When you learn a new word, you can expand your vocabulary quickly by learning

- other words with the same root.
- some common collocations.

journalism   journalist

political journalist   freelance journalist

1 Complete the chart with the areas of work and the jobs.

Area of work	Job
accounting	accountant
architecture	
	carpenter
counseling	
	dentist
design	
editing	
	engineer
financial analysis	

Area of work	Job
	interpreter
law	
	manager
	nurse
pediatrics	
	photographer
physical therapy	
	plumber

Area of work	Job
psychiatry	
	psychologist
	publisher
sales	
	surgeon
telemarketing	
	translator
	zoologist

2 **Word builder** Match the words in **A** with the words in **B** to make common collocations. How many jobs can you make? Can you add any more words to make different job combinations?

A	
civil	psychiatric
construction	social
laboratory	systems
pediatric	

B	
analyst	technician
engineer	worker
nurse	

On your own

Find a jobs website. Write the names of 20 different jobs in English.

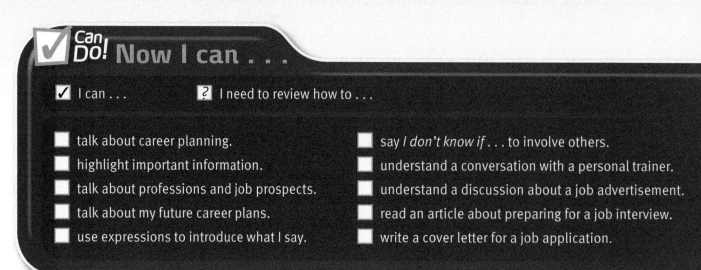

Now I can . . .

✓ I can . . .   ? I need to review how to . . .

- talk about career planning.
- highlight important information.
- talk about professions and job prospects.
- talk about my future career plans.
- use expressions to introduce what I say.

- say *I don't know if . . .* to involve others.
- understand a conversation with a personal trainer.
- understand a discussion about a job advertisement.
- read an article about preparing for a job interview.
- write a cover letter for a job application.

1 Talking about jobs

Match the two parts of each sentence. Then discuss them with a partner. Add ideas and expressions like *and so on*, *and so forth*, and *etc.*

1. Being a surgeon is very rewarding, __c__
2. Stockbrokers are under a lot of stress _____
3. It's easy to get health-care jobs these days _____
4. Workers are being brought into the country _____
5. Plan your career in five-year blocks _____
6. More students are taking media studies, _____
7. There are fewer telemarketing jobs _____

a. even though really good jobs are hard to get.
b. in order to fill all the jobs in construction.
c. in spite of the long hours you have to work.
d. so that you can set realistic goals.
e. because of the shortage of nurses.
f. as a result of outsourcing to other countries.
g. due to the constant changes in financial markets.

"I imagine being a surgeon is rewarding, in spite of the long hours and the stress and so on."

2 How many words can you think of?

A Add six words and expressions to each category, and compare with a partner.

Being famous	The environment
in the headlines	

B **Pair work** Choose four items from each category to use in a conversation. How many different expressions can you remember to introduce what you say?

A I don't know if you've heard, but Angelina Jolie is in the headlines right now.
B Oh, yeah. What I heard was she recently . . .

3 What will life be like in 2030?

A Complete the sentences using the future continuous or future perfect.

1. Hopefully, by 2030, people _will be buying_ (buy) more and more environmentally friendly products, and we _____ (find) new ways to save energy, so we _____ (live) in a cleaner environment.

2. Ideally, we _____ (slow) global warming by then. We _____ (not use) fuels like coal anymore. More countries _____ (start) to use cleaner, more efficient fuels.

3. By 2030, people _____ (eat) healthier food, and the number of obese people _____ (decrease).

4. Because we _____ (live) longer, the percentage of older people in society _____ (rise) by then.

B **Group work** Discuss the sentences. Refer back to what people say with expressions like *As you said*, *Like you were saying*, and *Going back to . . . .* Add your opinions.

4 What if . . . ?

"I applied for an internship at a public relations company after college. At the end of my interview, they offered me a job. Now, 20 years later, I'm still there, and I'm vice president."
– Alice

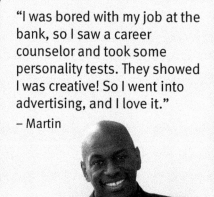

"I was bored with my job at the bank, so I saw a career counselor and took some personality tests. They showed I was creative! So I went into advertising, and I love it."
– Martin

"I was going to major in math at college, but I got sick the first week and had to drop out. In the hospital, I got interested in nursing, and so now, here I am – a pediatric nurse."
– Alfonso

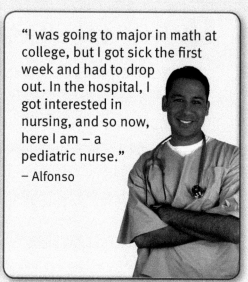

A Read the comments above. How might these people's lives have been different? Write sentences using *if* + the past perfect form and *would have*, *could have*, or *may / might have*.

If Alice hadn't applied for an internship at that company, she wouldn't have ended up working there.

B **Pair work** Talk about three big decisions you've made in life. Ask and answer hypothetical questions. If a question is difficult to answer, use an expression like *Good question*.

5 Check it out.

What do you know about your partner? Complete the sentences, adding tag questions. Then ask your partner.

1. You live in _____ , <u>*don't you*</u> ?
2. You've studied English for _____ years, _____ ?
3. You don't like _____ music, _____ ?
4. You're a _____ , _____ ?
5. You went to _____ on vacation once, _____ ?

6 Any suggestions?

Complete the sentences using the passive of the present continuous or present perfect. Then role-play with a partner. Take turns making suggestions.

1. "We *'re being given* (give) too much homework these days."
2. "I _____ (ask) to do volunteer work, but I'm too busy."
3. "I _____ (promote) at work, but I prefer my old job!"
4. "People _____ (lay off) at work recently. I'm worried because I _____ (pay) more than my co-workers."

A We're being given too much homework these days.
B You could talk to your teacher about it, couldn't you?

^{UNIT} **1** An interview with . . .

1 Think of interesting things to ask a classmate. Complete the questions below with your own ideas.

How long have you been _____ ?

When did you last _____ ?

What's your favorite _____ ?

Have you ever tried _____ ?

What do you like to _____ ?

Who do you _____ ?

What do you remember about _____ ?

What were you doing _____ ?

How did you end up _____ ?

2 **Pair work** Take turns asking and answering your questions. Give as many details as you can.

A *So, how long have you been living in this city?*
B *Oh, for about two years. My dad got a job here. He was working for this big company and . . .*

3 **Class activity** Share the most interesting questions and answers with the class.

^{UNIT} **2** What's popular?

Group work Discuss the questions. Do you agree on your answers?

TV	Fashion	Cars	Hairstyles
• What TV shows are popular?	• What's in fashion right now?	• Which cars are popular right now?	• Which hairstyles are trendy right now?
• Have TV shows gotten better or worse in the last five years?	• Do you like the new styles as much as last year's?	• What kind of car would you like?	• How have hairstyles changed over the last few years? Has yours?

Music	Food	Technology	Personal tastes
• What bands are popular right now?	• What diets and foods are popular?	• What gadgets are popular at the moment?	• How have your personal tastes changed over the last five years – for example, in fashion, music, and food?
• Have you downloaded any songs lately? Which ones?	• Is your diet as healthy as it could be?	• What are some popular apps for phones and tablets?	

"Well, talent shows are still popular, but I don't watch them as often as I used to."

129

UNIT 3 Traditions

1 You have two minutes. Write ideas that your classmates might not think of.

Think of . . .

- a traditional instrument. _____
- a national holiday. _____
- a national sport. _____
- a traditional handicraft. _____
- a festival. _____
- a folk song. _____
- a national food or dish. _____

2 **Pair work** Ask your partner questions. Try to guess the things on his or her list.

A *OK, so what is your instrument made from?*

B *It's made from wood.*

A *And where is it played?*

UNIT 5 Do you agree?

1 **Pair work** What is your opinion about the issues below? Think of two or more reasons to support your view on each topic.

"Well, to be honest, I think they should, for two reasons. First of all, . . . "

Do you think . . .	Name
1. manufacturers should be made to produce only energy-efficient appliances?	
2. consumers should be encouraged to stop using plastic bags?	
3. schools should be required to provide only healthy food for lunches?	
4. 16-year-olds should be allowed to vote in some types of elections?	
5. vending machines with candy and soda should be banned from schools?	
6. the speed limit should be reduced to 20 miles per hour (32 kilometers per hour) on all city streets?	
7. homework should not be given to students before high school?	
8. elementary school students should be required to take a national reading test?	
9. manufacturers should be forced to produce cars that don't use gasoline?	
10. the parents of children who regularly skip classes should be fined?	

2 **Class activity** Now survey your classmates. Find someone who answers no to each question. Find out why. Write his or her name in the chart above.

UNIT
4 Pass on the message

Class activity You are going to play a message game. Follow the instructions below.

STEP 1 Write your name on a piece of paper, fold it, and put it on your teacher's desk. Then pick another piece of paper from the pile. Read the name, but keep it a secret.

STEP 2 Think of a place you'd like to go with the person whose name you picked. Complete the chart with information about your plans.

a place you would like to go	
when you would like to go	
what you would like to do or see	
what the event is supposed to be like	
a time and a place to meet	
what the weather is supposed to be like	
what to wear	
how much it costs	
one thing to bring along	

STEP 3 **Pair work** Follow the instructions below, and then change roles.

Student A: Ask your partner to pass on a message to the person on your paper. Make sure you give all the details of your plans.

Student B: Listen carefully to your partner's message. You have to pass the message on later, so check your understanding!

A *Please tell Rodrigo I'd like to go to a concert in Riverside Park with him tonight. There's a band playing, and they're supposed to be really good. Tell him . . .*

B *Ok. Wait. So you're going to Riverside Park, right?*

STEP 4 Pass on the message you have just heard. Then listen to the message for you. Do you want to go to the event? Are you free?

"So, Rodrigo, Andrew would like you to go to a concert with him tonight. The band's supposed to be really good, and . . . "

UNIT **6** **What do you believe in?**

Group work Discuss the topics below. What are your views?

Childhood beliefs Children often believe in things that are not true (e.g., the tooth fairy). What did you believe in as a child? What do you think about parents who encourage their children to believe in these things?

Good fortune Some people seem to be luckier than others. Why is this? Are you a lucky person? Tell about a time you were lucky.

Aliens A lot of people believe that there is life on other planets. Do you? Do you believe the stories about alien spacecraft that have been sighted around the world?

Coincidences Some people say that coincidences are just events that we notice. Other people think that everything happens for a reason. Do you agree? What coincidences have you or your friends experienced?

Dreams Some people think that dreams are a way of making decisions about your life – and that they tell you important messages. Do you agree? Have you ever "listened" to a dream?

"I used to believe in the tooth fairy. Every time I lost a tooth, I'd put it under my pillow. Then, in the morning, the tooth was gone, and there would be some money. Of course, it came from my parents! It's funny. But I think it's nice to keep traditions like that."

UNIT **7** **Who gets help with something?**

Class activity Ask and answer the questions. Find someone who answers yes. Ask questions to find out more information.

Do you know anyone who . . .
- gets family photos taken professionally?
- got someone to run an errand for them recently?
- has something at home that needs to be fixed?
- is having their house decorated?
- often gets a friend to help with homework?
- likes to get pizza delivered at home?
- got a tech center to solve a computer problem recently?
- owns something that is old and needs replacing?

8 How did you react?

1 Think of a time an incident happened to you. Use the ideas below or one of your own.

something went wrong with a cab ride	someone got mad at you
you yelled at someone	you had to get out of a date or appointment
you were late for something	someone was rude to you

2 Prepare your story about the incident to tell the group. What happened? How did you react? How did the people around you react? Think of as many details as you can.

3 Group work Take turns telling your stories. Listen to your classmates' stories. Ask questions. Think about what happened and say why. Have you had a similar thing happen to you? Tell the group.

> So one time, I was driving with my friend, and this car was behind us, and the driver was trying to get past us. And he kept honking and flashing his lights. And my friend got really mad and called the police on his cell phone . . .

> The driver behind you must have been in a hurry. He could have been on his way to the hospital.

> Yeah, but he shouldn't have driven like that. It's dangerous.

> I had something like that happen to me one time. . . .

10 Quotations

1 Group work Look at the quotations below. Do you agree with them? Which one is your favorite?

> A man is a success if he gets up in the morning and gets to bed at night, and in between does what he wants to do.   — Bob Dylan

> Having a lot of money does not automatically make you a successful person. What you want is money and meaning. You want your work to be meaningful, because meaning is what brings the real richness to your life.
> — Oprah Winfrey

> You don't have to be famous. You just have to make your mother and father proud of you.
> — Meryl Streep

> Success is a state of mind. If you want success, start thinking of yourself as a success.
> — Dr. Joyce Brothers

> All you need in this life is ignorance and confidence; then success is sure.
> — Mark Twain

> Success is really about being ready for the good opportunities that come before you.
> — Eric Schmidt

2 Can you think up your own definition of "success"? Complete the sentence below.

Success is _____ .

3 Class activity Now go around the class and find out your classmates' definitions. Choose the two you like best, and write them down with your classmates' names. Then share your new "quotations" with the class.

9 Material things

1 Complete the questions below with your own ideas on the topic of "material things."

Material things

1. Can you imagine life without _____ ?
2. How many _____ do you own?
3. Have you ever bought _____ ?
4. Are you good at _____ ?
5. _____ money?
6. When did you last _____ ?
7. Do you think you'll ever own a _____ ?
8. Do you think people _____ ?

2 **Pair work** Ask and answer your questions. Remember the questions your partner asks.

3 **Pair work** Find a new partner. Tell each other the questions you were asked, and say how you answered them.

"Mario asked me if I could imagine life without the Internet. I told him I had to go without the Internet last weekend, and it was awful!"

^{UNIT} **11** **What's trending?**

1 **Pair work** Look at the topics below. What trends have you noticed in each of these areas? Brainstorm ideas and make a list.

education

lifestyle

communications

entertainment

> education
> online learning and webinars
> more testing

2 **Group work** Join another pair. Discuss the trends on your list. What are they a result of? What impact do you think they will have? Can you predict any trends for the future in these areas?

 A *Well, online learning is definitely being introduced into schools in this area.*

 B *It's interesting, don't you think? I mean, why is that?*

 C *I think it's a result of the demand for more flexible learning opportunities.*

UNIT **12** The best person for the job

1 Look at the different jobs below. Choose a job that you'd like to apply for, and prepare for a job interview. Think of answers to the following questions.

- Why are you interested in this job?
- What experience and qualifications do you have?
- What are your main strengths and weaknesses?
- What qualities do you think someone needs to do this job well?
- Where do you see yourself in five years?

Help Wanted

OFFICE ASSISTANT

Office assistant needed in busy head office of an international trading company. Needs good computer skills and customer service skills.

TUTORS

Tutors needed in English and Math to teach first-year college students who need extra help in these subjects.

STUDENT COUNSELORS

Student counselors needed by foreign student exchange agency to assist students from overseas with all aspects of life in a foreign country.

TECHNOLOGY STAFF

Major technology company needs part-time staff to set up exhibitions around the country, and explain the features of our new products, including cameras and cell phones.

2 **Group work** "Interview" each person for the job they want to apply for. Take turns asking the questions above. At the end of the interview, hold a group vote, and decide if the person should be hired.

"So, Amelie, why are you interested in a job as a student counselor?"

UNIT 1 🔊 **4.27** Listen and repeat the verbs. Is the stress in each verb like the stress in *bother*, *agree*, or *consider*? Write the words from the list in the correct columns below.

1. begin
2. continue
3. decide
4. expect
5. finish
6. happen
7. imagine
8. intend
9. offer
10. remember

• ● **bother**	• ● **agree**	• ● • **consider**
	begin	

UNIT 2 🔊 **4.28** Listen and repeat the pairs of words. Notice the underlined sounds. Are the sounds the same (S) or different (D)? Write *S* or *D*.

1. sh**oe** / c**ool** ___S___
2. b**oo**t / w**oo**l _____
3. fl**are**d / sc**ar**ves _____
4. atten**ti**on / styli**sh** _____
5. b**a**ggy / pl**ai**d _____
6. c**o**lor / s**o**lid _____
7. ca**sh**mere / fa**sh**ion _____
8. p**o**lka-dot / p**o**lyester _____
9. scr**u**ffy / c**o**mfortable _____

UNIT 3 🔊 **4.29** Listen and repeat the words. Notice the underlined sounds. Match the words with the same underlined sounds.

1. **a**ffection ___e___
2. b**ar**gain _____
3. d**ow**n _____
4. k**ee**p _____
5. p**oi**nt _____
6. sh**ow**ing _____
7. w**ear** _____

a. b**are**foot
b. b**ow**ing
c. c**ar**ved
d. h**o**lding
e. **o**ffend
f. p**eo**ple
g. v**oi**ce

UNIT 4 🔊 **4.30** Listen and repeat the expressions. Check (✓) the expressions in which the *t* in *get* sounds like a quick *d*. (Hint: Look at the sound that follows *get*.)

☑ 1. ge**t** around to
☐ 2. ge**t** away with
☐ 3. ge**t** going
☐ 4. ge**t** home
☐ 5. ge**t** off
☐ 6. ge**t** out of
☐ 7. ge**t** over
☐ 8. ge**t** ready
☐ 9. ge**t** the feeling

Sounds right

UNIT 5

🔊 **4.31** Listen and repeat the words. Notice the underlined sounds. Which sound in each group is different? Circle the word with the sound that's different.

1. ag̲ainst   arre̲st   freed̲om   (kidnapper)
2. inva̲s̲ion   proba̲t̲ion   puni̲sh   s̲hould
3. k̲illing   shopli̲ft   vandali̲sm   v̲iolent
4. c̲aught   l̲aw   o̲ught   y̲oung
5. j̲ail   leg̲al   maj̲ority   manag̲e
6. licen̲se   pri̲son   privac̲y   s̲entenced

UNIT 6

🔊 **4.32** Listen and repeat the words. Notice the underlined sounds. These words have the sound /y/ or /w/ before the underlined sounds, although the letters *y* and *w* don't appear. Circle the correct sound.

1. any̲one   /y/ or (/w/)
2. Austral̲ian   /y/ or /w/
3. be̲autiful   /y/ or /w/
4. co̲incidence   /y/ or /w/
5. comput̲er   /y/ or /w/
6. E̲urope   /y/ or /w/
7. lang̲uage   /y/ or /w/
8. m̲usic   /y/ or /w/
9. q̲uestion   /y/ or /w/
10. q̲uiet   /y/ or /w/
11. s̲uede   /y/ or /w/
12. unus̲ual   /y/ or /w/

UNIT 7

🔊 **4.33** Listen and repeat the words. Notice the underlined sounds. Are the sounds like the sounds in *enjo̲y*, *cho̲ose*, *do̲ne*, *s̲erviced*, *s̲traight*, or *t̲here*? Write the words from the list in the correct columns below.

1. adj̲ust
2. c̲urtains
3. decor̲ate
4. em̲ergency
5. fl̲ooded
6. h̲air
7. n̲oise
8. o̲il
9. p̲aint
10. rep̲air
11. r̲outine
12. scr̲ewdriver

enjo̲y	cho̲ose	do̲ne	s̲erviced	s̲traight	t̲here
		adjust			

UNIT 8

🔊 **4.34** Listen and repeat the pairs of words. Notice the underlined sounds. Are the sounds the same (S) or different (D)? Write *S* or *D*.

1. str̲essed / d̲ead   _S_
2. em̲otional / g̲otten ____
3. a̲ggressive / a̲ngry ____
4. j̲ealous / intelli̲gent ____
5. s̲hould / motiva̲tion ____
6. de̲cisive / di̲scipline ____
7. aggre̲ssion / depre̲ssed ____
8. sy̲mpathetic / g̲uilty ____
9. c̲onfidence / h̲onesty ____

UNIT 9 🔊 **4.35** Listen and repeat the words. Underline the silent letter in each word.

1. answer   3. debt   5. honest   7. sign   9. could   11. half
2. budget   4. gadget   6. should   8. walk   10. might   12. listen

UNIT 10 🔊 **4.36** Listen and repeat the words. Notice that one or more syllables in each word are unstressed. They have a weak vowel which sounds like the /ə/ sound in *person*. Circle the weak vowels.

1. album   4. confidence   7. famous   10. recently
2. amazing   5. connections   8. happened   11. seminar
3. career   6. extra   9. millionaire   12. talent

UNIT 11 🔊 **4.37** Listen and repeat the words. Notice the underlined sounds. Which sound in each group is different? Circle the word with the sound that's different.

1. consumption   natural   ocean   shortage
2. congestion   energy   garbage   gas
3. conserve   consume   recycle   rising
4. carbon   outsource   warming   warning
5. change   chemical   packaging   technology
6. because   brought   drought   talk

UNIT 12 🔊 **4.38** Listen and repeat the words. Notice the underlined sounds. Are the sounds like the sounds in *analyst*, *apply*, *construction*, *engineer*, *personality*, or *recruit*? Write the words from the list in the correct columns below.

1. advertising   7. experience
2. business   8. psychiatric
3. choose   9. publishing
4. career   10. research
5. civil   11. surgeon
6. love   12. school

analyst	apply	construction	engineer	personality	recruit
	advertising				

Extra practice

Lesson A Simple and continuous verbs (review)

> **✗ Common errors**
>
> Avoid continuous forms with verbs like *believe, know, like,* and *want.*
>
> ***Have you known*** each other for long?
> (NOT ~~Have you been knowing each other for long~~?)

A Complete the questions. Use the correct forms of the verbs given.

1. What _____were_____ you _____doing_____ (do) at this time last week?
2. _____Ded_____ you _____play_____ (play) a sport last weekend?
3. What kind of music _____do_____ you _____like_____ (like) nowadays?
4. How long _____have_____ you _____known_____ (know) your best friend?
5. Who _____do_____ you usually _____spend_____ (spend) time with on weekends?
6. How often _____do_____ you _____go_____ (go) to the movies?
7. _____Ded_____ you _____travel_____ (travel) somewhere interesting on your last vacation?
8. How long _____have_____ you _____been_____ (learn) English?
   _____learning_____

About you B Pair work Ask and answer the questions above with a partner.

Lesson B Verb complements: Verb + *-ing* or *to* + verb

A Complete the conversations with the correct forms of the verbs. Sometimes there is more than one correct answer.

> **ℹ Note**
>
> Notice the difference in meaning:
> *I remember paying the bill.*
> (I remember now – I paid it before.)
> *I remembered to pay the bill.*
> (I remembered, then I paid it after.)

1. A Why did you decide _____to study_____ (study) English?
   B I'm considering _____getting_____ (get) into hotel management, and hotels expect you _____to speak_____ (speak) English well.

2. A What are you planning on _____doing_____ (do) tonight?
   B Well, I'm thinking about _____going_____ (go) to the movies.
   A Well, if you go, remember _____to call_____ (call) me.

3. A Do you remember _____meeting_____ (meet) your best friend for the first time?
   B Let me think . . . I guess I don't remember the exact moment we met, but I know we really liked _____to play/_____ (play) together when we were little kids.
   _____playing_____

4. A What do you intend _____to do_____ (do) next summer?
   B I'm going to stop _____working_____ (work) at the beginning of August so I can spend a couple of weeks _____relaxing_____ (relax) at the beach.

5. A Are you going to continue _____taking_____ (take) English classes after you've finished this course?
   B Yes, I definitely want to keep on _____learning_____ (learn) English!

6. A Do you remember _____getting_____ (get) your first-ever job?
   B Yeah. I worked in this new store. Luckily, I remembered _____to show up_____ (show up) early, because they did the training an hour before we started.

About you B Pair work Take turns asking and answering the questions above.

UNIT 2 — Lesson A Comparisons with *(not) as . . . as . . .*

A Complete the *b* statements so they have the same meaning as the *a* statements. Use *(not) as . . . as . . .*

Common errors

Don't use *so* instead of *as*.

*She wears **as** many bright colors **as** she can.*
(NOT *She wears ~~so many bright colors as~~ she can.*)

1. a. Sneakers are more comfortable than boots.
   b. Boots _____ .
2. a. Women usually dress more fashionably than men.
   b. Men _____ .
3. a. I like pastels more than bright colors.
   b. I don't like bright colors _____ .
4. a. Long hair and short hair are equally stylish.
   b. Short hair _____ .
5. a. I spend very little money on clothes – the least possible.
   b. I spend _____ .
6. a. Women and men both have to work hard to look stylish.
   b. Men have to _____ .
7. a. When I buy shoes, I pay the most I can afford.
   b. When I buy shoes, I pay _____ .
8. a. Designer clothes and clothes from cheap stores can look equally stylish.
   b. Clothes from cheap stores _____ .

About you **B** **Pair work** Do you agree with the *b* statements above? Tell a partner.

UNIT 2 — Lesson B Negative questions

A Complete the negative questions in the conversations with *isn't*, *aren't*, *don't*, or *doesn't*. Then practice with a partner.

1. A _____ you love these shoes?
   B I'm not crazy about them, actually. I mean, _____ that style kind of boring?

2. A _____ these glasses cool?
   B Yeah, they're great. _____ they kind of expensive, though?

3. A I'm thinking about changing my hair. _____ this a great style?
   B I don't know. _____ it seem too short?

4. A _____ this sweater seem a little too bright for me? I'm afraid I'd never wear it.
   B Really? _____ you like bright colors?

About you **B** **Practice the conversations. Replace B's lines with your own opinions. Then change roles.**

Extra practice

UNIT 3 Lesson A The simple present passive

A Complete the conversations. Use the simple present active or passive form of the verbs given.

1. A What _____ people _____ (wear) during Carnival in Latin America?
   B Lots of people _____ costumes.

2. A What _____ Chinese children _____ (give) by their parents on New Year's?
   B They _____ red envelopes filled with money.

3. A What's the most popular sport that _____ (play) by men and women?
   B Well, soccer _____ by both men and women. So I guess it's soccer.

4. A What _____ people _____ (eat) on Thanksgiving in the United States?
   B Most people _____ turkey.

5. A In Korea, _____ Children's Day _____ (celebrate) in May or in June?
   B It _____ in May.

6. A What kinds of things _____ (buy) during the holidays in the U.S.?
   B It depends on the holiday. Like on the Fourth of July, people _____ fireworks and stuff.

7. A What kinds of events _____ (hold) during the traditional festivals in Japan?
   B Well, people _____ (dance), and lanterns _____ (put) in front of the houses. It's really pretty.

About you B Pair work Write five questions about holidays or festivals in your country. Use the passive. Then take turns asking a partner your questions. Can you answer your partner's questions?

A *So, when is the Dragon Boat Festival celebrated?*
B *That's easy. It's celebrated in June.*

UNIT 3 Lesson B Verb + -ing and to + verb; position of not

A Write the sentences about texting etiquette another way. Use verb + -ing or to + verb.

1. Texting during class is not acceptable. *It's not acceptable to text during class.*
2. It's impolite to text friends when you're having dinner with someone. _____
3. Texting too many times in a day can offend people. _____
4. Not responding to a text message immediately is acceptable. _____
5. It's appropriate to read text messages during a business meeting. _____
6. Letting your text messages beep during a meeting is not acceptable. _____
7. It's OK not to spell words out in full in emails. _____
8. Sending a lot of texts to someone is bad manners. _____

About you B Pair work Discuss the statements above. Do you agree with them? Why or why not?

UNIT 4

Lesson A *be supposed to; was / were going to*

A Rewrite the sentences with the correct form of *be supposed to* or *was / were going to*.

1. I expected my boyfriend to arrive at 7:00 tonight, but he didn't show up until 9:00.

    My boyfriend was supposed to arrive at 7:00, but he didn't show up until 9:00.

2. You should bring a small gift when you go to a friend's house for dinner.

    _____

3. I heard there'll be a storm this weekend.

    _____

4. I wanted to send out invitations to my birthday party, but I didn't have time.

    _____

5. My sister planned to have a party this weekend, but then she decided not to.

    _____

6. I'm planning to go to a concert tonight. My friends say it's going to be fun.

    _____

About you **B** Pair work Make a list of things you're supposed to do and not supposed to do in English class. Is there anything you were supposed to do last week for English class but didn't do?

UNIT 4

Lesson B Inseparable phrasal verbs

A Rewrite the underlined parts of the sentences using an expression in the box.

get along with	get away with	get over	get through to
get around to	✓ get out of	get through	look forward to

get out of them

1. I find work parties boring. I usually try to <u>avoid them</u>.

2. It takes me ages to <u>find time to return friends' calls</u>. I'm surprised I have any friends.

3. If a friend tells me a lie, I never <u>stop being upset by it</u>. I never trust that person again.

4. I'm not good at buying gifts for people, so I usually try to <u>avoid criticism and buy</u> gift cards.

5. It annoys me when friends can't <u>make it to the end of dinner</u> without looking at their phones.

6. My dad wants a big party for my twenty-first birthday. I hate parties, but he won't listen, and I can't <u>make him understand</u>.

7. My friends are all pretty easygoing. I <u>have a great relationship with</u> them all.

8. I like to spend Friday evenings all by myself. I <u>can't wait for</u> them.

i Note

Other inseparable phrasal verbs + prepositions are: *get along with, look forward to, get through to* (= make someone understand)

About you **B** Pair work Make the sentences above true for you. Then read your sentences to a partner.

Extra practice

Lesson A The passive of modal verbs

A Complete the conversations with the active or passive form of the verbs given.

1. A I think 15-year-olds _____ (should / allow) to have jobs. They're old enough.

    B Well, I think they _____ (should / spend) their time studying, not working.

    A Yes, but I still think they _____ (ought to / give) a choice about whether to work.
       Some kids _____ (need to / earn) money, and they _____
       (should / encourage) to work.

2. A People _____ (should / not / allow) to get credit cards until they're 21. They're not
       responsible enough.

    B But young people _____ (need to / learn) to manage their money, don't they?

    A Yes, but they _____ (not / have to / give) credit cards. They _____
       (could / use) debit cards instead.

3. A Something _____ (ought / do) about dangerous drivers who've caused an accident.
       Maybe their licenses _____ (could / take) away for life or something.

    B But people learn from mistakes. They _____ (should / not / lose) their licenses forever.

    A Well, maybe they _____ (should / required) to take a driving test every year, then.

About you **B** **Pair work** For each conversation above, do you agree with speaker A or speaker B? Give reasons
for your opinions.

UNIT
5 **Lesson B** *get* passive vs. *be* passive

A Complete the comments on transportation in other countries. Use
the *get* or *be* passive with the verbs given. Both forms are possible.

> **i Note**
> After a modal verb (e.g.,
> *can, should*, etc.), you can
> use a *get* passive, but *be*
> passives are over 90 times
> more frequent.

1. People who _____ (catch) speeding in Norway can
    _____ (fine) 10 percent of their annual income. Sometimes
    they _____ (sentence) to 18 days in jail, too. That's pretty
    harsh. I mean, they should just _____ (sentence) to
    community service instead. – *Lars, Norway*

2. Here in Germany, people _____ (not / arrest) for speeding on the freeway because many
    areas don't have a speed limit. I love to drive fast, so I definitely think these laws should
    _____ (not / change). But you know, people _____ (fine) for running out of gas on
    the freeway. I guess it's dangerous, so . . . – *Lena, Germany*

3. It's interesting, but in some European countries, if your car breaks down, and you get out of the car
    without a visibility vest, you could _____ (fine). I really think laws like that should
    _____ (not / enforce). Actually, things like that should _____ (not / make) into
    laws at all. It should be your own choice. – *Jill, United States*

About you **B** **Pair work** What do you think about the laws above? What laws are there about driving in your
country? Are they fair? Are there any laws that should be changed?

UNIT **6**

Lesson A The past perfect

A Complete the blog post with the simple past or past perfect. Sometimes both are possible.

www.adrianbowensblog...

Was it a just a coincidence?   posted by Adrian Bowen

I have some good news for everyone! It's a long story, but . . . in my last year of high school, in California, I _____ (have) a girlfriend named Sophia. We _____ (meet) two years earlier when we were both playing on the softball team. After we graduated, she _____ (move) to Texas because she _____ (get) a place at a culinary school there. After a few months, she _____ (break up) with me because she _____ (meet) someone else. I was very upset, but I accepted it because we _____ (not / see) each other since graduation. Eventually I _____ (get) a job in Chicago. Before I left California, I _____ (try) to contact Sophia and her family, but no one _____ (return) my calls. Then, last month, I _____ (go) to the grocery store, and there was Sophia, in line at the checkout. It turned out she _____ (get) a job in Chicago a month earlier, and she _____ (move) into an apartment on my street! It was weird because I _____ (spend) a whole year trying to contact her. And the best thing was that Sophia _____ (miss) me, too. Anyway, to make a long story short, we're now planning to get married. Maybe it wasn't a coincidence after all!

B **Pair work** Read Adrian's blog again. Then close your books. Take turns telling the story. How much detail can you remember?

UNIT **6**

Lesson B Responses with *So* and *Neither*

A Read the conversations. Circle the correct responses. There may be more than one. Then practice with a partner.

> **✕ Common errors**
>
> The past perfect is *had* + past participle. Don't use *had* + simple past.
>
> *I'd* just **seen** . . .
> (NOT *I'd* just ~~saw~~ . . .)

1. A When I was a kid, I never went anywhere without my good luck charm.
    B Really? That's funny. **Neither was I.** /**(Neither did I.)**/ **I did too.** /**(I didn't either.)**

2. A So many people claim they've seen UFOs, but I've never seen one.
    B **Neither have I.** / **I wasn't either.** / **I haven't either.** Actually, I don't believe they exist.

3. A I always make a wish before I blow out the candles on my birthday cake.
    B **I am too.** / **So do I.** / **I don't either.** But my wishes never come true!

4. A A few times, I've had the strange feeling I've been somewhere before – you know, like *déjà vu*.
    B **So have I.** / **I haven't either.** / **I am too.** It's weird, isn't it?

5. A I'm always losing things – my umbrella, my keys, and stuff like that.
    B **So am I.** / **So do I.** / **Neither did I.** / **I am too.** I guess we're both a bit forgetful.

6. A Something weird happened to me once. Like really weird. I had a dream, and it came true.
    B Really? **So did I.** / **Neither did I.** / **I did too.** / **I was too.** Actually, it scared me a little.

7. A Some people believe in telepathy, but not me. I don't believe you can read people's minds.
    B **Neither do I.** / **I'm not either.** / **I don't either.** I never know what other people are thinking.

About you **B** **Pair work** Practice the conversations again, this time making the sentences true for you and giving true responses.

Extra practice

Lesson A Causative *get* and *have*

A Complete the sentences. Use the verbs given.

1. I don't have my clothes ___cleaned___ (clean) professionally.
2. We usually have my brother _____ (repair) things around the house.
3. My friends get me _____ (fix) their computer problems.
4. I've never had my hair _____ (color).
5. I often get my sister _____ (cook) for me.
6. My neighbor gets his windows _____ (wash) every week.
7. When I throw a party, I get friends _____ (help) me.
8. I don't have my car _____ (service) regularly.
9. I always get people _____ (help) me when I try to fix anything in the house.
10. I don't buy new shoes very often. I like to get them _____ (repair). In fact, I'm having a pair of boots _____ (repair) right now.

About you **B** **Pair work** Are the sentences above true for you? How do you get these things done? Discuss with a partner.

Lesson B *need* + passive infinitive and *need* + verb + *-ing*

A Complete the list of things that need doing in Mia's apartment.

- *front door doesn't close — fix the lock*
- *some lights don't work — change the bulbs*
- *large crack in window — replace the glass*
- *shelves in kitchen aren't straight — adjust them*
- *TV making a strange noise — repair it*
- *leaking bathroom faucet — tighten the faucet*
- *dirty rug — clean it*
- *stain on kitchen wall — paint it*

1. The lock needs ___to be fixed / fixing___ .
2. Some bulbs need _____ .
3. The glass in the window needs _____ .
4. The shelves need _____ .
5. The TV needs _____ .
6. The faucet needs _____ .
7. The rug needs _____ .
8. The wall needs _____ .

> **In conversation**
>
> ***need*** + passive infinitive is more common than ***need*** + verb + ***-ing***.
>
> ***need*** + verb + ***-ing*** ▪▪
>
> ***need*** + passive infinitive ▪▪▪▪▪▪▪▪▪▪▪▪▪▪▪▪

About you **B** **Pair work** Do any of the things above need doing in your apartment? Tell a partner. What else needs fixing?

Lesson A Past modals *would have*, *should have*, *could have*

A ~~Cross out~~ the incorrect words. Then write answers to the questions.

1. Dan's daughter was sick and couldn't go to school. Dan took her to work with him.
   What <u>could</u> / ~~would~~ he have done instead? _____

2. Ashley had a meal at a restaurant. The food was tasteless, and the service was rude. She complained politely and left. What else <u>could</u> / <u>would</u> she have done? _____

3. There were six cartons of milk left at the grocery store. A man pushed in front of me and picked up all six. I really needed one. <u>Should</u> / <u>Would</u> I have said something? _____

4. Sara borrowed a dress of Kate's. She spilled coffee on it. She gave it back with a stain on it without saying anything. What <u>should</u> / <u>would</u> she have done? _____

5. Josh bought a camera. It should have cost $500, but the salesperson charged him the wrong price of $395. <u>Should</u> / <u>Would</u> Josh have said anything? _____

6. Hal had an important meeting that he hadn't prepared for. He said he wasn't feeling well and went home. <u>Would</u> / <u>Should</u> you have done the same thing? _____

About you **B** **Pair work** Discuss your answers to the questions above. Do you have the same views?

> **✗ Common errors**
>
> Use *should have*, not *must have*, + past participle, to talk about the right thing to do.
>
> She **should have** called me. (NOT ~~She must have called me.~~)

Lesson B Past modals for speculation

A Write a sentence to explain each situation. Start the sentences with the words given. There may be more than one correct answer.

1. You're stuck in a traffic jam, and you're sure there's been an accident.
   "There _must have been an accident_____."

2. You're in a nice restaurant, and the couple at the table next to you aren't talking to each other. You think it's possible they've had a fight.
   "They _____."

3. You don't think it's possible that you left your credit card at the store.
   "I _____."

4. When you arrive at the dentist for an appointment, they tell you that you are an hour late. You think it's possible you wrote down the wrong time.
   "I _____."

5. You call your sister, but someone else answers. You're sure that you called the wrong number.
   "I _____."

6. Your mother didn't send you a birthday card. It's not possible that she has forgotten.
   "She _____."

About you **B** **Pair work** Compare your answers. Have you ever been in situations like the ones above? Share stories.

C **Pair work** Imagine that you're at a coffee shop. You can't find your wallet to pay. Think of as many reasons as you can why this is possible. Tell your partner.

"I must have left my wallet at home."

UNIT **9** **Lesson A** Reported speech

A Read what Pablo says. Then complete the sentences to report what he said.

> **Note**
>
> Present continuous forms in direct speech shift back to past continuous forms in reported speech.
>
> "I**'m destroying** all my things."
> → He said that he **was destroying** all his things.

"I don't think that I'm very materialistic. I'm moving to a new apartment soon, and so I've been trying to get rid of the things I don't want. I actually think I'm very self-disciplined – I only spend money on things I really need. I mean, I've kept a few gifts that I've never used. You know, things that close friends gave to me. And I've kept some old family photos that I can't throw away, obviously. But over the years, I've bought a lot of books, and I'll probably give most of them away."

1. Pablo said that he ___didn't think___ that he _____ very materialistic.

2. He said he _____ to a new apartment, and so he _____ to get rid of the things he _____ .

3. He said he _____ that he _____ very self-disciplined and said he only _____ money on things he really _____ .

4. He said that he _____ a few gifts that he _____ _____ – things that close friends _____ to him.

5. He said he _____ some old family photos that he _____ throw away.

6. He said that over the years, he _____ a lot of books and that he _____ probably give most of them away.

About you **B** **Pair work** Ask your partner, "Are you materialistic? Could you give away your possessions?" Then find another partner and report the answers.

> **Common errors**
>
> Don't use *say* + *me*, *him*, *them*, etc.
>
> She said she wasn't materialistic.
> (NOT ~~She said me she wasn't materialistic.~~)

UNIT **9** **Lesson B** Reported questions

A Imagine a market researcher asked you these questions. Write the reported questions.

1. Are you saving up for anything special? *He asked me if . . .*
2. How much money have you spent today?
3. What's your favorite store?
4. Could you live without your smartphone?
5. How do you keep track of your money?
6. Does your bank account pay good interest?
7. How often do you check your bank account?
8. Do you ever spend too much on things?

> **In conversation**
>
> . . . asked **if** and . . . wanted to know **if** are much more frequent than . . . asked **whether** and . . . wanted to know **whether**.

> **Common errors**
>
> Don't use *tell* to report questions.
>
> She **asked** me if I owned any stocks.
> (NOT ~~She told me if I owned any stocks.~~)

About you **B** **Pair work** Ask and answer the questions. Then find another partner and report the questions and your first partner's answers.

Lesson A Talking hypothetically about the past

A These people are talking hypothetically about the past. Complete the sentences.

1. If I _had worked_ (work) harder at school, I might have gotten a better job.
2. If I hadn't quit my job, I _____ (would not meet) my new friends.
3. If my family _____ (not encourage) me, I wouldn't have had the confidence to apply for my current job.
4. If my neighbor _____ (take) different subjects, he would have had better job opportunities.
5. If I'd gotten better grades, I _____ (could get) into grad school.
6. If I had studied English at an earlier age, I _____ (might take) this class years ago.
7. If my parents hadn't set aside the money, they _____ (could not afford) a big house.
8. If we _____ (grow up) 50 years ago, our lives might have been very different.

About you **B** Pair work Make four of the sentences above true for you, and tell a partner. Give more information.

"If my friend Robin had worked harder in school, she would have passed more exams and she would have gotten a better job."

Lesson B Tag questions

A Complete the sentences with a tag question.

1. Celebrity couples often have problems with their marriages, _don't they_ ?
2. People are not really watching reality shows anymore, _____ ? They've lost interest in them.
3. You don't have to have a lot of confidence to go on a talent show, _____ ?
4. It's easier to become an Internet celebrity these days, _____ ?
5. Some actors don't deserve all the bad press they get, _____ ?
6. To be successful in Hollywood, you have to have connections, _____ ?
7. Some singers are just terrible when they perform live, _____ ? I'm not the only one who thinks that, _____ ?
8. The old black and white movies were much better than today's movies, _____ ?
9. Some actors have dropped out of sight completely, _____ ?
10. They're making a lot of violent movies these days, _____ ? I'm right about that, _____ ?

About you **B** Pair work Start conversations with the sentences above. Do you agree? Give your own views.

> **i Note**
>
> Notice how to make tag questions when the verb in the statement is *have* or a continuous verb.
> You **have** a guitar, **don't you?**
> She **didn't have** connections, **did she?**
> He**'s doing** really well, **isn't he?**
> They **were getting** bad press, **weren't they?**
> Notice how to make tag questions with *I'm . . .* and *I'm not . . .*
> I'm right, **aren't I?**
> I'm not wrong, **am I?**

UNIT 11 Lesson A Passive of present continuous and present perfect

A Which of the sentences below need a passive, not an active, verb? Correct the sentences.

being created
1. Fewer jobs are ~~creating~~ in the construction industry.
2. Fast food chains are providing healthier meals.
3. Skilled workers have recruited from other countries.
4. Smoking has banned in public places.
5. A lot of older houses have knocked down to make room for new buildings.
6. In the last few years, young people haven't encouraged to go to college.
7. Plans to address water shortages have not discussed.
8. More and more life-saving medicines have developed in the last ten years.
9. A large number of bank employees have laid off because their jobs have outsourced to other countries.
10. New gyms and swimming pools are building in some neighborhoods because people are demanding better facilities.

> **✖ Common errors**
>
> Don't forget to use the passive when you don't know who is doing the action.
>
> *More roads **are being built** every year.* (NOT ~~More roads are building every year.~~)

About you **B** **Pair work** Which of the sentences above are true where you live? Discuss with a partner.

UNIT 11 Lesson B Linking ideas

A Rewrite the sentences using the expressions given.

1. I think it's better to get around by bicycle than to drive your car everywhere. (instead of)
   I think it's better to get around by bicycle instead of driving your car everywhere.

2. I'm concerned that carbon dioxide levels are rising because of increased burning of fuels. (due to)
   _____

3. I'm worried that congestion on the roads is still a problem, even though there have been improvements. (in spite of)
   _____

4. It's annoying that people often throw away plastic bottles when you can recycle them. (even though)
   _____

5. I think we should use things like lemon juice as a cleaning product – then we won't need to buy so many toxic chemicals. (so that)
   _____

6. We should reduce our energy use so we can protect the environment. (in order to)
   _____

7. It worries me that obesity in children is becoming more of a problem because of unhealthy eating habits. (as a result of)
   _____

About you **B** **Pair work** Do you agree with any of the concerns above? Brainstorm solutions to the problems.

UNIT 12 Lesson A *What* clauses and long noun phrases as subjects

A Rewrite these sentences to give someone advice about starting a new job. Start with the words given.

1. Making a good impression is really important.
   What _____ .

2. A friend of mine offered to help the manager.
   Something _____ .

3. My sister introduced herself to everyone.
   What _____ .

4. Smile – that's the best thing you can do.
   The _____ .

5. I would try to listen and learn from your co-workers.
   What _____ .

6. I like to find out as much about the job as possible before starting. Then you feel prepared.
   What _____ .
   The advantage of that _____ .

About you B Pair work Do you agree with this advice? What other advice do you have for someone on their first day at work?

UNIT 12 Lesson B The future continuous and future perfect

A Read what Natalie says about her future. Then complete the sentences.

"I'm finishing my degree in math right now. I hope I do well on my exams because I've applied to go to medical school next year. The program lasts four years, and then there are three to seven years of internship to do after that. I don't know what type of medicine I want to work in yet, but I have a lot of time to decide. I might go and work in another country. Who knows?"

1. In a few months, Natalie _____ (finish) her degree in math, and she _____ (get) ready to go to medical school.

2. Five years after that, she _____ (leave) medical school, and she _____ (do) an internship somewhere.

3. She probably _____ (not decide) which area of medicine she'd like to work in by then.

4. She doesn't know who she _____ (work) with or where she _____ (live).

5. She _____ (might move) to a different country to work.

About you B Pair work Think of three ideas for each question. Tell your partner.

What will you be doing . . .
- 24 hours from now?
- in three months?
- in five years?

What will you have done by then?

Illustration credits

Harry Briggs: 7, 31, 55, 68, 69, 95 **Bunky Hurter:** 14, 36, 54, 77, 100 **Scott Macneil:** 71 **Q2A studio artists:** 24, 47, 57, 79, 89 **Lucy Truman:** 10, 20, 30, 42, 52, 62, 74, 84, 94, 106, 116, 126

Photography credits

Back cover: ©vovan/Shutterstock **38, 39, 58, 59, 90, 91, 112, 113** ©Cambridge University Press **6, 7, 12, 26, 27, 70, 71, 80, 102, 103, 118, 122, 123** ©Frank Veronsky **viii** *(left to right)* ©RubberBall/SuperStock; ©Cultura Limited/SuperStock **1** *(clockwise from top left)* ©Marmaduke St. John/Alamy; ©Exactostock/SuperStock; ©Nicola Tree/Getty Images; ©Steven Robertson/istockphoto **2** ©Thinkstock; *(top background)* ©monticello/Shutterstock **3** ©Masterfile/RF **4** ©blackred/istockphoto; *(background)* ©ruskpp/Shutterstock **8** ©Jordan Strauss/Invision/AP; *(utensils)* ©Martin Kemp/Shutterstock **9** ©2010 AFP/Getty Images **11** *(clockwise from top left)* ©Blend Images/SuperStock; ©Radius/SuperStock; ©Transtock/SuperStock; ©Blend Images/SuperStock **12** *(all photos)* ©Frank Veronsky **13** ©Thomas Barwick/Getty Images **15** *(all photos)* ©Cambridge University Press **16** ©Imagemore/SuperStock **17** ©Imagemore/SuperStock **18** *(left to right)* ©quavondo/Getty Images; ©Dreampictures/Media Bakery **21** *(clockwise from top left)* ©Pixtal/SuperStock; ©miker/Shutterstock.com; ©Pixtal/SuperStock; ©Steve Vidler/SuperStock; ©Pacific Stock - Design Pics/SuperStock; ©windmoon/Shutterstock.com **22** *(clockwise from top left)* ©Gregory Johnston/age fotostock/SuperStock; ©Linzy Slusher/istockphoto; ©Thinkstock; ©Juanmonino/Getty Images; ©Thinkstock; ©Kerrie Kerr/istockphoto; ©Steve Kaufman/CORBIS; ©Marco Maccarini/istockphoto **25** ©Bill Sykes Images/Getty Images **28** *(background)* ©Shutterstock **29** *(all backgrounds)* ©Shutterstock **32** *(top to bottom)* ©Blend Images/SuperStock; ©4kodiak/istockphoto **33** *(clockwise from top left)* ©Chris Whitehead/Getty Images; ©Thinkstock; ©Thinkstock; ©PYMCA/SuperStock **34** *(clockwise from top left)* ©Thinkstock; ©Fancy Collection/SuperStock; ©Thinkstock; ©Jupiterimages/Thinkstock; ©Edward Bock/istockphoto; ©Mie Ahmt/istockphoto; ©Exactostock/SuperStock; ©Silvia Jansen/istockphoto **35** ©Image Source/SuperStock **40** *(hole)* ©Fotana/Shutterstock **41** ©Nicole S. Young/istockphoto **43** *(clockwise from top right)* ©Transtock/SuperStock; ©Thinkstock; ©Exactostock/SuperStock **44** *(clockwise from top left)* ©Thinkstock; ©Thinkstock; ©Jupiterimages/Thinkstock; ©Jupiterimages/Thinkstock; ©Thinkstock **48** *(people)* ©Blaj Gabriel/Shutterstock *(bus stop)* ©Joy Rector/Shutterstock; *(sign)* ©Rob Wilson/Shutterstock **49** *(top)* ©Blaj Gabriel/Shutterstock *(bottom)* ©Jack Hollingsworth/Getty Images **50** ©Olivier Lantzendörffer/istockphoto; *(background)* ©Hluboki Dzianis/Shutterstock **51** *(background)* ©Hluboki Dzianis/Shutterstock **53** *(clockwise from top left)* ©The Power of Forever Photography/istockphoto; ©PhotoAlto/SuperStock; ©Thinkstock; ©Thinkstock; ©Ingram Publishing/SuperStock **54** *(left to right)* ©Paul Hakimata/Fotolia; ©Jupiterimages/Thinkstock **56** *(top section, top to bottom)* ©Eric Isselee/Shutterstock; ©Flavia Morlachetti/Shutterstock; ©Eric Isselee/Shutterstock; ©ULKASTUDIO/Shutterstock; ©Coprid/Shutterstock *(bottom row, left to right)* ©Morgan Lane Photography/Shutterstock; ©Peter Waters/Shutterstock; ©Eric Isselee/Shutterstock; ©Yu Lan/Shutterstock; *(background)* ©sunil menon/istockphoto **60** Photo Courtesy of Mary E. Holmes **63** *(left to right)* ©Arcady/Shutterstock; ©Arcady/Shutterstock; ©Miguel Angel Salinas Salinas/Shutterstock; ©Arcady/Shutterstock; ©Olga Anourina/istockphoto **64** ©altrendo images/Getty Images **65** *(clockwise from top left)* ©Yuri Arcurs Media/SuperStock; ©Exactostock/SuperStock; ©Niels Busch/Getty Images; ©Blend Images/SuperStock; ©baranq/Shutterstock; ©moodboard/SuperStock **66** *(clockwise from top left)* ©Michael Hitoshi/Getty Images; ©Jupiterimages/Thinkstock; ©Catherine Yeulet/istockphoto; ©Jupiterimages/Getty Images **67** *(invitation)* ©mark wragg/istockphoto *(photographer)* ©Marcin Stefaniak/istockphoto *(cake)* ©Dean Turner/istockphoto *(dress)* ©fStop/SuperStock *(flowers)* ©RubberBall/SuperStock *(passport)* ©Lana Sundman/age fotostock/SuperStock **73** ©Dfree/Shutterstock **75** *(clockwise from top left)* ©Thinkstock; ©Thinkstock; ©Thinkstock; ©Photo and Co/Getty Images **76** ©digitalskillet/istockphoto **81** ©BanksPhotos/istockphoto **82** ©Michael Rosenwirth/Alamy; *(background)* ©argus/Shutterstock **85** *(clockwise from top right)* ©Thinkstock; ©Jamie Grill/Getty Images; ©Fotosearch/SuperStock; ©Dmitry Kalinovsky/istockphoto **86** *(top, left to right)* ©WireImage/Getty Images; ©Julian Stallabrass/Flickr; *(bottom)* ©Photocrea/Shutterstock **88** *(background)* © photolinc/Shutterstock **91** ©Bruce Glikas/Getty Images **92** ©stevecoleimages/istockphoto; *(background)* ©Loskutnikov/Shutterstock **97** *(clockwise from bottom left)* ©Getty Images; ©Indigo/Getty Images; ©Getty Images; ©GYI NSEA/istockphoto; ©GYI NSEA/istockphoto **98** *(top to bottom)* ©Featureflash/Shutterstock.com; ©Thinkstock; ©Ciaran Griffin/Thinkstock; ©Comstock Images/Thinkstock; *(background)* ©Henning Riemer/Shutterstock **99** ©Paul A. Hebert/Getty Images **101** *(top to bottom)* ©Getty Images; ©Time & Life Pictures/Getty Images **104** *(left to right)* ©GYI NSEA/istockphoto; ©Featureflash/Shutterstock.com; ©GYI NSEA/istockphoto **107** *(clockwise from top left)* ©Edward Bock/istockphoto; ©TIM MCCAIG/istockphoto; ©Johner/SuperStock; ©Thinkstock **108** *(top row, left to right)* ©Thinkstock; ©Comstock Images/Thinkstock; ©Thinkstock *(bottom row, all photos)* ©Thinkstock **110** ©Thinkstock **114** *(top to bottom)* ©Debby Wong/Shutterstock.com; ©Stockbyte/Thinkstock; *(background)* ©Itana/Shutterstock **115** ©Thinkstock; *(background)* ©Itana/Shutterstock **117** *(clockwise from top left)* ©Jack Hollingsworth/Thinkstock; ©Andrew Rich/istockphoto; ©Alexander Podshivalov/istockphoto; ©Blend Images/SuperStock **120** *(clockwise from top left)* ©Thinkstock; ©ViviSuArt/istockphoto; ©Neustockimages/istockphoto; ©Don Bayley/istockphoto; ©Thinkstock **124** ©age fotostock/SuperStock **128** *(left to right)* ©Rich Legg/istockphoto; ©daniel rodriguez/istockphoto; ©Stephanie Swartz/istockphoto **130** *(left to right)* ©Martijn Mulder/istockphoto; ©Corbis/SuperStock **131** ©Oliver Gutfleisch/ima/imagebroker.net/SuperStock **132** ©Ghislain & Marie David de Lossy/Getty Images **134** ©Monkey Business Images/Shutterstock **135** *(clockwise from top left)* ©hxdbzxy/Shutterstock; ©Sandra Baker/Alamy; ©bikeriderlondon/Shutterstock; ©ArtFamily/Shutterstock **136** *(background)* ©Gunnar Pippel/Shutterstock **141** *(top to bottom)* ©Thinkstock; ©Thinkstock; ©Lorraine Kourafas/Shutterstock; ©Chamille White/Shutterstock **145** ©Jupiterimages/Thinkstock

Text credits

The authors and publishers acknowledge the following sources of copyright material and are grateful for the permissions granted. While every effort has been made, it has not always been possible to identify the sources of all the material used, or to trace all copyright holders. If any omissions are brought to our notice, we will be happy to include the appropriate acknowledgments on reprinting.

8 Text adapted from "Blind Chef Christine Ha Crowned 'MasterChef' in Finale" by Ryan Owens and Meredith Frost, *ABC News*, September 11, 2012. Reproduced with permission of ABC News.
40 Quotes from *Quiet: The Power of Introverts in a World That Can't Stop Talking* by Susan Cain, Penguin Books, 2012. Copyright ©Susan Cain. Reproduced by permission of Penguin Books Ltd.

SECOND EDITION

TOUCHSTONE

WORKBOOK 4

MICHAEL MCCARTHY

JEANNE MCCARTEN

HELEN SANDIFORD

CAMBRIDGE
UNIVERSITY PRESS

Contents

Interesting lives

Lesson A / Interviews

1 Meet Alex. . . .

Grammar | Claire is interviewing Alex, a successful photographer, for a news website. Circle the correct verb forms to complete the conversation.

Claire   When (did you start) / **were you starting** taking photos?

Alex   Gosh, **I'm taking** / (I've been taking) photos since I was about six.

Claire   Really? So, what kind of camera (did you use) / **have you used** back then?

Alex   Well, when I was young, my uncle (showed) / **was showing** me how to use this old camera and how to develop the prints. I still use it!

Claire   That's amazing. So, what projects **do you work** / (are you working) on currently?

Alex   I just started this nature series (I'm taking) / **I was taking** photos of trees. You know, trees that have interesting shapes.

Claire   That's great. How many tree photos (have you taken) / **have you been taking** so far?

Alex   A lot. Hundreds.

Claire   Really? And how has your work changed? I mean, what kind of photography (were you doing) / **have you been doing** five years ago?

Alex   Well, I (was working) / **'ve worked** on some color portraits for a competition. I (didn't win) / **wasn't winning**, but it was a good experience.

2 About you 1

Grammar | Write the questions using a correct verb form. Then write true answers.

1. What / you take / photos of lately ? _What have you been taking photos of lately?_
   I've been taking photos of my friends and interesting buildings in my hometown.

2. How long / you / have / a camera ? _____
   How long have you had a camera.

3. your parents / take / many photos of you when you were a child ? _____
   Did your parents take ? _Yes they did._

4. you ever / be / to a photographer's studio ? _____
   Have you ever been to a photographer's studio? Yes I have

5. When / you last take a photo ? _____
   When did you last take a photo? It was at New Year time

6. What / social networking sites / you / post / your photos on currently ? _____
   What social networking sites are you posted your photos on currently,

3 Questions and answers

Grammar | Complete each conversation with the correct form of the verb given.
Sometimes more than one answer is possible.

1. (watch)
   Ben   What kinds of movies ____have____ you _been watching_
          lately?
   Kumi   Well, mostly I_'ve been watching_ horror movies. I usually
          ___watch___ three or four horror movies a month.
          Actually, I _watched_ a great horror movie last night.

2. (live)
   Ana   _Have_ you ever _lived_ in another country?
   Joel   Yes, I_'ve lived_ in two other countries. I _lived_
          in Canada for three years after I left college, and I
          lived/was living in Kenya until last June.

3. (eat)
   Christa   You look great. What's your secret?
   Jalila   Thanks. I_'ve been eating_ a lot of vegetables and whole
             grains lately. And I always ___eat___ six small
             meals a day. I just ___ate___ a salad for lunch.

4. (write)
   Vito   How long _have_ you _been writing_ poetry?
   Kim   Um. I guess I _'ve wrote_ poetry for about four years.
          I ___write___ _'ve been writing_ almost every day if I can. Yesterday,
          I ___wrote___ for almost three hours nonstop!

4 About you 2

Grammar | Answer the questions with true information.

been? / lived

1. How long have you been studying English? _I've been studying English for five years._
2. Have you ever lived in another country? _Yes, I've living in Hongkong for many years._
3. What kinds of music are you listening to these days? _____
4. What kinds of TV shows do you watch? _____
5. What did you do during your last vacation? _____
6. What were you doing at this time last week? _____

1 Dream jobs

Grammar and vocabulary | Circle the correct words to complete the paragraphs.

1. LEIGH HUDSON tells us how she **seemed** / (**ended up**) / **decided** being an editor.

Well, after I **imagined / finished / bothered** taking my law school entrance exams, I still wasn't sure if I wanted to be a lawyer. I already had a degree in English and was **considering / expecting / agreeing** training to be a journalist. Then one day, I saw an ad for an editorial assistant on a publishing company's website, and I **offered / expected / decided** to apply for it. After the interview, the manager said I was right for the job and **offered / ended up / considered** to pay me a good salary. I immediately **agreed / finished / missed** to take the job. Anyway, I've been working at the company for over five years, and now I'm a senior editor. I absolutely love my job – I can't **agree / expect / imagine** doing anything else!

2. GEORGE ALLEN explains how he became a chef.

I wasn't really **agreeing / missing / planning on** being a chef. I **spent / bothered / decided** four years in college studying electrical engineering. After I graduated, I **agreed / happened / started** working at an engineering firm and had a great salary, but a lot of responsibility. After six months, I **intend / remember / miss** thinking, "Am I really happy being an electrical engineer?" I decided I wasn't happy at all, so I quit my job and applied to a local cooking school. After I finished training, I opened a small restaurant. I've never **ended up / missed / offered** working at my old job – not once. And that was 15 years ago now!

3. CELIA MENDEZ tells us how she became a dancer.

Well, a few years ago, my friends and I **happened / seemed / missed** to go on vacation to a Caribbean resort that put on a great show every night with singing and dancing and everything. I was taking dance classes at the time, and I was actually **finishing / bothering / considering** becoming a dancer. Anyway, one night, the resort had a talent competition for the guests. I didn't **imagine / happen / bother** to sign up. But my friends said, "Celia, this **seems / spends / expects** to be a perfect opportunity for you. You're such a good dancer. You should do it!" Well, to make a long story short, I won the talent competition, and the resort offered me a position as a dancer! I never **happened / expected / ended up** to be a successful professional dancer, least of all at a Caribbean resort! Dreams really do come true!

2 How I ended up living in New York City

Grammar and vocabulary **Complete the paragraph with the correct form of the verbs.**

A lot of people ask me how I ended up ___living___ (live) in New York City. Well, actually, I wasn't planning on _being_ (be) here. It's just that the opportunity came up when my friend Samuela happened _to move_ (move) here for college. She needed a roommate, so I agreed _to share_ (share) an apartment with her in the city. We were only in the apartment a couple of months when Samuela started _missing / to miss_ (miss) home. She said she missed _being_ (be) with her family. I guess she couldn't imagine _staying_ (stay) three more years and _being_ (be) happy. So, she decided _to complete_ (complete) the semester, and then she transferred to a college back home. Anyway, I kept the apartment and found a great job. I've been here for over six years now, but Samuela and I are still great friends. We've never stopped _to email_ (email) each other, and we call each other all the time. We just live in different cities – that's all!

3 About you

Grammar and vocabulary **Answer the questions with true information.**

1. Where do you think you'll end up living in a few years?
   I think I'll end up living in Paris after I finish school.

2. What are you planning on doing when you finish this English course?
   _____

3. Have you started reading a new book recently?
   _____

4. What's something fun you remember doing as a child?
   _____

5. Have you ever decided to do something and then regretted it?
   _____

6. Do you expect to get a good grade in this class?
   _____

7. What do you intend to do this weekend?
   _____

8. Is there anything you can't imagine doing in life?
   _____

Lesson C — We're both getting scared. . . .

1 When I was little, . . .

Conversation strategies | Read the conversation. Change the underlined verbs to the simple present to highlight the key moments.

Freda	This pie reminds me of the time my sister made me eat a mud pie.
Chris	You're kidding! What happened?
Freda	Well, when I was very little, she and I used to play together, and we would always play outside, you know?
Chris	Yeah. We always played outside, too. Not like kids nowadays.
Freda	Well, anyway, one day, I <u>was</u> *'m / am* in the yard, and she <u>made</u> me eat a mud pie. Here she <u>was</u>, seven years old, in the yard with three beautiful mud pies. She <u>said</u>, "Freda, try this. It's so good." And she <u>acted</u> like she put some in her mouth. I was three years old, so what did I know?
Chris	Oh, no! What did it taste like?
Freda	I don't remember.
Chris	Really?
Freda	No. But I remember being sick afterward.

2 I'll never forget . . .

Conversation strategies | Read the conversation. Change some verbs in Sarah's story to the simple present or present continuous to highlight key moments in the story.

Sarah	Did I ever tell you about the time I ran out of cash in South Korea?
Lisa	No. What happened?
Sarah	Well, I was traveling through South Korea, way out in the middle of nowhere, and I ~~ran out~~ *run out* of cash and I had no way of getting back to Seoul.
Lisa	Really? You didn't have any traveler's checks or anything?
Sarah	Well, I had one check for 50 dollars, but I was in the mountains, and there was nowhere to exchange it.
Lisa	Oh, no! So, what did you do?
Sarah	Well, I was getting pretty nervous. I was walking around and couldn't find a bank or anything. Anyway, finally, I met this really nice French man. So I explained the situation, and he agreed to take my traveler's check in exchange for Korean money. So at least I had enough money to get a bus to the nearest town. And so yeah, I went to the most expensive hotel.
Lisa	Why the most expensive hotel?
Sarah	Well, back then, small hotels didn't accept credit cards. And it was a holiday, so the banks were closed.
Lisa	So you stayed there?
Sarah	Yeah. I ended up booking a room for the night, and then the next day, I found a bank and got some cash. So it all worked out in the end.

3 This great bike path

Complete the story with *this* or *these*.

My friends went bike riding one day on ___*this*___ great bike path in
the country. The bike path is really _____ old railroad track that
isn't used by trains anymore. Anyway, it goes through all _____
beautiful old farms. But, you see, my friends are from the city, so
they're not used to seeing farm animals and fields and stuff. So, my
friends are riding along, and they see all _____ goats in a field.
Well, they stop to take photos, but they have no idea that goats can be
a little unfriendly. Suddenly, they see _____ big goat running
toward them, so they jump back on their bikes and ride away, you
know, really quickly. Then _____ guy starts yelling at them. It
turns out it's the farmer, and they're riding their bikes on his field.

4 Really?

**Rewrite these stories. Use the simple present or present continuous to highlight
some key moments in each story. Use *this* and *these* to highlight important people,
things, or events.**

1. You know, a friend of mine is always seeing famous people when she's out. One time,
   she was checking out a computer in a computer store. And all of a sudden, she looked
   up and saw her favorite basketball player. He was standing next to her – checking out
   the same computer!
   You know, this friend of mine is always seeing famous people when she's out.
   One time, she was checking out this computer in a computer store. And all
   of a sudden, . . .

2. You know, my cousin Adam met his fiancée because of his dog. He has an enormous
   dog named Scruffy. Well, one day they were in the park. Anyway, Scruffy started chasing
   a squirrel and pulled my cousin right into a woman. So, Adam apologized, and he and
   the woman started talking. And to make a long story short, now they're engaged!

   _____

   _____

   _____

3. I remember one time my friend Linda had a party. It was for her graduation, I think, and
   we were all outdoors. Anyway, the weather was beautiful at first, but after an hour or so,
   some dark clouds started coming in, and it started to rain really hard. So, she just turned on
   a radio, and we all started dancing in the rain. We had so much fun. It was the best party ever.

   _____

   _____

   _____

Lesson D / Against the odds

1 Super man

Reading | **A** Read the article. What do you think an *activist* is?

- [ ] a successful actor
- [ ] someone who is physically active
- [ ] a motivational speaker
- [ ] someone who works for a cause

Inspiring in Life and Death

Until 1995, Christopher Reeve was living a life most people only dream about. He was a successful actor – famous for his roles in the *Superman* movies – and happily married with three children. He had everything to live for.

Then on May 27, 1995, his life changed dramatically. Reeve fell off his horse while riding in a horse-jumping competition. The accident left him with serious injuries – a fracture in the second vertebra of his neck – and Reeve was left paralyzed from his neck down.

Reeve was confined to a wheelchair and had to depend on his wife, nurses, doctors, and therapists to do everything for him. He could no longer walk, hold anything in his hands, or feed or wash himself. He also relied on a respirator to help him breathe.

Many people may have given up hope and felt sorry for themselves. But not Christopher Reeve.

Shortly after his accident, Reeve said, "The only limits you have are the ones you put on yourself." With this positive attitude, he began adjusting to his new life.

Amazingly, he continued to act in movies and direct them. But most importantly, he became an activist for people with spinal cord injuries. He raised money for research and started the Christopher & Dana Reeve Foundation, which awards money to people researching cures for paralysis. He wrote an autobiography, *Still Me*. He even testified before the U.S. Senate to encourage funding for stem-cell research.

Although Reeve never recovered from his injuries, he remained hopeful throughout his life about finding a cure for paralysis. By not giving up hope, he gave other people with disabilities hope that in the future, recovery won't be against all odds.

Christopher Reeve
September 25, 1952–October 10, 2004

B Read the article again. Then answer the questions.

1. What movies did Christopher Reeve star in? _____

2. What was Reeve doing when he hurt his neck? _____

3. Who did Reeve have to rely on for help? _____

4. What does the Christopher & Dana Reeve Foundation do? _____

8

2 How I overcame stage fright

Writing | **A** Read the anecdote. Then put the story in the correct order by writing each number in the correct box.

1. Set the general time or place.	3. Describe what happened.
2. Set the particular time or place.	4. End the story. Link the events to now.

☐ So, with that memory in my mind, I calmed down and walked on stage. I looked at the audience, and I thought, "I know you want me to do well." I closed my eyes and played a great recital.

☐ Today, remembering my teacher's words helps me to be confident when I perform. And it helps me with a lot of other things, too!

☐ I'm a musician, and when I was in graduate school, I had to give a final violin recital to get my degree. I was nervous because there were so many talented students at my school.

☐ On the night of the recital, I was so nervous that my hands were shaking. But I remembered what my very first teacher said to me years before: "People are here because they want you to do well."

B Use the steps above to write an anecdote about something you were nervous about doing and how you overcame it.

Unit 1 Progress chart

What can you do? Mark the boxes. ✓ = I can . . . ? = I need to review how to . . .	To review, go back to these pages in the Student's Book.
☐ use the simple and continuous forms of verbs.	2 and 3
☐ use verbs that are followed by verb + -ing or to + verb.	4 and 5
☐ use at least 10 new verbs.	2, 4, and 5
☐ use the present tense to highlight key moments in a story.	6
☐ use this and these to highlight key people, things, and events.	7
☐ write an anecdote.	9

Grammar — rows 1–2
Vocabulary — row 3
Conversation strategies — rows 4–5
Writing — last row

Personal tastes

Lesson A / Makeovers

1 Confessions of a fashion queen

Grammar and vocabulary | Complete the sentences with the words in the box.

| hard | important | much | nice | ✓often | quickly |

1. I go shopping as __often__ as I can. I go almost every other day.
2. You can't look your best if you get ready as _____ as possible. It's better to take your time.
3. Jeans can look just as _____ as pants if you wear them with a cool top.
4. For me, comfort isn't as _____ as style when it comes to choosing clothes.
5. I try as _____ as I can to look great every day. I pay a lot of attention to how I look.
6. I don't like bright colors as _____ as dark colors. I almost always wear black.

2 Dear Vera, . . .

Grammar and vocabulary | Complete the letters with the words and expressions in the box.

| fast | ✓interested in fashion | little time | many things | much attention | scruffy |

❶ Dear Vera,

My boyfriend isn't as __interested in fashion__ as I am, and he wears the same clothes all the time. He really needs a makeover. How can I help him look better? – *JB, Vancouver*

Dear JB,

Lots of people don't pay as _____ to their appearance as their partners would like. Gently let your boyfriend know that you want to help him look better. Help him pick out clothes that aren't as _____ as the ones he wears now. Your boyfriend might not want your help at first, but he'll be glad when people start noticing how good he looks. – *Vera*

❷ Dear Vera,

It takes me so long to get ready in the morning, and I always end up being late for work. I need to get ready as _____ as possible. What should I do? – *CN, Taipei*

Dear CN,

Mornings are always difficult. You need to spend as _____ as possible organizing yourself. So, to save time, do as _____ as you can the night before. Pick out your clothes before you go to bed, and put everything you need for the day in your bag. That way, your mornings won't be as rushed. – *Vera*

3 She isn't as . . .

Grammar and vocabulary Look at the pictures of Sachi and Nell. How are they alike or different? Write sentences with
as . . . as or *not as . . . as.*

1. (tall) *Sachi isn't as tall as Nell.*

2. (hair / short) _____

3. (many dark clothes) _____

4. (skirt / long) _____

5. (shoes / comfortable) _____

6. (much jewelry) _____

7. (earrings / big) _____

8. They both love fashion. (interested in fashion)

   _____

   _____

4 About you

Grammar and vocabulary Answer the questions with true information. Use *as . . . as* or *not as . . . as.*

1. Do you generally wear bright colors as often as dark colors?
   I don't wear bright colors as often as dark colors. I'm most comfortable in black.

2. Do you spend as much money on clothes as your friends?

   _____

3. Do you try as hard as you can to be trendy and fashionable?

   _____

4. Do you have as many accessories as your best friend?

   _____

5. Do your parents care as much about their appearance as you do?

   _____

6. Do you find stylish clothes to be as comfortable as casual clothes?

   _____

7. Do you spend as little time as possible getting ready in the morning?

   _____

1 Isn't that dress awful?

Grammar | Complete the conversations with *isn't, aren't, don't,* or *doesn't.*

1. A Oh, look at that dress. ___*Isn't*___ it awful?

   B Oh, I don't know. It's what's in style. _____ you interested in fashion?

   A Not really. Are you?

   B Kind of. But look at this dress. _____ it have something special about it?

   A Yeah, it has something all right – a $5,000 price tag! _____ that a little expensive for a dress?

   B Yeah. But being fashionable isn't cheap.

2. A Are you ready yet?

   B Yes, almost. I . . . um . . . just need to find a tie.

   A _____ you have lots of ties?

   B Yeah, but they're all dirty.

   A You should wear a jacket, too, _____ you think?

   B But it's warm outside. _____ this outfit look good?

   A Well, . . . um, _____ your socks different colors?

   B Oh, yeah. You're right. I need to find socks now, too!

2 Don't you think . . . ?

Grammar | Rewrite the sentences as negative questions.

1. Leather jackets are cool.
   Aren't leather jackets cool?

2. Most sneakers cost way too much nowadays.
   _____

3. A tie is a great way to complete a man's outfit.
   _____

4. Plaid looks great with floral prints.
   _____

5. It's hard to find jeans that fit well.
   _____

6. Neon green and orange are great colors.
   _____

❸ What's in fashion?

Vocabulary | **A** Look at the picture and read the comments. Two things in each description are wrong. Underline the wrong word(s) and correct the sentences.

1. Luis looks very stylish in his denim jeans and a <u>short-sleeved</u> shirt. His <u>neon striped</u> tie looks cool, too.
   Luis looks very stylish in his denim jeans and a long-sleeved shirt.
   His polka-dot tie looks cool, too.

2. Kate looks great in that plaid silk skirt. Her cashmere turtleneck sweater goes with it really well, too.

   _____

   _____

3. Tiana's wearing dark blue skinny jeans – as usual – with a leather jacket. That look never goes out of fashion.

   _____

   _____

4. Ravi's light gray scarf goes perfectly with his suede jacket. Those fitted casual pants look great, too.

   _____

   _____

B Look at the pictures. Write descriptions of Angelo's and Risa's clothing.

1. Angelo _____

   _____

   _____

2. Risa _____

   _____

   _____

1 So, you must like . . .

Conversation strategies | **Circle the response that best summarizes what A says.**

1. A I like music that's calm – music that helps me unwind after a crazy day.
   a. So, you have broad tastes, then.
   b. Uh-huh. You like music that's relaxing.

2. A I love Passion Pit. I've seen them in concert five times, and I have all their albums.
   a. So, you're a big fan.
   b. You like a lot of bands, then.

3. A I have a laptop, a smartphone, a tablet, and an e-reader.
   a. You don't know much about electronics.
   b. So, you have every gadget you need.

4. A I don't like the school cafeteria. They have the same things on the menu day after day.
   a. Yeah. I don't like it, either.
   b. Yeah. There's not much variety.

2 Summing it up

Conversation strategies | **Complete the conversation with the sentences in the box.**

> ✓ You have definite tastes, then.
> You like clothes that you can wear every day.
> You like songs that you know the lyrics to.
> You want to understand what you're looking at.

Russ So anyway, you asked me what kind of music I like. Well, I like jazz, but I don't like blues. And I like rock, but I'm not really into pop. I guess I listen mostly to classical music, though not new stuff.

Liza *You have definite tastes, then.*

Russ Yeah. I guess. I just know what I like and what I don't. What about you?

Liza Well, I like music I can dance to – music that makes me feel good. I love it when I can sing along.

Russ I know what you mean. _____

Liza Exactly. I like music that puts me in a good mood.

Russ Yeah, I know what you're saying.

Liza It's the same with art. I like to be able to look at a picture and recognize what it is. Is it a flower or a car? Is it a man or a woman? You know what I mean?

Russ I know. _____

Liza That's right. I don't like art that's too weird.

Russ That's kind of how I feel about fashion. I like all the new fashions, but I'm not sure I'd ever wear them. Some styles are a little too weird for my taste, you know? They're just not practical.

Liza Right. _____

Russ Yes. I'm just conservative, I guess.

3 Now, what do you like?

Conversation strategies Add *Now* to the conversation in two appropriate places. Change the capital letters and add commas where necessary.

Avery   I guess I'm pretty traditional, you know. I have conservative tastes in most things, like music and fashion.

Mike   Really? I guess you don't listen to techno music, right?

Avery   No way!

Mike   _____ Are you the same about food, too?

Avery   Actually, I like trying different foods. _____ I guess I'm not as conservative when it comes to eating.

Mike   Interesting! _____ Have you tried sushi?

Avery   Yes, I have. _____ And I love it!

4 Now, is there . . . ?

Conversation strategies Read Kay's comments about her likes and dislikes. Use the cues to complete each conversation with a summarizing response and a follow-up question with *Now*.

1. Kay   I listen to all kinds of music – jazz, classical, hip-hop, rock.

    You   (you / have / pretty broad tastes in music)   *So, you have pretty broad tastes in music.*

    Kay   Yeah, I guess I do!

    You   (you / have a favorite)   *Now, do you have a favorite?*

    Kay   No, I pretty much like everything!

2. Kay   Isn't this weather terrible? It's been over 90 degrees for at least eight days in a row! I can't stand it.

    You   (you / not like / hot weather)   _____

    Kay   No, I don't like hot weather at all.

    You   (you / like / cold weather)   _____

    Kay   Absolutely! I'm a skier, so I love cold weather.

3. Kay   My car is really old, so I always worry that it's going to break down. I never know if it's going to start or not.

    You   (it / be / pretty unreliable)   _____

    Kay   Yeah, it is. Maybe I need a new one.

    You   (what kind of car / you / like)   _____

    Kay   I'm not really sure. Anything, if it's reliable.

1 Street fashion

Reading | **A** Read the interviews.

Which person is the most interested in fashion? _____
Who is the least interested? _____

How would you describe your style?

My style? It's casual and easy. I wear things that aren't too fussy – things that are comfortable and easy to wear. It's a little plain, but not too plain – I always wear a little color.

What does your style say about you?

My style says I'm easygoing. I like to look good, but I'm not going to spend a lot of time in front of the mirror. It says you should try to get to know me in a deeper way than just looking at the outside. There are other things more important than clothes.

How do you express yourself through the clothes you wear?

I don't, really. I don't spend a lot of time thinking about my clothes. I'd rather express myself in other ways, like talking to people or writing.

Sadie

How would you describe your style?

I wear casual but stylish things that don't stand out, or aren't too different. I like my clothes to be simple, but I usually take more of a risk with my shoes.

What does your style say about you?

It reflects my desire to be fashionable, but is not a demand for attention. For example, at parties I usually talk to one person at a time, rather than trying to be really outgoing. I'm more laid-back.

How do you express yourself through the clothes you wear?

My clothes are a way of showing the outside world what to expect. When I go out, people can guess that I'm relaxed and friendly. My clothes make me look approachable.

Carlos

How would you describe your style?

Unique. I mix lots of different styles together to make my individual style. Some days I'll wear a lace skirt with a plaid wool vest and tights in a cool pattern. And sometimes I'll put on a vintage hat to complete the look.

What does your style say about you?

My style says I'm unpredictable. I change from one day to the next. You can't put a particular label on me, like "She's preppy," or "She's classic," or "trendy," or whatever.

How do you express yourself through the clothes you wear?

It's fun to wear things that make people guess about you. People don't know who I am when they see my clothes, because I don't look just like everyone else. I like to be a little mysterious, to keep a few secrets about myself.

Michi

B Find the words below in the interviews and circle the best meaning.

1. fussy a. simple b. very detailed or decorated
2. stand out a. look different b. look the same
3. a desire a. something you really want b. something you don't want
4. approachable a. easy to talk to b. unfriendly or shy
5. unpredictable a. conservative and average b. strange and difficult to guess

16

C Read the questions. Check (✓) the names in the chart.

	Sadie	Carlos	Michi
1. Who likes to stand out in a crowd?	☐	☐	✓
2. Who likes to wear comfortable clothes?	☐	☐	☐
3. Who thinks their clothes shouldn't reveal their true personality?	☐	☐	☐
4. Who likes to change their look the most?	☐	☐	☐
5. Who likes to look nice, but not too different?	☐	☐	☐

2 Fashion tips

Writing **A** Read the fashion tips and add the appropriate punctuation: commas (,), dashes (–), or exclamation marks (!).

1. If you want to take care of your clothes you should wash them regularly dry them carefully and store them properly.

2. Choose clothes that make you feel good clothes that reflect your individual style.

3. Buy clothes that you can wear for more than one season that way you will get the most out of your new clothes.

4. Mix classic designs with trendier pieces wear simple black pants with a fun belt a trendy shirt and a classic jacket. You'll never be out of style.

B What is your fashion advice? Write three of your own fashion tips.

Unit 2 Progress chart

What can you do? Mark the boxes. ✓ = I can . . . ? = I need to review how to . . .	To review, go back to these pages in the Student's Book.
Grammar ☐ make comparisons using *as . . . as* and *not as . . . as*. ☐ ask negative questions when I want someone to agree with me.	12 and 13 14
Vocabulary ☐ use at least 20 new words and expressions to talk about fashion.	12, 13, and 15
Conversation strategies ☐ show understanding by summarizing what someone says. ☐ use *Now* to introduce a follow-up question on a different aspect of a topic.	16 17
Writing ☐ use commas (,), dashes (–), and exclamation marks (!).	19

17

World cultures

UNIT **3**

Lesson **A** / Traditional things

1 Traditions

Grammar | Complete the conversation with the simple present passive.

Ken What's your favorite tradition from when you were a child?

Kerstin Hmm . . . let's see . . . I'd say Santa Lucia's Day.

Ken Santa Lucia's Day? I've never heard of it. Is it a Swedish festival?

Kerstin Yeah. It *'s celebrated* (celebrate) on December thirteenth. It's the darkest time of winter, and Santa Lucia _____ (consider) to be the symbol of light. So, it reminds everyone that the days will get longer and sunnier after December.

Ken Oh, I see. So what do you do to celebrate?

Kerstin Well, in schools, for example, one girl _____ (choose) to be Santa Lucia. She wears a white dress, and a crown of candles _____ (place) on her head. Then the Santa Lucia song _____ (sing) by everyone. And in some families, the girl serves her parents breakfast in bed. That _____ (not do) in all homes, though.

Ken So, is there a special kind of food that _____ (eat), or anything?

Kerstin Yeah, they have these sweet buns that _____ (make) with spices. They _____ usually _____ (serve) with coffee – or juice for the kids.

Ken Huh. It sounds nice.

2 Did you know?

Grammar | Rewrite each sentence using the simple present passive. Use *by* when the "doer" of the action is given.

1. Some Native Americans carve totem poles out of wood.
   Totem poles are carved out of wood by some Native Americans.

2. They make the traditional Spanish dish, *paella*, with chicken, seafood, and saffron.
   _____

3. In Mexico, they celebrate the Day of the Dead on the first two days in November.
   _____

4. In Taiwan, parents give children red envelopes with money inside on New Year's Day.
   _____

18

So you want to know about Ireland . . .

Grammar | Complete the web page with the verbs in the boxes. Use the simple present passive.

○○○   About Ireland

ABOUT IRELAND

SPORTS   ✓call   call   hold   play   use

The Irish love international sports like soccer and rugby, but they have their
very own national sports, too. One traditional sport in Ireland _is called_
hurling. Sticks, or *hurleys*, _____ to hit a ball, a *sliotar*. Matches are
usually 70 minutes long and _____ between two teams. Women play a
similar sport, which _____ *camogie*. The final match _____ every
September in Dublin.

MUSIC   call   learn   not use   perform   sing

Music is a strong tradition in Ireland. A typical musical event _____ a
"session." Sessions _____ in pubs, clubs, and homes, where musicians
and singers get together to play Irish music in an informal setting. Sheet music
_____ at a traditional session because the tunes and songs _____ by
heart. Some of the oldest songs _____ without musical accompaniment.

FOOD   boil   make   mash   mix   serve

One of Ireland's dishes, *colcannon*, _____ traditionally on Halloween. It
_____ with potatoes and cabbage, which _____ in separate pots.
The potatoes _____ until creamy, and then they _____ with the
cabbage, leeks, milk, spices, and butter, and baked in a pan.

 About you

Grammar | Complete the questions with the verbs in parentheses. Then answer the questions with true
information using the simple present passive.

1. What sport _is considered_ (consider) a traditional sport in your country?
   Kite flying is considered a traditional sport in South Korea.

2. What handicrafts _____ typically _____ (make)?

   _____

3. What drinks _____ traditionally _____ (serve)?

   _____

4. What kinds of traditional games _____ (play)?

   _____

5. What special occasions _____ (celebrate)?

   _____

6. What traditional songs _____ (sing)?

   _____

19

1 Mind your manners!

Grammar and vocabulary

Use the words in the box to complete the sentences with either verb + -ing or to + verb.

1. Italy: It's customary _to kiss_ friends and family when you meet.
2. South Korea: _____ your bare feet to elderly people is disrespectful.
3. Indonesia: _____ and drinking before you are asked to by your host is rude.
4. The U.S.A.: It's impolite _____ at a bus stop or in a bank, for example.
5. Mexico: _____ is the normal way to greet people in a business situation.
6. Japan: It's important _____ your shoes before you enter someone's home.
7. Saudi Arabia: _____ in public is a sign of friendship.
8. Germany: If you're sitting, it's polite _____ when greeting people and shaking their hands.

> cut in line
> eat
> hold hands
> ✓ kiss
> shake hands
> show
> stand up
> take off

2 Manners dos and don'ts

Grammar and vocabulary

Look at the pictures and complete the sentences.

1. In the United States, you should try _to keep_ your voice down in a library.

2. In Japan, _____ is a way of showing respect.

3. _____ an argument in public in Vietnam is considered bad manners.

4. _____ around barefoot in Belize is an acceptable custom.

5. It's acceptable not _____ waiters in Australia, unless you're at a very fancy restaurant.

6. It's bad manners in Indonesia _____ at someone with your finger.

3 Good manners

Grammar | Complete the sentences with the correct form of the verbs. Then check (✓) the sentences that are true in your country. Circle the six most important ones.

GOOD MANNERS CHECKLIST

1. ____ You can offend people by _reaching_ (reach) across a table for something.
2. ____ It's polite _____ (say) hello to your teacher when you arrive in class.
3. ____ _____ (eat) on the subway is considered rude.
4. ____ _____ (be) five minutes late for a meeting is acceptable.
5. ____ It's considered rude _____ (shout) at someone.
6. ____ It's not acceptable _____ (go) to a party uninvited.
7. ____ People are expected _____ (be) on time for medical and dental appointments.
8. ____ Be careful not _____ (leave) work without _____ (say) good night to your co-workers.
9. ____ _____ (give) money for a wedding gift is common.
10. ____ _____ (ask) about someone's age might be offensive.
11. ____ When a train stops, it's better _____ (wait) for people to get off before _____ (get) on yourself.
12. ____ It's bad manners _____ (talk) loudly on a cell phone in public places.

4 About you

Grammar | Rewrite the sentences using _not_ to give them an opposite meaning. Then check (✓) the sentences that are true in your country.

1. ____ It's OK to point at people in public places.
   ____ _It's not OK to point at people in public places._

2. ____ It's customary to walk in someone's house without taking off your shoes.
   ____ _____

3. ____ Try to stand close to people you're talking to.
   ____ _____

4. ____ Opening a gift in front of the person who gave it to you is considered rude.
   ____ _____

5. ____ You can annoy people by saying you're sorry if you bump into them.
   ____ _____

6. ____ It's customary to tip hairstylists.
   ____ _____

7. ____ Being early for a party is considered polite.
   ____ _____

8. ____ Talking on a cell phone in a public place is acceptable.
   ____ _____

To be honest, . . .

1 I really like it.

Conversation strategies | **Rewrite each response using the best expression to make the response sound more direct.**

1. A Do you like your new dorm?
   B Yeah. I like it.
   ((really)/ sort of) _I really like it._

2. A What's your new roommate like?
   B Well, I don't really like her.
   (to be honest / I guess) _____

3. A Do you miss anything about your old school?
   B No. I hated my old school.
   (absolutely / a little bit) _____

4. A Do you ever think about studying abroad?
   B Yes! I would like to do that.
   (kind of / definitely) _____

5. A If you moved away, would you miss your family?
   B Oh, I'd miss my family, especially my brother.
   (in a way / certainly) _____

2 About you 1

Conversation strategies | **Rewrite the sentences so that they are true for you. Use different expressions from the box. Add more information.**

| absolutely | certainly | honestly | really | to tell you the truth |
| actually | definitely | in fact | to be honest | |

1. I love learning about new cultures.
   I really love learning about new cultures. I'd absolutely love to go to Kenya.

2. I don't think it would be exciting to live in a new city.
   _____

3. I'd miss home cooking if I lived in another country.
   _____

4. I'd hate to live with a roommate. I'd prefer to live by myself.
   _____

5. I'd like to live all over the world. I can't imagine living in just one place.
   _____

6. I'm sure I'd get homesick if I lived a long way from home.
   _____

3 Of course . . .

Conversation strategies Use *of course* twice in each conversation where it is appropriate and not rude. Leave one blank in each conversation empty. Add commas where necessary.

1. **Bruno** I hear you decided to study abroad next year. Where are you going?

   Kara _____ I'm going to Mexico!

   Bruno You must be so excited! I know I would be.

   Kara Yeah, I'm definitely excited, but I'm really nervous, too.

   Bruno Just think about all the cool experiences you'll have.

   Kara Yeah, I know. But I'm going to miss you _____ !

   I mean, who am I going to talk to when I have a problem?

   Bruno Well, *me* _____ . We can always chat over the Internet!

   Kara Right. . . . I forgot about that!

2. **Yumi** Hi, Brad. How was your business trip?

   Brad To tell you the truth, it was awful. The day I left, the
   traffic was really bad, so I got to the airport late.
   And _____ I missed my flight.

   Yumi So, you were probably late for the sales meeting, then?

   Brad Yeah _____ . Then, because I was so stressed
   out, I forgot to give Mr. Yamamoto my business card.

   Yumi I'm sure he understood.

   Brad Yeah, and I apologized right away _____ .

   Yumi So, it doesn't sound like your trip was that bad.

4 About you 2

Conversation strategies Answer the questions directly and confidently with true information.
Then add a follow-up sentence with *of course*.

1. Would you jump at the chance to study in another country?

   I'd absolutely jump at the chance to study in another country.

   Of course, I'd have to learn the language first.

2. What would you miss about your country if you lived abroad?

   _____

   _____

3. If you had the opportunity to live someplace else, where would it be?

   _____

   _____

4. What would be the first thing you'd do after moving to a new city?

   _____

   _____

1 Proverbs for everyday living

Reading | **A Read the article. Which sentence best states the writer's attitude toward proverbs?**

1. Proverbs are fun but not meaningful.
2. Proverbs about love are truer than proverbs about sports or money.
3. Proverbs can help and guide us in different life situations.
4. Proverbs are never true.

Timeless wisdom

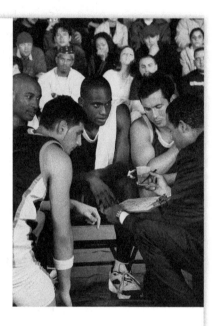

No matter what problem we have or what issue we are discussing, there always seems to be a memorable proverb that neatly sums up the situation, provides some wisdom, or simply makes us feel better. We find a selection that will inspire us, make us wiser, and console us through hard times. Sports, money, and love are just three of the areas that have inspired a number of well-used proverbs.

SPORTS There are probably few coaches who haven't called on a proverb or two to motivate their players. Players who aren't working to their full potential might benefit from hearing "no pain, no gain" and understand that increasing performance on the field requires more hard work and effort. During intense parts of a game, a coach might yell, "No guts, no glory!" to push his or her players into scoring a goal. "There is no *I* in *team*" encourages teamwork and reminds players that not being the "star" of the team might be hard, but it could mean a stronger winning team.

MONEY The proverb "A fool and his money are soon parted" describes a person who has money but squanders it on poor choices. A person who doesn't understand that it takes hard work to make money might benefit from the proverb "Money doesn't grow on trees." If it did, it would be easy to find and everyone would have an abundance of it. On the other hand, it's important to remember that money isn't always the answer to our problems. Sometimes we have to remind ourselves that "the best things in life are free" – for example, good health, family, and friends.

LOVE The proverb "Love is blind" means that if you are in love with someone, you overlook all their negative points. It's often said when you don't approve of a friend's partner; it offers an explanation for what you see as a poor choice. Then, when relationships go through sad or emotional times, the proverb "Love conquers all" reminds us that it's wise to approach these problems with love because they will be easier to handle. Love will get you through most difficult situations.

B Find these words and phrases in the article. Match them with their definitions.

1. sums up ___f___	a. waste
2. console ____	b. ability
3. potential ____	c. an amount that is more than enough
4. squander ____	d. defeats, beats
5. abundance ____	e. give comfort or sympathy to
6. conquers ____	✓f. explains without detail

2   If at first you don't succeed, . . .

Writing   **A   Read about an athlete's favorite proverb. Fill in the blanks with the expressions in the box.**

I like this proverb because	it means that
it's often said that	one of my favorite proverbs is

As a college wrestler, I compete with some of the toughest and most disciplined athletes. _____ "fall seven times, stand up eight." To me, _____ you should never give up on your goals and dreams no matter how hard practice is every day or how many important matches you lose. _____ athletes can't win unless they believe in themselves. _____ it reminds me that no matter how many times I fail, if I don't stand up after my failure, I'll never succeed.

B   Describe a proverb that you use for motivation in your life. Use the expressions above.

Unit 3 Progress chart

What can you do? Mark the boxes. ✔ = I can . . . ? = I need to review how to . . .	To review, go back to these pages in the Student's Book.
☐ use the simple present passive to talk about cultural traditions.	22 and 23
☐ use verb + -ing as a subject, and as an object of a preposition.	24 and 25
☐ use to + verb after It's.	24 and 25
☐ use at least 10 expressions to talk about different customs and manners.	24 and 25
☐ use expressions like to be honest to sound more direct.	26
☐ use of course to give information that is not surprising or to agree.	27
☐ use expressions like It means . . . to talk about culture or proverbs.	29

Grammar

Vocabulary

Conversation strategies

Writing

Socializing

Lesson A — Party time

1 What are you supposed to do?

Grammar and vocabulary | Look at the pictures. Complete the sentences with *be supposed to* and an appropriate verb. Use negatives where necessary.

1. You *'re not supposed to park* on the street.
   You *'re supposed to park* in the parking lot.

2. They _____ shoes inside.
   They _____ their shoes.

3. She _____ at the dentist.
   She _____ home.

4. He _____ his room.
   He _____ on the phone.

2 It was supposed to be a nice weekend.

Grammar | Complete the email with the correct form of *be supposed to* or *was / were going to*. Sometimes more than one answer is possible.

New Message

Hey Jane,

    I had a terrible weekend. On Saturday morning, I _was going to / was supposed to_ go running with a friend because the weather _____ be nice. But it rained, and she didn't come. She emailed me and wrote, "I _____ come, but when I saw the weather, I decided to stay in bed. Sorry."

    Then my parents came over to my apartment – they were two hours early. They _____ come at 1:00, but they came at 11:00. The apartment was a complete mess! They took me to that new Mexican place on Oak Street. Have you been there? It _____ be really good. But it was completely booked – I didn't realize that you _____ make reservations.

    So then we tried an Italian place across the street. That was nice, but I didn't know my pasta dish had shrimp in it. I'm allergic to shrimp, and I _____ avoid it. So I got sick. Now here's the worst part. I _____ go to a party on Saturday night, but I couldn't because I still felt sick. I sure hope next weekend will be better.

Take care!
Allie

3 I was supposed to . . .

Grammar | **Complete the conversation with the correct form of *be supposed to* or *was / were going to*. Sometimes more than one correct answer is possible.**

Christy   Hi, Zach. Are you going to Isabelle's party tonight?

Zach   Yeah, I am, actually. I *was supposed to meet / was going to meet*

(meet) my parents for dinner, but they canceled. So, now I can go.

Christy   Great! I _____ (pick up) Sanjay at 7:00.

Do you need a ride?

Zach   Sure, thanks. Now, I can't remember. . . . _____

we _____ (bring) anything like food or drinks?

Christy   No, only if you want to. I _____

(not / make) anything, but maybe I will if I have time.

Zach   You should make those chocolate chip cookies you brought

to the last party. They were awesome.

Christy   Yeah, they are pretty good. But they have nuts in them.

Isabelle _____ (not / eat) nuts

because she's allergic to them.

Zach   Right. Maybe you should just make a chocolate cake or something.

Christy   Good idea. Oh, and don't forget to bring your bathing suit and a towel.

The weather _____ (be) great tonight, and Isabelle's

pool is beautiful.

Zach   Sounds like a plan to me!

4 About you

Grammar | **Answer the questions with your own information. Use *be supposed to* or
was / were going to. Use negatives and contractions where necessary.**

1. Is there anything you have to do to prepare for your English class?
    For our next class, we're supposed to bring in some photos.
    _____

2. What's the weather forecast for tomorrow?
    _____

3. What do you have to do tomorrow?
    _____

4. What plans do you have for this week?
    _____

5. What appointment or plans did you cancel last month?
    _____

6. What exciting future plans do you have?
    _____

1 Get away with . . .

Vocabulary | **A** Complete the sentences with the appropriate *get* expression.

1. In some companies, you can <u>g</u> <u>e</u> <u>t</u> <u>a</u> <u>w</u> <u>a</u> <u>y</u> <u>w</u> <u>i</u> <u>t</u> <u>h</u>
   wearing casual clothes to work. In my company, you have to dress more formally.

2. I'm so busy at work that I don't have time to answer all my emails right away, but I always
   ____ ____ ____ ____ ____ ____ ____ ____ ____ ____ ____ them eventually.

3. I have a business trip next week, but I'm going to try to
   ____ ____ ____ ____ ____ ____ ____ ____ it. I'm tired of traveling so much.

4. Someone else got the promotion I wanted at work. I'm upset, but I'll
   ____ ____ ____ ____ ____ ____ ____ it soon.

5. My friend's always late for work. I just don't ____ ____ ____ ____ ____! How does he keep his job?

6. My office doesn't have windows. It's depressing. I don't think I'll ever
   ____ ____ ____ ____ ____ ____ ____ ____ ____ not having sunlight.

7. During the summer, my company has new hours – we ____ ____ ____ ____ ____ ____
   work at noon on Fridays!

8. My boss never returns my phone calls. I ____ ____ ____ ____ ____ ____
   ____ ____ ____ ____ ____ ____ that he's avoiding me.

9. Tonight there's a company party so new employees can ____ ____ ____ ____ ____
   ____ ____ ____ ____ everyone. I really hope to ____ ____ ____ ____ ____ ____ ____ early.
   I hate these functions. But, the good food should help me
   ____ ____ ____ ____ ____ ____ ____ ____ ____ ____ it OK.

10. I have a meeting in ten minutes! I really have to ____ ____ ____ ____ ____ ____ ____ ____ .

B Complete the conversations with some of the *get* expressions from part A.

1. A Oh, I can't believe it's already 8:30! I'd better <u>get going</u> if
      I want to catch the 9:00 train.

   B Yeah, I don't think you can _____ being late again.

   A I know, but it's so hard to get up in the morning. . . .

   B I don't _____ . How can you complain?
      You _____ work so early. I'd love your job!

2. A What time do you think you'll finish work tonight? Do you think
      you can _____ from work a little early?

   B Sure, I have a late meeting, but I can probably _____
      it. Why? I _____ you have something planned. . . .

   A Did you _____ reading yesterday's restaurant review?

   B Yeah, for that amazing restaurant with the six-month waiting list?

   A Well, we're going tonight!

2 ▶ I get the feeling . . .

Grammar
and
vocabulary

Complete the anecdotes. Put the words in order and use the correct form of the verbs.

1. Melanie was very superstitious. She couldn't _get over her fear_
   (over / her fear / get) of seeing black cats. She thought they were so
   unlucky. Now she can't _____
   (get / a day / through) without running into one.

2. Gary was supposed to meet Tracy at the movies, but he really wanted to
   _____ (get / of / go / out) with her. He called Tracy and said
   he couldn't _____ (work / off / get) early on Friday night.
   Instead, Gary made arrangements to go to the movies with Marissa.
   He really thought he could _____ (it / away / get / with).
   But he didn't – as he found out when he ran into Tracy at the
   movie theater!

3. John didn't _____ (pay / around / to / get) his
   electricity bill. He thought he could _____
   (get / with / away / make) the payment a few days late. Now he has
   to _____ (to / used / eat / get) dinner in the dark!

3 ▶ About you

Grammar
and
vocabulary

Answer the questions with true information.

1. What haven't you gotten around to doing this week?
   I haven't gotten around to cleaning my room.

2. Have you bought anything new that took time to get used to?
   _____

3. What's a chore you always try to get out of doing?
   _____

4. What events do you find it hard to get through?
   _____

5. What time do you get off work?
   _____

6. How long did it take you to get over your last cold?
   _____

1 So, you're throwing a party?

Conversation strategies **A** Unscramble these statement questions.

1. right / you, / is / It ?
   It is you, right?

2. teenagers, / huh / So / teach / you ?
   _____

3. them / haven't / So / told / you / yet ?
   _____

4. that software company, / working / still / You're / at / right ?
   _____

5. know / then / here, / don't / So / they / you're ?
   _____

6. huh / about / didn't / You / hear / that, ?
   _____

B Complete the conversation with the statement questions from part A.

Eva   Oh, my gosh. Dan? I haven't seen you in ages!

Dan   Eva? *It is you, right?* _____ You look great!
       How are you?

Eva   Oh, I'm fine. Thanks. So, what are you up to?
       _____

Dan   Cyber-trex? Actually, no, not anymore. They went out of
       business. _____

Eva   No, I didn't. I'm sorry.

Dan   Oh, it's OK. I'm at Micro-com now. I like it a lot better.
       So, what's up with you?

Eva   Um, I teach history at the local high school.

Dan   Wow! _____ What's that like?

Eva   It's really good. The students are great. Anyway, what brings you back here?

Dan   Well, I'm in town to throw my parents a surprise party for their
       40th wedding anniversary.

Eva   _____

Dan   No, not yet! In fact, my brother and sister don't even know I'm here.

Eva   _____ About the party, I mean.

Dan   No, I couldn't. They can't keep a secret to save their lives!

2 So, you're having a birthday party?

Conversation strategies | Find three more places where you can use *so* in the conversation. Change the capital letters and add commas where necessary. Then write which meaning of *so* you are using: 1 = to start a topic with a question; 2 = to check your understanding; 3 = to pause or let the other person draw a conclusion; 4 = to close a topic.

Rita   _So, ~~Y~~ᵧou're having a birthday party this year?_   _1_

Craig   I don't know. _____ My birthday is going to fall right in the middle of final exams.   _____

Rita   _____ You think people won't come if they're studying?   _____

Craig   Yeah, I mean, these are important exams, _____ . . .   _____
you know, everyone is working hard to get good grades.

Rita   _____ Well, maybe you could wait until after the   _____
exams are over.

Craig   Yeah, I guess I could.

Rita   Then you can have a double celebration: for your   _____
birthday *and* the end of exams. _____

Craig   That's a good idea.

Rita   _____ Don't forget to invite me!   _____

Craig   I won't!

3 A late night

Conversation strategies | Complete the conversation with the sentences in the box.

So you're not too tired to go out tonight?	You're going out again tonight?
You didn't do anything?	✓You stayed out pretty late, huh?
You had a good time, right?	

Keith   Oh, . . . I'm so tired. That was a long night last night.

Phil   _You stayed out pretty late, huh?_ _____

Keith   Yeah, until about 2:30 in the morning. But it was fun.

Phil   _____

Keith   Oh, definitely. The band was great – just awesome.
So, anyway, what about you? Did you go out?

Phil   No. . . . I just stayed home. That's all.

Keith   _____

Phil   No. I was just here all night.

Keith   Too bad. Do you want to come out tonight? Are you doing anything?

Phil   I don't have any plans yet. _____

Keith   Well, I was thinking about it. But I don't want to be out too late.

Phil   _____

Keith   Too tired to go out? No way! I'll be fine later.

Phil   Sounds good to me.

1 First impressions

Reading | **A** Read the article. Then add the correct heading to each section.

> Be fearless.   Pay attention to your body language.   Use your ears.
> Maintain eye contact. ✓Smile!

SOCIALIZING 101

Whether you are an extrovert or an introvert, one thing is certain: Almost everyone experiences some degree of stress when it comes to being sociable in new situations. It doesn't matter if you're starting a new job, going back to school, or if you're waiting in line at a coffee shop. The next time you're out and about, try one of these tips to help you become better at socializing.

_____*Smile!*_____ One of the easiest and most effective ways to be more sociable is to smile. Remember: You're supposed to be having fun. When you strike up a conversation, a warm smile will make you seem more approachable and friendly. Don't be surprised when the person you start a conversation with reciprocates with an equally warm smile!

_____ Once you've started a conversation, make sure you keep your eyes focused on the person you're talking to. There's nothing more off-putting than talking to someone whose eyes are wandering around the room rather than paying attention to the conversation. Not every conversation is interesting, but there's no reason to be rude.

_____ When you cross your arms in front of you while standing or you cross your legs while sitting, you are literally keeping people at a distance. Try to keep an open, relaxed position, and people will feel more comfortable approaching you.

_____ Having a conversation is a two-way street. Ask engaging questions, and then really listen to what your conversation partner says. Who knows? You may discover you have common musical interests, or you might even get a recommendation for a great restaurant. You'll never know if you don't listen closely.

_____ Don't stand around waiting for someone to start talking with you. Get over your fear and be the person who initiates conversations. Most people are open to having a warm, meaningful conversation, especially when they are out in a social situation. Walking up to a stranger may seem daunting at first, but once you've done it a few times, it will seem natural and maybe even fun!

B Find these words and expressions in the article. Match them with their meanings.

1. reciprocate _e_
2. off-putting _____
3. wandering _____
4. literally _____
5. engaging _____
6. initiate _____
7. daunting _____

   a. interesting
   b. actually
   c. slightly frightening
   d. annoying or unpleasant
✓e. behave in the same way
   f. going around with no clear purpose
   g. start, cause something to begin

C Read the article again. Check (✓) the statements that the writer of the article would agree with. Cross (✗) the ones that the writer wouldn't agree with.

1. __✗__ There's no reason to be nervous when you socialize.

2. __✓__ Socializing is easier when you smile.

3. _____ People are supposed to enjoy socializing.

4. _____ It's not rude to look around the room when you're talking to someone.

5. _____ Crossing your arms is a good idea because it helps you feel comfortable.

6. _____ Socializing is more difficult when you only listen.

7. _____ Conversations with strangers can lead to all kinds of new possibilities.

8. _____ You can get used to socializing, and then it will be easier.

2 As an introvert

Writing **A** Read the short article about meeting new people. Replace each underlined *as* with *because*, *being*, or *while*.

> <u>As</u> an introvert, I have a hard time meeting new people. I usually don't like to go to parties where there are lots of people I don't know.
>
> When I travel, though, I am less shy. I find I can talk to people <u>as</u> I wait to get on a plane or train. Maybe I feel more comfortable <u>as</u> I'm away from home and I can be who I want to be. But when I get back home, I'm shy again!

B Write a short article about how you meet new people.

Unit 4 Progress chart

What can you do? Mark the boxes. ✓ = I can . . . ? = I need to review how to . . .	To review, go back to these pages in the Student's Book.
Grammar	
☐ use *be supposed to* to say what should happen.	34 and 35
☐ use *be supposed to* to talk about things I should do.	34 and 35
☐ use *was / were supposed to* and *was / were going to* for things that didn't happen.	34 and 35
☐ use inseparable phrasal verbs with and without prepositions.	36 and 37
Vocabulary	
☐ use at least 10 new expressions with *get*.	36 and 37
Conversation strategies	
☐ use statement questions to check understanding.	38
☐ use *so* to start or close topics, pause, or check understanding.	39
Writing	
☐ use three different meanings of *as*.	41

Lesson A / Rules and regulations

1 Something ought to be done.

Grammar | **Rewrite the sentences in the passive form, starting with the words given.**

1. They must change the law.
2. They should ban fireworks.
3. They ought to fine people who litter.
4. They shouldn't allow smoking on the street.
5. They could encourage healthy eating in schools.
6. They have to do something about violent movies.

The law _must be changed_ .

Fireworks _____ .

People who litter _____ .

Smoking _____ on the street.

Healthy eating _____ in schools.

Something _____ about violent movies.

2 What's your opinion?

Grammar and vocabulary | **A Circle the correct words to complete the opinions.**

1. People should not be (**encouraged**) / **changed** / **passed** to keep dangerous pets like snakes and spiders.
2. Cell phones shouldn't be **fined** / **allowed** / **given** in museums.
3. People who litter should be **encouraged** / **allowed** / **fined** at least $100 for each item they drop.
4. People should be **given** / **made** / **changed** to vote.
5. Laws have to be **passed** / **arrested** / **done** to ban smoking in all public places.
6. Young people ought to be **banned** / **made** / **given** a driving test every year until they are 21.
7. Smoking on city streets could easily be **made** / **passed** / **banned**.
8. People should be **arrested** / **made** / **changed** for not carrying an ID.

B Do you agree or disagree with the opinions in part A? Answer with your own opinions.

1. _I agree completely. I don't think people should be allowed to keep dangerous pets at all._
2. _____
3. _____
4. _____
5. _____
6. _____
7. _____
8. _____

3 What should be done?

Grammar | **Read the situations and complete the comments. Use the passive of the verbs given.**

1. A woman is facing a large fine because her neighbor complained to the police about her messy yard. The angry woman then dumped her garbage in the neighbor's yard.

   A I think the fine is absolutely right. You shouldn't _be allowed_ (allow) to have a messy yard.

   B I don't agree. She shouldn't _____ (fine). It's her own property, and she should be able to do what she wants.

   C The woman should _____ (arrest) for dumping garbage in her neighbor's yard!

2. A motorcycle rider was arrested by the police for refusing to wear a helmet. The motorcyclist said that he couldn't wear the helmet because of his traditional headdress.

   A I agree with the motorcyclist. He shouldn't _____ (make) to wear a helmet.

   B People shouldn't _____ (arrest) for not wearing a helmet. It's their choice.

   C Well, everyone has to obey the law. People shouldn't _____ (treat) differently.

3. A foreign exchange student who failed to show his ID was given a warning after a local storeowner called the police. In an unrelated incident, a young woman riding her bike to work was fined for failing to carry her ID.

   A I didn't know you could _____ (fine) for not carrying an ID.

   B It's a new law, but I think it ought to _____ (change).

   C I wonder why the police stopped the woman. People shouldn't _____ (stop) for no reason.

4 About you

Grammar | **Read the situations and give your own opinion. Use passive modal verbs.**

1. A 13-year-old boy sneaks into an R-rated movie. What ought to be done?
   He ought to be made to tell his parents.

2. A man throws a soda can out of his car window. Should he be arrested or fined?

   _____

3. A 16-year-old student wants a part-time job. Should she be encouraged to get one?

   _____

4. A 15-year-old girl applies for a credit card. Should she be given one?

   _____

5. A 12-year-old boy spends three hours a day online. Should he be given a time limit?

   _____

6. An 85-year-old man was in six minor car accidents this year. Should he be allowed to drive?

   _____

1 What's the crime?

Vocabulary | Match the words in Column A with the words in Column B to make expressions for crimes and punishments. Write the expressions under the appropriate heading in the chart.

Column A
put
armed
lose
break into
kill
take someone
send
minor
clean up
go to

Column B
a house
offense
on probation
robbery
graffiti
to prison
captive
jail
your license
someone

Crime	Punishment
	put on probation
‘	

2 News flash

Vocabulary | Complete the news flashes with the words in the box.

jaywalker	penalties	sentence	stealing
kidnapper	robbers	✓ shoplifters	vandals

1. A TV actress was caught stealing in a designer store. The manager said ___shoplifters___ will be punished even if they're famous.

2. The number of robberies has declined. Police say more _____ are getting caught.

3. A murderer who was convicted of killing his boss receives a _____ of life in prison.

4. Three _____ were caught on camera spray-painting graffiti on office buildings. All three were put on probation for two years.

5. _____ for a first-time speeding offense now include a $500 fine.

6. A _____ was arrested after crossing in the middle of a busy street.

7. A _____ demands $10,000,000 after taking a politician's daughter from her home.

8. A teen was arrested for _____ money from a neighbor's house. Police say the 17-year-old broke into the neighbor's house while she was at work.

3 In the news

Grammar | Imagine you are telling a friend about the excerpts from the newspaper below. Rewrite each sentence in the passive. Change the underlined verbs to the *get* passive, or use the *be* passive with *should*. Make any other necessary changes.

> **1** Police <u>arrested</u> three teenagers yesterday for stealing a car.   **2** The officers <u>caught</u> them joyriding along a busy street.   **3** The owner of the car thinks they should <u>fine</u> the teens.

1. " *Three teenagers got arrested yesterday for stealing a car.* "
2. "_____"
3. "_____"

> **4** Fans think a TV network should <u>make</u> reality-TV star Lulu Maxwell give a public apology.   **5** The county court <u>fined</u> Maxwell $500 and <u>put</u> her on probation for six months.   **6** Store detectives <u>caught</u> her shoplifting in a department store downtown in March of this year.

4. "_____"
5. "_____"
6. "_____"

> **7** Car owners <u>caught</u> a man writing graffiti on their cars last Wednesday.
> **8** The judge <u>convicted</u> Jim Hillman yesterday of vandalism.   **9** The owners of the cars believe they should <u>make</u> Hillman pay for the damage done to their vehicles.

7. "_____"
8. "_____"
9. "_____"

4 About you

Grammar | Answer the questions with true information. Use the *get* passive.

1. What happens if you get caught shoplifting in your country?
   You get fined and perhaps put in jail.

2. What's the punishment for writing graffiti on a public building?
   _____

3. What's the punishment for murder?
   _____

4. What happens if you jaywalk?
   _____

5. What happens if you get caught speeding too many times?
   _____

1 Basically, I don't think . . .

Conversation strategies | Choose the best expressions to complete the conversation.

Roy   Did you know that Sam got caught cheating on the test?

Helen   Yeah, it's about time. He cheats on all his tests.
I wonder what the teacher's going to do about it.

Roy   I don't know. What do you think they should do?

Helen   Hmm. Well, **another thing is** / (**basically,**) I don't think
he should get away with it.

Roy   Well, no, I guess not.

Helen   I mean, **for a couple of reasons** / **the point is**. First of all, it's
not fair to the other students, and **number one** / **second of all**, it doesn't help the
person who cheats. I mean, **the thing is** / **another thing is**, I don't think Sam's really learning.

Roy   I know what you mean.

Helen   And **for two reasons** / **another thing is**, if they don't punish him, it might make other students
think they can cheat, too.

Roy   Yeah. I guess you're right.

2 I mean, the thing is, . . .

Conversation strategies | **A**   Read what Carl has to say about carrying ID cards. Number the lines in the
correct order from 1 to 7.

_____ I mean, ID cards make things easier for two reasons.

__1__ What do I think about having to carry an ID card?

_____ And then, secondly, if you have an accident or something, people can find out
who you are right away.

_____ And finally . . . um, I guess I just don't mind. You have nothing to be afraid of
if you have nothing to hide. Don't you think?

_____ First, they help the police identify criminals more easily.

_____ Well, I guess basically, I'm in favor of carrying them.

_____ And another thing is, people who work in movie theaters and other places can
easily check who is old enough to go in and stuff.

B   What do you think about carrying an ID card? Write four sentences. Use words
and expressions from part A and Exercise 1 to organize your ideas.

_____

_____

_____

_____

3 That's true, but . . .

Conversation strategies **Match Diego's opinions with his friends' responses. There is one extra response.**

1. I don't think jaywalking should be a crime. I mean, if I'm in a hurry, I should be able to cross the street wherever I want to! _____

2. I think couples that are getting married should be made to take marriage classes before they actually get married. You know, to help lower divorce rates. _____

3. I think it's the parents' responsibility to make sure their kids know right from wrong. I mean, if the kids do something wrong, their parents should be punished, too. _____

4. You know, there are just too many laws for everything! The thing is, most people are sensible enough not to need all these laws. _____

a. You've got a point there, but don't you think that parents with kids that are always in trouble should be helped, not punished?

b. Well, you've got a point, but society would be a big mess without them! I think people actually need them.

c. That's true – maybe it shouldn't be a crime – but you still need to be careful, especially if you're in a hurry.

d. That's true, but on the other hand, kids are kids, and we have to treat them all the same.

e. I never really thought of it that way. It's not such a bad idea, but I'm not sure that taking classes would help.

4 The point is, . . .

Conversation strategies **Complete the conversation with the words and expressions in the box.**

another thing is	I never thought of it that way	number two	there are two reasons
basically	number one	✓ their point is	you've got a point

Pam   Did you hear they won't let students bring snacks to class anymore? Some teachers complained that students spend too much time eating when they should be taking notes. I guess _their point is_ , students aren't paying enough attention.

Roger   I don't think that's right. I mean, _____ , you should be allowed to bring a snack.

Pam   Why do you think that?

Roger   Well, I mean, . . . _____ . I guess, _____ , you don't always have enough time between classes to get something to eat. And _____ , some classes are three hours long! You really need to eat just to stay awake! And, _____ , the teachers sometimes have drinks and things while they're teaching.

Pam   Hmm. . . . _____ there, but in some classes, students just leave the garbage from their snacks and drinks all over the desks. It's really disgusting.

Roger   Yeah, that's true. I must admit, . . . _____ .

Your right to privacy

1 Dumb criminals

Reading | **A** Read the article below. Then match the stories with the pictures.

Dumb Criminals

We all know that crime is serious and that criminals should be punished. However, it's hard not to smile when you hear about criminals like the ones in these stories, who made some dumb mistakes.

1. A thief stole 27 shoes from a store, without realizing that they were all right-footed. He wasn't arrested, but he certainly didn't get what he wanted.

2. A burglar was caught sleeping in an armchair of the house he was burglarizing when the owners came home.

3. Robbers stole $1,221 of electronics from a store. All the goods were faulty items returned by customers.

4. A man stole a police car in order to get to work. He was discovered when he stopped to help someone on the side of the road who flagged him down for help.

5. A woman walked into a fast-food restaurant early one morning and demanded money. The clerk said he couldn't open the cash drawer without a food order. When the woman grudgingly ordered onion rings, the clerk said they weren't available for breakfast. The woman became frustrated and walked out.

6. A man walked into a convenience store and asked for change, putting a twenty-dollar bill on the counter. When the cashier opened the drawer, the man demanded all the money in it. Then he ran out, leaving his twenty on the counter. The cashier reported that the man fled with about $17 in cash.

B Answer the questions about the criminals above.

Criminal 1: What didn't he notice? *He didn't notice all the shoes were right-footed.* _____

Criminal 2: Why was he caught? _____

Criminal 3: Why weren't these robbers happy? _____

Criminal 4: What was his mistake? _____

Criminal 5: What did she need to order? _____

Criminal 6: How much did his crime cost him? _____

2 A bad landing . . .

Writing **A** Read the police report. Add *because*, *since*, or *as*. Sometimes more than one answer is possible.

> ## POLICE REPORT
>
> A woman was arrested for trying to rob a convenience store. _____ she didn't
> know the store was open 24 hours a day, she broke in through the roof. Unfortunately for
> her, she fell through the roof and landed on top of a coffee machine. A police officer was
> inside the store, and he didn't have to go far to make the arrest _____ he was
> right there getting his coffee! _____ the woman was slightly injured, she went to
> the hospital first before going to jail. She was treated for minor cuts and coffee burns.

B Write a short story or article about something funny that has happened to you.
Use *because*, *since*, or *as* to give reasons for the events.

Unit 5 Progress chart

What can you do? Mark the boxes. ✓ = I can . . . ? = I need to review how to . . .	To review, go back to these pages in the Student's Book.
Grammar □ use the passive of modal verbs.	44 and 45
□ use the *get* passive.	46 and 47
Vocabulary □ use at least 25 expressions to talk about rules, regulations, crimes, and punishments.	44, 45, 46, and 47
Conversation strategies □ organize what I say with expressions like *First of all*, etc.	48
□ use expressions like *That's a good point* to show someone else has a valid argument.	49
Writing □ give reasons using *because*, *since*, and *as*.	51

Strange events

Lesson A / Coincidences

 My strange experiences

Vocabulary | **Complete Ava's blog with the words and expressions in the box.**

coincidences	out of the blue	sticks in my mind	✓UFO
déjà vu	ran into	telepathy	unexpectedly

Ava's Blog

Nothing really strange has ever happened to me. I've never seen a
_____UFO_____ . And I don't believe in _____ – you know,
that you can tell what someone else is thinking. I've never even had
that strange feeling of _____ , like I've been someplace
before. The only weird thing that _____ is meeting someone
with the same birthday as mine. But that's about it.

However, I absolutely believe strange _____ happen all the
time. In fact, last week, I called a friend completely _____ at
the same time she was calling me. That was pretty funny. A couple of
years ago, I _____ that same friend at a restaurant while I
was on vacation – completely _____ . Oh, and another time,
I was on the Internet and typed in the wrong URL. I found a website
about my old high school science teacher. He'd invented a new type
of vacuum cleaner and had become a millionaire! Cool, huh?

2 What a coincidence!

Grammar and vocabulary | **Complete the story. Use the simple past or the past perfect. Sometimes more than one answer is possible.**

One night about a year ago, I went out with some friends. I didn't really want to
go out because I _had broken up_ (break up) with my girlfriend a week or so earlier.
Anyway, I met this great girl, and we _____ (start) talking. We had a great time
and danced all night. So, we _____ (decide) to meet the next day, and to make a
long story short, we started dating.

We _____ (date) for about four months when she _____ (invite)
me to a party at her apartment. I was looking at the pictures of her college friends
around her apartment, and I _____ (notice) that my cousin Ciara from Chicago
was in one of her photos. It turns out that my girlfriend and my cousin _____ (be)
roommates for over three years in college, but they _____ (not see) each
other for about a year. What a coincidence!

3 A mystery ride

Grammar
and
vocabulary | **Read the story. Then answer the questions below using the past perfect.**

Last Tuesday, Peter got ready for his interview with a company called Compu-com. He left class and went to an ATM to get cash, but he didn't have time to get gas. He decided to get it early Wednesday morning. That night, he read over his cover letter and résumé. He felt confident. He always wrote good letters, and he had a great résumé with a nice photo. He had paid a professional to help him put it together.

Before going to bed, he got his things ready: his suit, shirt and tie, his best shoes. He set his alarm for 7:00 and went to sleep. But his cell phone was in silent mode, and he didn't hear it go off. Peter woke up at 8:30, but he left the house in two minutes flat! He didn't have enough gas to drive to Compu-com, so he decided to take a taxi. Of course, they were all occupied. After 15 minutes, a taxi stopped. There was a woman in the backseat. She asked, "Do you want a ride to Compu-com?" Peter didn't know her, but she obviously recognized him.

1. Why was Peter feeling confident? *He had written a good cover letter and résumé.*
2. Why was his résumé very strong? _____
3. Why did he sleep late on Wednesday morning? _____
4. Why was he able to leave home so quickly? _____
5. Why didn't he have enough gas to drive to the interview? _____
6. Why did he have enough money for a taxi? _____
7. Had Peter met the woman before? _____
8. How do you think the woman recognized Peter? _____

4 About you

Grammar | **Write about a strange experience or coincidence that happened to you or someone you know. Use the simple past and past perfect. Use the ideas in the box or your own ideas.**

> You received an email or a text from a friend you were thinking about.
>
> You ran into an old friend on vacation in another part of your country.
>
> You met someone with the same birthday as you.
>
> You found an item that belonged to a friend in a strange place.
>
> You gave a friend or family member the same present that he or she gave you.

_____
_____
_____
_____
_____
_____

Lesson B | Superstitions

1 Super superstitions

Vocabulary | **What superstitions do these pictures illustrate? Write the superstition below each picture.**

1. *If you put your clothes on inside out, you'll get a nice surprise.*

2. _____

3. _____

4. _____

5. _____

6. _____

2 More world superstitions

Vocabulary | **Complete the superstitions with the expressions in the box.**

broom	come into	come true	make	snake	sweep

1. Thailand: It's lucky to dream of a _____ because it means you'll meet the man or woman of your dreams.

2. China and Vietnam: It's bad luck to _____ the floor on New Year's Day with a _____ . You'll take away your good fortune.

3. Turkey: If you stand between two people with the same name and _____ a wish, your wish will _____ .

4. Ireland: If the palm of your right hand itches, it might mean you'll _____ money.

3 Are you superstitious?

Grammar | **Complete the conversation with responses with *So* and *Neither*.**

Junya   Are you superstitious?

Marta   I'm not sure, actually.

Junya   *Neither am I.*

Marta   Do you believe in bad luck?

Junya   Oh, do you mean like believing you'll have bad luck
if you buy just one pillow? Well, I never buy just one.

Marta   _____

Junya   I mean, I don't believe it's unlucky. Still, I always buy two,
just in case . . .

Marta   _____ Anyway, why do you ask?

Junya   Well, a friend of mine told me it's unlucky to sneeze only once.

Marta   I didn't know that!

Junya   _____ . . . But I *am* interested in all that stuff.

Marta   _____ . . . So, does that mean we are superstitious, then?

4 I agree! . . . Or do I?

Grammar | **Write two responses to each statement – one response with *So* or *Neither*,
to show you are the same, and another showing you are different.**

1. I always make a wish when
I see a falling star.

   So do I, if I see one.
   Really? I've never heard of that superstition.

2. I believe in telepathy.

   _____
   _____

3. I never cut my fingernails on Fridays.

   _____
   _____

4. I always pick up pennies for good luck.

   _____
   _____

5. I didn't know it was unlucky to spill salt.

   _____
   _____

1 Funny and hilarious

| **Choose the best word to repeat the underlined idea in each sentence.**

1. I have the <u>funniest</u> dreams, like one about me teaching a class in my robe and hair curlers. I mean, isn't that **frustrating / (hilarious)**?

2. I don't usually dream, so I find other people's dreams <u>interesting</u> to listen to. It's really **fascinating / scary** to listen to them.

3. I sometimes have this <u>amazing</u> dream that I can fly. It's just a **comical / wonderful** dream.

4. Every once in a while, I have this really <u>scary</u> dream. I'm driving along a road, and suddenly, I don't know how to drive! It's **disappointing / frightening**.

5. About once or twice a year, I have this <u>strange</u> dream that I'm back in college taking an important test. I mean, isn't it **weird / fascinating** to dream about something like that?

6. I wish I could remember my dreams, but it <u>isn't easy</u>. I mean, it's **difficult / important**. I heard you should write them down the moment you wake up.

2 How many ways can you say *beautiful*?

Conversation strategies | Complete each sentence by using a word to repeat the main idea in the first sentence.

1. I often dream about a very attractive woman. She's
   really ___beautiful___ .

2. She's very easygoing. She's a really _____ kind of person.

3. She never gets annoyed. She never gets _____ .

4. In my dream, we do some fun things together. You know, we
   do _____ stuff, like play games in the clouds.

5. They're always happy dreams. They're never _____ .

3 Strong or soft

Conversation strategies | Read the comments. Does *just* make what the people say stronger or softer? Write *stronger* or *softer*.

1. I didn't sleep well last night. I guess I just ate too much spicy food before I went
   to bed. ___softer___

2. Last night, I dreamed I won ten million dollars! It was just the most incredible
   dream. _____

3. I don't really believe in superstitions. They're just a bit of fun. _____

4. I went to bed early last night. I was just exhausted. _____

5. I had a terrible nightmare last night. It was just the worst dream I've
   ever had. _____

4 About you

Conversation strategies | Write answers to the questions below. Use *just* to make your answers stronger or softer as necessary.

1. Do you believe in telepathy? _Yes, I do. I think some people can really tell what others_
   are thinking. It's just amazing. **or** _No, I don't. I just don't believe you can ever tell_
   what others are thinking.

2. Do you like to watch TV shows about UFOs? _____
   _____

3. Do you think you can make something happen by wishing for it? _____
   _____

4. Do you believe that aliens exist? _____
   _____

5. Do you believe that dreams give us clues about our past or our future? _____
   _____

Lesson D / Amazing stories

1 How strange is that?

Reading | **A** Read the stories. Write the number of the title that best describes each story.

1. I Really, Really Love You!
2. Special Delivery . . . to Jail
3. Not a Book, but My Daughter
4. Reluctant Movie Star

Would You Believe . . . ?   　　　　　　　　　▢ ▢ ✕

WOULD YOU BELIEVE . . . ?

☐ Charles McLean, who works for a New York shipping company, wanted to visit his parents but didn't want to spend $320 on a plane ticket. Instead, he packed himself into a shipping crate and express-mailed himself to DeSoto, Texas. When the crate was delivered to his parents' home, he broke out of the box and shook hands with the delivery person. Unfortunately, the frightened woman did not have a sense of humor. She called the police, and McLean was arrested and charged as a stowaway.

☐ Christina Hudson of Denver, Colorado, is such a fan of Stephenie Meyer's *Twilight* books that she changed her name to include all four titles in the series. Hudson is now legally known as Christina Twilight New Moon Eclipse Breaking Dawn Hudson. Christina's mother and father don't mind that she changed her name to honor the *Twilight* books. They are just happy that she didn't choose to rename herself as a series of reality TV shows!

☐ Julianne Clark, a makeup artist at a Hollywood movie studio, was working one Sunday afternoon. When she tried to drive home from the studio, she discovered that the exit gate was locked. As she tried to find another exit, she saw a bus full of people. She followed the bus, thinking it would lead her to an exit. But the bus was part of a movie. Clark followed the bus onto a ramp and slid into a large pool of water after the bus. No one was hurt, but it took security guards three hours to get her car out of the water!

☐ Tim Wilson was worried about being late for his wedding when he crashed his car and broke his arm and leg. Refusing to stay in the hospital, he jumped into a taxi and arrived at the church just in time for the ceremony. But by the time he had cleaned himself up, his painkillers had worn off, and he passed out. He was rushed back to the hospital with his fiancée and the preacher, who married the couple as Wilson lay in his hospital bed.

B Read the article again and answer the questions. Then find words in the article to replace the underlined words.

　　　　　　　　　　an exit
1. Who couldn't find a way out from her workplace? _Julianne Clark_
2. Who was the person that hid on a plane to avoid paying the fare? _____
3. Who took some medicine to stop pain, which then stopped working? _____
4. Who got into a large delivery box? _____
5. Who wanted to show her respect for a series of books? _____

2 Happily ever after . . .

Writing **A** Read the story. Add *soon after, after,* or *before.*

Steven Park and his wife Susan were having financial problems. One day, they each decided, without telling the other, to buy a lottery ticket. _____ buying these tickets, they had never spent money on the lottery. They both used numbers that were their anniversary date and address. That night, they were watching the news on TV, and the winning numbers were drawn. _____ hearing the familiar numbers, they started jumping up and down. They were shocked to find out that they each held a winning ticket! The Parks were $450,000 richer _____ picking up their winnings.

B Write an amazing story you know, or make one up. Use prepositional time clauses.

Unit 6 Progress chart

What can you do? Mark the boxes. ☑ = I can . . . ❓ = I need to review how to . . .	To review, go back to these pages in the Student's Book.
Grammar ☐ use the past perfect. ☐ give responses with *So* and *Neither*.	54 and 55 57
Vocabulary ☐ use at least 12 expressions to describe strange events and superstitions.	54, 55, and 56
Conversation strategies ☐ make my meaning clear by repeating ideas. ☐ use *just* to make what I say stronger or softer.	58 59
Writing ☐ use prepositional time clauses.	61

49

Problem solving

 Get someone else on the job!

Grammar | Read each sentence. Then circle the correct verbs to complete the sentences.

1. My sister never **gets** /(**has**)a mechanic check her oil. She just **gets** / **has** her brother to do it.

2. My boss always **gets** / **has** someone at the copy shop make his copies.

3. When my friend sold her small house, she **got** / **had** a famous architect design and build her a new one.

4. I hate doing the dishes, so I **get** / **have** my little sister to do them.

2 **Get a professional.**

Grammar | Complete the radio advertisements with the correct form of the verbs.

1. When your car is dirty, get a professional _to wash_ (wash) it at Jake's Car Wash. Cheap prices. Friendly service. Get your car _washed_ (wash) at Jake's today!

2. Have you always done your own decorating or gotten a friend _____ (do) it? This spring, why not have your home _____ (redecorate) by Paint Works? No job too big or too small.

3. Need a new image? Come to Alice's Salon to have your hair _____ (cut) by an expert. Get our stylists _____ (help) you choose the style that's right for you.

4. Don't pay a fortune to have your car _____ (repair). When your car breaks down, call Joe's Garage and get it _____ (fix) for less.

5. With your busy lifestyle, you don't have time for chores. From now on, get Helping Hands _____ (do) them for you. Whether you want to have the whole house _____ (clean) or just some shirts _____ (iron), we're here to help.

3 Get some advice online.

Grammar | Jerry just moved to a new city. He posted these questions on an online forum. Complete the answers with the pairs of words in the box. Add appropriate pronouns.

get / clean   have / deliver   have / paint
✓get / repair   have / fix

Forum

Jerry85	My camera's making a funny noise. I can't afford a new one. Does anyone repair cameras these days?
StanP	You can _get it repaired_____ at Mick's Repairs. They're pretty cheap.
Jerry85	My TV's not working. Can someone recommend a good shop?
LilyRose	I like Gus's TV Shop. It won't cost a lot to _____ there.
Jerry85	Help! I need to find a really good dry cleaner's. I spilled spaghetti sauce all over my silk shirt last night.
JuanJ	When my clothes are stained, I always _____ at Main Street Cleaners. It's expensive, but they do a great job.
Jerry85	Where can I buy really fresh fruits and vegetables near Fry Street?
Hwatanabe	There's a health-food store on the corner of Fry and Middle Streets. You can also buy your groceries online and _____ .
Jerry85	My apartment needs painting. Does anyone know a professional painter?
Psmith89	It will cost a lot to _____ professionally. Could you paint it yourself?

---

4 About you

Grammar and vocabulary | Answer the questions with true information.

1. What's something you usually pay to have someone do for you?
    _I usually pay to have someone fix my motorcycle._____

2. What's something you get a family member to do for you?
    _____

3. How much does it cost to get your hair cut?
    _____

4. What's something you would have done by a professional?
    _____

5. What's the last thing you had repaired?
    _____

6. If the screen on your laptop got damaged, would you get it fixed or buy a new laptop?
    _____

1 What's wrong?

Vocabulary | Circle the best words to complete April's thoughts.

1. The mouse isn't working. I'll have to **recharge** / **fix** the battery.
2. I should really **tighten** / **upgrade** this software. I don't have the latest version.
3. Something's wrong with the monitor. I've tried **adjusting** / **replacing** the settings, but it's just not right.
4. Maybe I just need to **clean** / **recharge** the screen.
5. If it can't be fixed, I wonder if the store will **replace** / **adjust** it.

2 A fixer-upper

Grammar and vocabulary | Look at the picture. Describe the problems. Write eight sentences with *need* + verb + *-ing* or *need* + passive infinitive. Use the verbs in the box.

adjust
clean
fix
paint
repair
replace
throw away
✓ tighten

1. *The lightbulb needs to be tightened.*
2. _____
3. _____
4. _____
5. _____
6. _____
7. _____
8. _____

3 Leaks and dents

Vocabulary **Complete the conversations with the words and phrases in the box.**

dead	get a shock	making a funny noise	torn
✓dent	hole	slow	won't turn on
fall off	leaking	stain	
flickering	loose	stopped	

1. A What happened to your car? There's a big _____*dent*_____ in the door.
       And look, the oil is _____ .

    B Well, I was driving to school, and the car started _____ .
       So, I pulled over to the side of the road and hit a tree by accident.

2. A What happened? You're 15 minutes late.

    B Am I? My watch must be _____ . Uh-oh. It looks like it's _____ .

3. A Oh, no! The computer's not working. It's completely _____ .

    B You know, yesterday the screen kept _____ on and off.

    A Well, now it _____ at all. Maybe I should check the cables.

    B OK. Just be careful. You don't want to _____ .

4. A I had a horrible day. First, I spilled coffee on my new jeans.

    B Ooh. I bet that left a terrible _____ .

    A It did. Then, on the way home from work, I tripped and fell. Now my pants are stained, *and* they
       have a big _____ in them.

    B Well, _____ jeans are fashionable right now!

5. A Look at this old cabinet I found. I think I can fix it up nicely.

    B Really? All the knobs are _____ . And the legs – they all look like they're about to
       _____ . Are you sure you can fix it?

    A Oh, yeah. I repair furniture all the time.

4 About you

Grammar **Write true answers. Use *need* + verb + *-ing* or *need* + passive infinitive.**

1. What's something in your home that needs cleaning?
    My kitchen always needs cleaning.

2. What's something in your home that needs to be tightened sometimes?

    _____

3. What's something in your home that sometimes needs to be adjusted?

    _____

4. What's something you own that needs to be recharged?

    _____

5. What's something you own that needs replacing?

    _____

1 Like it?

Conversation strategies

A Match each sentence with its shorter version.

1. Do you like it? _d_
2. I'm ready! ____
3. I'd love to! ____
4. Do you want me to help you? ____
5. Do you need some help moving it? ____
6. Do you want me to get it? ____
7. Do you want one? ____
8. Have you got any chips? ____
9. Are you ready? ____

    a. Want me to help?
    b. Ready?
    c. Want one?
✓d. Like it?
    e. Ready!
    f. Got any chips?
    g. Need some help moving it?
    h. Want me to get it?
    i. Love to!

B Complete the conversations with the shorter sentences from part A.

1. A Oh, that looks heavy. _Need some help moving it?_

   B No. I think I can carry it by myself. But thanks anyway.

2. A _____

   B Yes. I'm all ready to go.

   A Wow. That's a beautiful dress!

   B _____

   A Yeah, I really do!

3. A Gosh, I'm hungry. _____

   B No, but I have some cookies. _____

   A Sure. Thanks.

4. A Oh, I can't figure out how to use this new computer program.

   B _____

   A Oh, yeah. That would be great!

5. A Oh, there's the phone. I'm busy washing the dishes.

   B _____

   A Yes, please. Could you just take a message? Thanks.

6. A Are you hungry? Want to get some sushi?

   B _____

   A Great. Are you ready to go now?

   B Yeah. _____

2 Ooh!

Circle the best word to begin each sentence.

1. (**Ooh!**)/ **Ouch!** I see why it isn't working!

2. **Yuck!** / **Ow!** That hurt!

3. **Ugh!** / **Whoops!** I poured too much!

4. **Yuck!** / **Oops!** This tastes awful!

5. **Shoot!** / **Ouch!** I missed the bus.

6. **Uh-oh!** / **Ow!** The sink is leaking.

3 Scrambled conversations

Number the lines of the conversations in the correct order.

1. _____ OK, put it down. How does it look?
   _1_ Need some help moving the table?
   _____ Hmm. Don't like it there. Let's move it back.
   _____ Yes, please. It's heavy. I can't move it by myself.
   _____ Ready. OK. . . . Ooh! . . . It's heavy.
   _____ OK. Let's lift it together. Ready?

2. _____ How about that new horror movie – *Monster Girl*?
   _____ Love to. What movie do you want to see?
   _____ OK. What time is it playing?
   _____ Too bad! Want to go out for dessert instead?
   _____ Let me check. Shoot! We just missed the 7:00 show.
   _____ Want to go to the movies tonight?

Brainteasers

Reading | **A** Read the puzzles. How many can you answer without looking at the solutions?

Here are some problems to solve,
JUST FOR FUN!

1 There are 20 people in an otherwise empty room. Each person can see everything in the room without moving in any way (other than his or her eyes). Where can you place an apple so that all but one person can see it?

2 A man was taking a walk outside when it started to rain. He didn't have an umbrella, and he wasn't wearing a hat. When he got home, his clothes were soaked, but not a single hair on his head got wet. How is this possible?

3 A painting hangs on the wall at a person's house. When the person is asked who is in the painting, the person replies, "I don't have a brother or a sister, but my mother's daughter is that man's mother." Who is the portrait of?

4 How can you throw a ball so that it reverses direction and comes back to you without bouncing off or touching any other object?

5 If it takes two men four hours to dig a hole, how much time does it take them to dig half a hole?

6 You are walking through a field, and you find something to eat. It doesn't have legs, and it doesn't have meat. You take it home and put it someplace warm. Three days later, it gets up and walks away. What is it?

7 Rearrange these letters into one long word: doornonegwl.

B Match each puzzle above with its solution.

a. "one long word" _7_

b. Throw it straight up in the air. _____

c. The man is bald. _____

d. An egg. _____

e. The owner's son. _____

f. On someone's head. _____

g. You can't dig half a hole! _____

C Find these words and expressions in the puzzles. Match them with their definitions.

1. (puzzle 1) but _c_

2. (puzzle 2) soaked _____

3. (puzzle 2) not a single _____

4. (puzzle 3) portrait _____

5. (puzzle 4) reverses direction _____

6. (puzzle 4) bouncing off _____

a. not one

b. hitting something and moving away quickly

✓c. except

d. a painting of a person

e. goes in the opposite direction

f. very wet

56

2 Interesting proposal

Writing **A** Read the proposal below. Circle the problem. Underline the solution and benefits. Then put parentheses ( ) around how the solution will be implemented.

I find that there is sometimes a lack of understanding and respect between students and teachers.

In order to solve this problem, we should have a teacher–student swap day once a semester. On this day, students would be the teachers, and teachers would be the students. The reason for this is so that students and teachers can learn from the challenges the others face. This could benefit the school in several ways. First, students could see what teachers have to do to prepare for a class. Second, teachers could learn new ideas from students and how students learn best. Another advantage would be that students could find out if teaching is something they'd like to do as a career.

This could easily be put into practice. Each semester, every teacher would become a student and let two students take over the class – one in the morning and one in the afternoon. Students who are interested would volunteer to teach a subject they feel comfortable with. They would then be chosen at random.

B Write about a solution to a problem. Explain its benefits and how it can be implemented. Use these ideas or your own.

- Too much litter in the city
- Not enough opportunities to practice English outside the classroom
- Ineffective public transportation

Unit 7 Progress chart

What can you do? Mark the boxes. ☑ = I can . . . ? = I need to review how to . . .	To review, go back to these pages in the Student's Book.
Grammar ☐ make sentences using causative *get* and *have*.	66 and 67
☐ use *need* + passive infinitive and *need* + verb + *-ing*.	68 and 69
Vocabulary ☐ use 5 new verbs to talk about fixing problems.	68
☐ use at least 10 new expressions to describe everyday problems.	69
Conversation strategies ☐ use "shorter sentences" in informal conversations.	70
☐ use at least 6 expressions for when things go wrong.	71
Writing ☐ present a solution to a problem.	73

Behavior

Lesson A / Reactions

 It's not nice to sulk.

Vocabulary | **What are these people doing? Write sentences using the words and expressions in the box.**

| hang up | hug | laugh out loud | lose his temper | ✓sulk | yell |

1. _He's sulking._   2. _____   3. _____

4. _____   5. _____   6. _____

2 I wouldn't have yelled at him.

Grammar and vocabulary | **Read each comment. Say what you would have done and what you wouldn't have done. Use the ideas in Exercise 1, or add your own.**

1. "Last night, a guy cut in line and bought the last two tickets for the movie I wanted to see!"
   I would have been annoyed. I wouldn't have yelled at him, though.

2. "Yesterday, my aunt gave me $100 for my birthday."
   _____

3. "My best friend told me a really funny joke in the middle of science class."
   _____

4. "Last week, I failed my math exam."
   _____

5. "My little brother accidentally deleted all the phone numbers from my smartphone."
   _____

3 What would you have done?

Grammar **A Complete the conversations with past modal verbs. Use the words given.**

1. **Rita** My uncle gave me this painting last year. It's not really my taste.

   Leah Hmm. Well, you _could have taken_ (could / take) it back to the store.

   Rita I _____ (could not / do) that. He painted it himself. And anyway, I _____ (would not / want) to upset him. He's such a nice guy.

   Leah Well, I guess the only thing you _____ (could / do) was smile and say thank you.

   Rita That's exactly what I did. I _____ (would not / say) anything else. Though I guess I _____ (should / sound) a little more enthusiastic.

2. **Luz** You know, I was upset that Cora didn't come to my party last month.

   Jon Yeah, I think I _____ (would / be) upset, too.

   Luz I was, but I guess I _____ (should / call) her to see if she was coming.

   Jon Maybe. But she still _____ (could / contact) you. Although maybe she was sick and couldn't call.

   Luz Yeah, I didn't think about that. But she _____ (should / get) her mother to call and tell me. That's what I _____ (would / do).

   Jon Yeah, but you never know. Why don't you call and find out what happened?

B Write questions with past modals that Rita and Luz could have asked in the conversations in part A. Then write your own answers.

Questions   **Answers**

Conversation 1

1. What else / I / say ?

   What else could I have said?   _____

2. How / you / react ?

   _____   _____

3. you / hang / it up ?

   _____   _____

Conversation 2

4. you / feel / angry ?

   _____   _____

5. you / call her ?

   _____   _____

6. What / Cora / do ?

   _____   _____

1 What's your personality?

Vocabulary | Read what each person says about himself or herself. Write three words that best describe each person.

aggressive	decisive	flexible	honest	jealous	sensitive
confident	determined	✓ happy	impulsive	realistic	sympathetic

1. I enjoy life. I'm pretty easygoing. If my friends want to do something, I'll usually go along with their plans, unless they're really crazy. I know what I'm capable and not capable of.

   _____happy_____   _____   _____

2. My friends often call me when something is worrying them. They say I'm a good listener, and I always tell them the truth. I don't like to see my friends upset or depressed.

   _____   _____   _____

3. I'm a pretty motivated person. I always know what I want. Once I decide to do something, I do it. I always try my hardest to achieve my goals.

   _____   _____   _____

4. What are my worst qualities? Well, I always want things that other people have. I sometimes lose my temper in stores and can shout if I don't get what I want. I guess I often do things without thinking about the consequences.

   _____   _____   _____

2 Positive or negative?

Vocabulary | Which words have a positive meaning for you, and which ones have a negative meaning? Complete the chart with the words in the box.

aggression	determination	happiness	motivation	sensitivity
anger	flexibility	hate	realism	shame
✓ confidence	grief	honesty	sadness	sulking
depression	guilt	jealousy	self-discipline	sympathy

Positive		Negative	
confidence			

3 She must have!

Grammar | **Rewrite the sentences in parentheses using past modal verbs. Use the modal verbs given.**

1. A There's no answer. (must) _She must have left by now._
   (I bet she left by now.)

   B Do you think she's coming by bus?

   A Um, I don't know. (may) _____
   (Maybe she decided to drive.)

   B I don't think so. Her car broke down. It was in the garage last night.
   (could not) _____
   (It's not possible she got it back yet.)

2. A Did I tell you someone robbed Dana last week and stole her purse?

   B How awful! (must) _____
   (I bet she was scared.)

   A Well, she was scared at first. The funny thing was, she knew the thief.
   She went to school with him! But Dana looks really different now.
   (might not) _____
   (So it's possible he didn't recognize her.)

   B Did she tell him that she knew him?

   A (may) _____ I don't really know.
   (Maybe she told him.)

   B Well, I hope she reported him to the police!

4 About you

Grammar | **Read each situation. Use past modals to complete the sentences with possible reasons why these situations happened.**

1. Your roommate overslept and missed an important meeting at work.
   She could _have stayed up too late the night before_ .
   She might _not have set her alarm_ .

2. Your best friend hasn't called you in a week.
   He / She may _____ .
   He / She couldn't _____ .

3. Your grandparents forgot your birthday.
   They may not _____ .
   They might _____ .

4. Your sister can't find her favorite earrings.
   She must _____ .
   She could _____ .

1 Rude behavior

Conversation strategies | **Complete the conversation with the expressions in the box.**

I had a similar thing happen to me,	That reminds me of the time
✓I had that happen to me	That's like
That happened to my friend Nancy,	Speaking of

A She just cut in line! It drives me crazy when people do that.

B _I had that happen to me_ last week. Same thing. This woman in the store just pushed her cart right in front of me. I looked at her, and she was like, "Too bad." She was so rude.

A Don't you hate that? _____ people who push right past you in the street. You know, when it's busy. It can really hurt.

B I know. _____ a guy walked right into me on Main Street. He never even apologized.

A Wasn't he looking?

B I guess not. Has that ever happened to you – someone walking directly into you?

A Well, not quite. I mean, _____ but with a door – and I walked into *it*!

B No way! _____ too. She walked into a glass door and knocked herself out! She was in a hurry and wasn't looking where she was going.

A _____ being in a hurry, I have to get going myself. I'll see you tomorrow!

2 Like, what?

Conversation strategies | **Read the sentences. Which meaning of *like* is used? Write the letter.**

a. to give an example	d. to report what someone said
b. to highlight something	✓e. to say *approximately*
c. to say something is similar	

1. I've known Giovanni for like ten years. _e_

2. My mom asked me to look for her car keys, and I was like, "Again!?" _____

3. I'm always like so tired in the morning, and it's so hard to get out of bed. _____

4. I'm just like my father – we're both tall, athletic, and easygoing. _____

5. My little sister loves TV. Like, she's always watching cartoons or game shows. _____

6. I've been studying for like weeks so that I do well on my final exams. _____

7. I wanted to leave work early tonight, but my boss was like, "You can't leave until you finish your report." _____

8. I'm always forgetting things. Like, I went to the supermarket the other day, and I forgot what I was supposed to buy! _____

I was like, "I'm sorry."

Conversation
strategies | **What does each speaker say next? Write the letter.**

1. One of my friends is really sensitive. __d__
2. My sister forgot to call me again. _____
3. My aunt is pretty old. _____
4. My mom is like really impulsive. _____
5. My friend is very motivated, just like me. _____
6. A co-worker got so upset with me. _____

a. She like never remembers!
b. She's like 80 years old!
c. We're both determined to do well in school.
✓d. Like, she's always crying about nothing.
e. I was like, "I'm sorry. I didn't realize."
f. Like, she does things without thinking.

4 Like, I had a similar experience!

Conversation
strategies | **Respond to each statement and describe a similar experience. Use the expressions in the box. Can you add a sentence using *like* with one of the meanings in Exercise 2 on page 62?**

I had that happen to me.
That happened to me.
I had a similar experience.
That reminds me (of) . . .
That's like . . .
Speaking of . . . ,

1. I went to a new hairdresser, and the guy did a terrible job with my hair. I looked ridiculous.

   I had a similar experience at the hairdresser last year. I asked for like curly hair, and when I left, I looked terrible.

2. A guy called last night while I was eating dinner. He wanted me to send money to a charity or something.

   _____
   _____
   _____

3. I was supposed to meet a friend at the movies last night, but she never showed up.

   _____
   _____
   _____

4. Last night I was at this restaurant, and a man at a table near me talked on his cell phone the whole time.

   _____
   _____
   _____

5. I have a friend who always interrupts me when I tell a story. It drives me crazy.

   _____
   _____
   _____

1 I'm peeved!

Reading | **A** **Read the blogs. What do the two stories have in common?**

☐ The problems were solved by yelling at the person.
☐ Both bloggers yelled at someone.

☐ The problems weren't solved.
☐ Both bloggers took action to solve the problems.

○○○   Pet Peeves

Pet Peeves

We asked our bloggers to write in with their pet peeves and tell us how they deal with the things that annoy them the most.

MARGARET, 32, OTTAWA If there's one thing that upsets me, it's people who throw their trash on the street. It really makes me angry when I see people toss their food wrappers and empty soda cans on the sidewalk. They should be ashamed of themselves, but people don't seem to feel at all guilty about it. I see it happen all the time, and afterward I always say to myself, "I should have said something." So finally I did.

I was walking down my block the other day, and this guy was coming toward me, and he threw his cup right into my neighbor's garden! What nerve! Now, I could have ignored it and carried on walking without saying a thing – as I usually do – but I know I would have regretted it. I was determined to do something this time because it was right there in my neighborhood! So I yelled at him. I probably shouldn't have done that, but I kind of lost my temper! I said, "You know, Mrs. Tweedy worked really hard on that garden, and you just threw your trash in it. And there's a garbage can right on the corner!" He seemed pretty embarrassed and said, "You're right. I'm sorry." Then he went and got his cup. I was really surprised, but I'm glad it turned out like that – he could have gotten mad at me or turned aggressive or something. Anyway, I felt great for the rest of the day, and in the future, I'll always stop and tell people to pick up their trash – though I probably won't yell like that!

ZACH, 21, MIAMI I can't stand it when people send me links to silly video clips. I'm talking about those cat videos or clips of blurry concert footage. It's so time-consuming because you feel obliged to watch them and send a comment back. Sometimes it makes you kind of question your friends' tastes and why they think these videos are funny. They just post links on everybody's social networking pages without thinking. I mean, sometimes I see something funny and post it on someone's wall, but I always include a personal comment. And I don't send things to everybody I'm friends with online.

I have this friend who used to post links on my wall all the time – like at least once a day. Some of them were funny, but some of them were kind of weird. In the end, I sent her a private message asking her – in a very nice way – to stop. She apologized and stopped. She said she sympathized because someone was sending her game requests up to four times a day, so she knew how annoying it could be. I thought, "So why do it, then?"

B **Find these words and phrases in the blogs. Match them with their definitions.**

1. pet peeves __f__
2. toss _____
3. What nerve! _____
4. carried on _____
5. time-consuming _____
6. obliged _____

a. continued
b. How rude!
c. forced
d. taking a lot of time
e. throw
✓ f. frustrations; irritations

C Read the blogs again. Then answer the questions.

1. What does Margaret usually do when she sees people throw trash on the street? _____

_____

2. Why did she decide to respond differently this time? _____

3. What does she think she should have done differently? _____

4. Why doesn't Zach like getting links from his friends? _____

5. Why did Zach's friend finally sympathize with him? _____

2 Apologies

Writing **A** Read the apology letter. Fill in the blanks with the expressions in the box.

I feel I should apologize for	I just hope	I promise not to	it was my fault entirely

Dear Mr. Feaster,

_____ letting my dog run in your garden the other day. I was talking on my cell phone, and I didn't notice he was digging up your flowers. I should have paid more attention. I know _____ . _____ let my dog into your garden again. _____ that you can accept my apology.

Sincerely,
Janice Brown

B Think of something you've done in the past and write a note of apology.

_____

_____

_____

_____

Unit 8 Progress chart

What can you do? Mark the boxes. ✓ = I can . . . ? = I need to review how to . . .	To review, go back to these pages in the Student's Book.
Grammar ☐ use past modals to talk hypothetically about the past.	76 and 77
☐ use past modals to speculate about the past.	79
Vocabulary ☐ use at least 6 words and expressions to discuss behavior.	76 and 77
☐ use 15 new words to talk about emotions and personality.	78
Conversation strategies ☐ use expressions like *Speaking of* and *That's like* to share my experiences.	80
☐ use *like* in different ways.	81
Writing ☐ use expressions to apologize.	83

Material world

Lesson A / Possessions

1 Things and stuff

Vocabulary **A** Complete the questions with the words and expressions in the box.

| accumulated | materialistic | part with |
| goals | ✓ own | possessions |

1. Do you _____own_____ a lot of valuable things?
2. How attached are you to the things you own – especially your most valuable _____ ?
3. What things do you find hard to throw away or _____ ?
4. What kinds of objects have you collected or _____ over time?
5. What are your main aims or _____ for this coming year?
6. How _____ are you?

B Answer the questions from part A with your own information.

1. _I don't own anything of great value, really, but I want to start collecting art._
   I have a lot of personal items, like clothes and books, though.

2. _____

3. _____

4. _____

5. _____

6. _____

2 What did they say?

Grammar and vocabulary **Read the statements. Then complete the sentences to report what the people said.**

1. "I think I'll clean out my closets soon."
   My sister said that she ___*thought*___ she *'d clean out* her closets soon.

2. "I've been saving money to buy a new car."
   My friend said that he _____ money to buy a new car.

3. "I haven't found a new dress for the wedding yet."
   My mom said that she _____ a new dress for the wedding yet.

4. "I can't part with my favorite jeans, even though they're torn."
   My cousin said he _____ his favorite jeans, even though they _____ torn.

5. "My goal is to pay off my credit card debt by next year."
   My older brother said that his goal _____ to pay off his credit card debt by next year.

6. "I'm always buying shoes. I think I have 30 pairs."
   My dad said that he _____ shoes and that he _____ he _____ 30 pairs.

7. "I won't ever throw out my favorite photographs."
   My grandma said that she _____ her favorite photographs.

8. "My parents bought me a beautiful pearl necklace."
   My aunt said that her parents _____ her a beautiful pearl necklace.

3 Her mother's a millionaire.

Grammar **Rewrite the direct speech as reported speech.**

Mel Did you have a good time on your date with Ariel last week?
I saw her at a café yesterday, and she said _she'd enjoyed it a lot_ .
  ("I enjoyed it a lot.")

Eric Yeah, it was fine. The only thing was I had to pay for everything.
Ariel said _____ . Then she said
  ("I'm broke.")
that _____ .
  ("I've been spending too much lately.")

Mel So you paid for the movies and dinner, too?

Eric Yes. She said _____ .
  ("I can't afford to buy the tickets.")

Mel Are you going to see her again?

Eric I don't know. She told me _____
  ("I'm going away for a week.")
and that _____ .
  ("I'll call you when I get back.")

Mel I hope she doesn't get back before your next paycheck!
Where's she going anyway?

Eric Well, she said _____ .
  ("It's a surprise.")
Her mother was sending her someplace exotic.

Mel Yeah. She once told me _____ .
  ("My mother's a millionaire.")

1 Money matters

Vocabulary | Circle the correct words to complete each money expression.

1. get into	a. money	(b.) debt	c. payment
2. pay good	a. account	b. budget	c. interest
3. pay in	a. cash	b. check	c. credit card
4. invest	a. account	b. money	c. debt
5. keep track	a. off	b. aside	c. of
6. charge to	a. a credit card	b. a loan	c. a budget
7. set _____ money	a. away	b. aside	c. off
8. pay _____ a loan	a. off	b. away	c. aside
9. take out	a. an interest	b. a debt	c. a loan

2 Smart money tips

Vocabulary | Complete the sentences and puzzle below with the words in the box.

away	bills	✓charge	debt	income	monthly	out	savings	stocks

1. Don't __charge__ too much to your credit card, unless you can pay it off in full every month.
2. It's important to pay your _____ on time. You shouldn't let them pile up.
3. Sticking to a _____ budget can save you money.
4. Many people take _____ loans to pay for cars or homes.
5. Try to put _____ some money every month for emergencies.
6. Shop around for a _____ account that pays good interest.
7. People sometimes take several jobs to increase their _____ .
8. You can invest in a company by buying _____ .
9. It's important to get out of _____ to avoid paying large sums of interest.

1. c h a r g e
2. __ __ __ __ __
3. __ __ __ __ __ __ __
4. __ __ __ __
5. __ __ __ __
6. __ __ __ __ __ __ __
7. __ __ __ __ __ __
8. __ __ __ __ __
9. __ __ __ __

When children do chores around the house, they often get an _____ .

3 He asked me . . .

Grammar | **Imagine you met with a financial adviser to talk about your spending habits.
Read the financial adviser's questions. Then complete the reported questions.**

1. "How much money do you save each month?"

   He asked me _how much money I saved_ each month.

2. "Do you have any credit card or other debt?"

   He wanted to know _____ any credit card or other debt.

3. "Can you stick to a monthly budget?"

   He wanted to know _____ a monthly budget.

4. "How many times have you taken money out of your savings account this month?"

   He asked _____ money out of my savings account this month.

5. "What do you spend most of your money on?"

   He wanted to know _____ most of my money on.

6. "Have you taken out a loan recently?"

   He asked me _____ a loan recently.

4 Where did the money go?

Grammar | **Read what Amy says and the questions her family asks her. Then change the
direct questions into reported questions by completing the sentences below.**

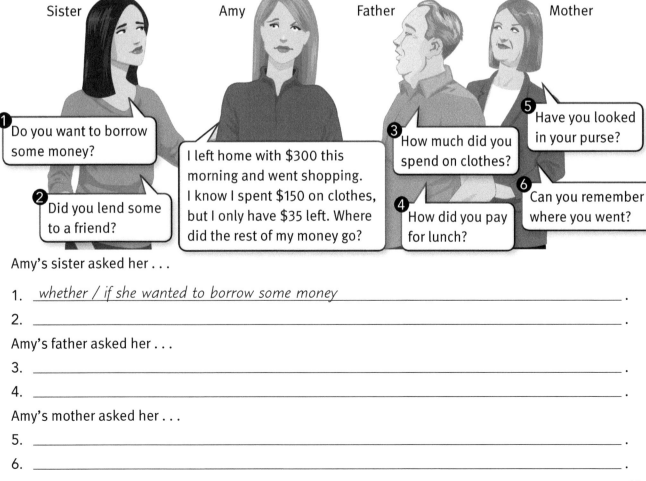

Amy's sister asked her . . .

1. _whether / if she wanted to borrow some money_____ .

2. _____ .

Amy's father asked her . . .

3. _____ .

4. _____ .

Amy's mother asked her . . .

5. _____ .

6. _____ .

1 What was she telling you?

Read these reports of conversations. Rewrite the underlined sentences as reported speech using past continuous reporting verbs.

I was talking with my neighbor yesterday. (1) <u>She told me about her son</u>. He's planning to do some community work for a few years. (2) <u>She said it doesn't pay much</u>. But he thinks it'll be a good experience anyway.

(3) <u>A co-worker of mine told me our boss just won the lottery</u>. I can't believe it! She never buys lottery tickets! But she bought one on impulse, and she won! (4) <u>My co-worker said she won $5,000</u>. So, hopefully, she'll buy us lunch today.

(5) <u>My friend told me she needs a new car</u>. Her car is always breaking down, and she's been late to work five times this month. (6) <u>She said that she might lose her job if she's late again</u>.

I was talking to my brother on the phone last night. (7) <u>I told him what to do while I'm on vacation</u>. So, he's going to feed my cat and water my plants. And I told him where things were.

1. _She was telling me about her son._

2. _____

3. _____

4. _____

5. _____

6. _____

7. _____

70

2 Who told you?

Conversation
strategies **Complete the conversations with the expressions in the boxes.**

✓evidently   I've heard   told me

1. A Wow! We have so much stuff in our closets. There's no more room.

    B I know. ____Evidently____ , there's a new TV show where this woman
       helps you get rid of all the stuff you don't want anymore.

    A Really?

    B Yeah, Seth _____ about it. They take everything you own
       and put it outside your house. You have to sell or throw away more
       than half of it!

    A Oh, yeah. _____ it's a fun show.

according to the report   they say   was saying

2. A Did you hear the news about interest rates?

    B Yeah, I did. _____ on TV last night,
       they're going up – again!

    A That's right. _____ we'll have to pay
       around 25% on our credit cards.

    B I know. Isn't that terrible?

    A Yeah. But, as my friend _____ ,
       it might stop us from spending so much.

apparently   he was telling me   I was told

3. A Did you get tickets for the school concert tonight?

    B It's tonight? _____ it was next week.

    A No, it's tonight. _____ , it's going to
       be a great show. I talked to Henry earlier today, and
       _____ it's already sold out.

    B Oh, no. I guess I'm not going, then.

3 About you

Conversation
strategies **Answer the questions with true information. Use past continuous reporting
verbs and expressions from Exercise 2.**

1. What's an interesting TV show you've heard about recently?

    _____

2. What's something you learned from the news?

    _____

3. What's some good or bad news someone just told you this week?

    _____

1 Books – pass them on!

Reading | **A Read the article. What do book swappers do with their books?**

☐ sell them to charities
☐ share them with fellow readers
☐ add them to wish lists

The Web Is Your Library!

What do you do when you've finished reading a book? Do you put it back on your bookshelf and forget about it, or do you pass it on to other readers through book swapping – exchanging books with friends, colleagues, book groups, or members of online book-swapping sites? Book swapping solves a number of problems for people who still love to read print books, such as how to find space to store their books and how not to spend lots of money purchasing new ones.

Over the years, dozens of book-swapping sites have popped up on the Internet. Each site has its own rules and regulations, but the basic idea is the same. Members register the books they wish to swap on the site. Other members browse through the postings and then make contact if they are interested in a particular book. The book is then mailed by the person who posted it. Once the book is mailed, the person who posted it earns points, which then allows him or her to acquire a book from another online member.

Some online book-swapping sites let members keep a wish list of books they'd like to acquire. When one of the books on a member's wish list is posted on the website, that member will receive a message generated by the website saying who the book can be acquired from. Another feature of many book-swapping sites is the ability to donate your books to a charity. Donating books earns the same number of points as swapping with another member.

If you're not keen on using the Internet as a means of obtaining cheap books, second-hand bookstores and public libraries often offer book-swapping services. Or, if you prefer to know where your books come from, you can also set up a book swap in your own community.

B Read the article again. Then read the sentences below. Write _T_ (true) or _F_ (false) for each sentence. Then correct the false sentences.

1. Book swapping ~~creates~~ *solves* a number of problems for book lovers. __F__

2. All book-swapping sites have the same basic rules. _____

3. The person who requests a book on a book-swapping site earns points. _____

4. When a book on your wish list is posted, the person who posts it will contact you. _____

5. You earn the same number of points for a book when you donate it to a charity. _____

6. There are book-swapping schemes in some public libraries. _____

2 So many books

A Read the article about a book lover. Fill in the blanks with the expressions in the box.

she added	she concluded	✓she explained	she recalled

Eunjoo Park has more than 5,000 books in her one-bedroom apartment. "I can't live without my books," _she explained_ . Her living room and bedroom are filled with bookshelves, and she is always buying more shelves. "It's better to buy more shelves than get rid of any books," _____ .

"Once, I decided to sell some books in a street sale," _____ . "When a woman came by and tried to buy a book, I couldn't sell it to her! I took my books back inside and put them away."

Now she knows better. "I just refuse to get rid of my books," she told me. "There seems to be only one solution – I just have to get a bigger apartment," _____ .

B Write an article about someone you know. Use reporting verbs to tell the person's story. Use an idea below or one of your own.

Someone who . . .

- collects something.
- often sells his or her things.
- is materialistic.

Unit 9 Progress chart

What can you do? Mark the boxes. ✓ = I can . . . ? = I need to review how to . . .	To review, go back to these pages in the Student's Book.
☐ report things that people said. ☐ report questions that people asked.	86 and 87 89
☐ use 25 new expressions about possessions and money.	86, 87, 88, and 89
☐ use past continuous reporting verbs to tell about a conversation. ☐ use expressions like *They say, I've heard*, and *Evidently*.	90 91
☐ use different reporting verbs to quote other people.	93

Grammar

Vocabulary

Conversation strategies

Writing

Fame

Lesson A / The rise to fame

1 Kelly Clarkson's rise to fame

Grammar | **Read the information about pop star Kelly Clarkson. Then complete the sentences below using the past perfect and past modals.**

Kelly Clarkson was chosen from among hundreds of competitors to win *American Idol*, a TV talent show that lets viewers vote on the winner. Since winning, she has recorded a number of top-selling "hits" and has become a household name. Yet, her rise to fame came somewhat unexpectedly, as she had always dreamed of being a marine biologist.

1. If Kelly _had followed_ (follow) her career dream, she _might have become_ (might become) a marine biologist.

2. If a music teacher _____ (not hear) Kelly singing in the hall of her middle school, she _____ (not join) the school chorus.

3. If Kelly _____ (not learn) to sing classically in her school chorus, she _____ (might not be able) to use her voice in so many different ways.

4. If Kelly's friend _____ (not tell) her about *American Idol*, Kelly _____ (not try out) for the show.

5. If Kelly _____ (receive) 47% and not 57% of the final vote on *American Idol*, she _____ (not win) the competition.

2 More pop idols

Grammar | **Complete the interviews with the runners-up of a TV talent competition with the past perfect or past modal form of the verbs given. Sometimes more than one answer is possible.**

a Pop magazine EXCLUSIVE **THE POP ARTISTS YOU VOTED FOR!**

THE RUNNERS-UP

PM Why do you think you came in second, Beth?

Beth I definitely chose the wrong song. The judges didn't like it at all.

PM So, if you _____ (not sing) that song, _____ you _____ (win), do you think?

Beth Who knows? I _____ (have) a better chance. But it doesn't really matter because I had a great time.

PM How are you feeling, Ian?

Ian Well, I didn't realize how hard it would be. If I _____ (know), maybe I _____ (work) harder on my singing.

PM _____ you _____ (take) more singing lessons?

Ian Yeah, I _____ (look) for a voice teacher and maybe a dance teacher, too!

Beth Simon

Ian Wong

3 She might have become a famous ballerina.

Grammar | **Complete each story with your own ideas. Use past modals.**

1. Emma was a top student in high school and in her dance classes. But then she dropped out of dance class to focus on her schoolwork. She then went on to study at Harvard University. If Emma hadn't stopped taking dance classes, _she might have / could have become a famous ballerina_
   or _she wouldn't have gone to Harvard_ .

2. Maemi always wanted to be a doctor, but on her 13th birthday, her parents gave her a camera. That was the start of her interest in photography, and she later became a professional photographer. If Maemi hadn't gotten a camera for her birthday, _____ .

3. Stephanie loved to build things when she was younger. She even helped her father design an addition to their house. But when she was in high school, she was spotted by a modeling agency and became a model. She always says that _____ if she hadn't become a model.

4. Martin loved farming, but he had no interest in cooking. His grandmother nevertheless made him help her cook dinner every Sunday. Martin just opened his second organic restaurant. If his grandmother hadn't taught him how to cook, _____ .

5. Hao-xing, a trombone player, was taking part in a competition. As he stepped on stage, he noticed a beautiful woman in the front row of the audience. While he was playing his piece, he became distracted by the woman. He forgot the music and didn't win the competition. If he hadn't seen the woman, _____ .

4 About you

Grammar | **Complete the sentences with past modals and your own ideas.**

1. If I had left school at the age of 16, _I might not have met the teacher who inspired me the most_ .
2. If I hadn't taken English, _____ .
3. _____ if I hadn't worked so hard.
4. If I had been born into a famous family, _____ .
5. _____ if I had practiced more.
6. If my parents hadn't _____ , _____ .

1 Making headlines

Vocabulary | **Complete the magazine article with the expressions in the box.**

bad press	in the headlines
drop out of sight	in the right place
go downhill	made headlines
got discovered	take off
have connections	✓ up-and-coming

LUCKY STAR

Up-and-coming movie star Gianna LaRose was seen having lunch with her boyfriend of two years, Rich Marsh, in Los Angeles earlier this week. The couple seemed relaxed and happy, even after the _____ their relationship has gotten recently. Ms. LaRose denied rumors of a split and happily signed autographs for her fans.

After losing last year's Best Breakthrough Performance Award, many people thought LaRose's career could only _____ , but just the opposite has happened. Ms. LaRose _____ recently when she was offered the lead role in director Rick Callahan's new blockbuster. This young actress has everything going for her. It's unlikely she will _____ anytime soon. Her career is just getting started and is sure to _____ .

Ms. LaRose _____ five years ago while working at a movie theater. Talent agent Erica Menken saw LaRose and thought she had "star qualities." The rest is history, as they say. Ms. LaRose says she was lucky to meet Ms. Menken. She was studying to be an actress, but she didn't _____ in the movie industry. "Meeting Erica was an example of being _____ at the right time," Ms. LaRose said.

Expect to see Ms. LaRose's name _____ for a long time.

2 A movie date

Grammar | **Complete the sentences below with the tag questions in the box.**

1. It's great to go out and see a movie, _isn't it_____ ?

2. We're not going to be late for the movie, _____ ?

3. You haven't seen this movie yet, _____ ?

4. You liked the movie, _____ ?

5. It was interesting, _____ ?

6. That actor has been in a lot of movies, _____ ?

are we
didn't you
hasn't he
have you
✓ isn't it
wasn't it

3 Stars among us

Grammar | **Complete the conversations with tag questions.**

1. A Ben Affleck gives a lot of money to charity, _doesn't he_ ?

    B I didn't know that. You don't see it in the press very much, _____ ?

    A No, but then, people often do charitable things quietly, _____ ?

    B Maybe. But it's great to see someone who's so wealthy give money to good causes, _____ ?

    A Sure, but I wish someone would give some to me!

2. A Oh, my goodness. That isn't Taylor Swift, _____ ?

    B I don't think so. She doesn't hang out at this coffee shop, _____ ?

    A I don't know. I think it's her. She just let that girl take a picture of her, _____ ?

    B Hmm. It does kind of look like her, _____ ?

    A See, I was right, _____ ? Come on. Let's go over and take her picture, too!

4 Tell us about yourself.

Grammar | **Imagine you are going to interview actor Reese Witherspoon. Write tag questions you can ask her to check the following facts.**

Facts	Questions
1. raised in Nashville, Tennessee	*You were raised in Tennessee, weren't you?*
2. started acting at the age of seven	
3. first major role was in *The Man in the Moon*	
4. appeared in over 25 movies by the age of 30	
5. has produced several movies	
6. married to a talent agent	
7. has three children	

1 Comic advice

Conversation strategies **Complete the conversation with tag questions.**

Tina Hey, Max. How was the comedy workshop you went to last week?

Max Great. I'd like to be a comedian someday, but I'm not sure I'm ready.

Tina Well, you could take another comedy workshop, _couldn't you_ ?

Max Yeah. . . . There's another one next month.

Tina Sounds good. You just need to call and sign up, _____ ?

Max Yeah. I wonder how all the famous comedians on TV got started.

Tina It would help to read some books about them, _____ ?

Max I guess. I'll look online tonight. You know, the hardest thing is writing new and original jokes.

Tina Well, you could look for some books on joke writing, too, _____ ?

Max Yeah. I mean, I learned a little bit about it in the workshop, but you never can tell what people will find funny.

Tina It would be a good idea to call some of the local comedy clubs, _____ ? And ask them if you could try out some of your jokes. They always need people to perform, _____ ? I'm sure the club owners could give you some advice, too. I mean, you need all the help you can get, _____ ?

Max Hey, that's not funny!

2 What's your advice?

Conversation strategies **Your friend is having a lot of bad luck lately. Read each situation, and give your best advice and encouragement using tag questions.**

1. I didn't do well on the last English test. I'm worried about my final grade.
   I'm sure you could ask to take the test again, couldn't you?

2. I want to practice my English, but I don't know any English-speaking people.
   _____

3. I got in a horrible fight with my best friend. I don't know what to do.
   _____

4. I've gained some weight over the holidays. I don't fit into my jeans!
   _____

5. I forgot my boyfriend's birthday and never got him a present.
   _____

6. I lost my mother's necklace. What am I going to do?
   _____

3 That's a good question.

Conversation strategies | **Match each question with the best response.**

1. What's the hardest thing about being famous? _b_

2. What do you plan to do next in your career? _____

3. Who inspires you in your work? _____

4. Do you consider yourself a role model? _____

5. What would you do if you weren't an actor? _____

a. That's a good question. I think I'd like to do some roles in theater.

✓ b. That's a tough one. I'd say it's probably always being in the public eye. You have no privacy.

c. Good question. Actually, I can't imagine doing anything else, really.

d. It's hard to say. There are so many good actors. I admire a lot of them.

e. Oh, definitely. I try to set a good example for young people.

4 To be famous or not to be famous . . .

Conversation strategies | **Number the lines of the conversation in the correct order.**

_____ But if you were famous, you would be hanging out with other famous people, wouldn't you? That sounds like fun to me!

_____ It's hard to say. Even if you're famous, you might not make a lot of money. Some politicians are famous, but they aren't rich – and they don't wear expensive clothes!

_1_ You want to be an actor, right? You *would* like to be famous someday, wouldn't you?

_____ I'm not saying that wouldn't be fun. I just kind of like my privacy, that's all.

_____ Oh, that's a tough question. Being famous would be nice, but I don't know if I'd like all the stuff that goes with it. I like acting. But that doesn't mean I want to be famous!

_____ I know what you mean, but just think, you'd make a lot of money. Then you could buy all kinds of cool clothes, couldn't you?

1 Rap image

Reading | **A** Read the article. Why do you think rap stars maintain their "bad boy" image?

From Rap to Riches

From **RAP** to *Riches* ◆

While rap music is now a mainstream part of the music industry, it began in the 1970s in a poor part of New York City, where life was often difficult and dangerous because of crime, unemployment, and violence. At that time, rappers like Grandmaster Flash and the Furious Five created rap as a form of poetry that reflected the way people like themselves lived in hard, inner-city neighborhoods. Soon, hanging out with friends and rapping became a way for many teenagers living on such tough city streets to express themselves creatively. Rap quickly spread to other cities in the United States and then became a worldwide phenomenon.

Even after its global success, many rap stars, such as 50 Cent, Jay Z, Lil Wayne, Nicki Minaj, and Wiz Khalifa, still come from poor urban neighborhoods. Moreover, as rap artists become rich and famous,

many choose to keep their tough "street image." Their songs continue to reflect the language of the neighborhoods where they grew up, and their clothes and accessories reflect – and influence – the style of urban youth around the world. However, some music fans are uncomfortable with the "bad boy" image of rap, and are critical especially of gangsta rappers, who often include violent lyrics in their songs.

Rap is now part of a larger cultural phenomenon known as hip-hop, which has become a successful and profitable industry. Hip-hop has influenced movies like *Hustle & Flow*, which follows an aspiring musician from his disadvantaged youth through his eventual success. It has also influenced fashion design, such as Sean John (Sean Combs' fashion line) and G-Unit (50 Cent's fashion line). Even professional sports teams are influenced by rap stars – Jay Z is now a part owner of the Brooklyn Nets, an NBA basketball team in New York City.

It's hard to imagine that rap stars haven't always been rich, famous, and influential, or that their early lives may have been difficult or even tragic. However, with some luck, a lot of hard work, and talent, rappers have entered the mainstream, providing not only entertainment, but reminding us of the tough environment that created it.

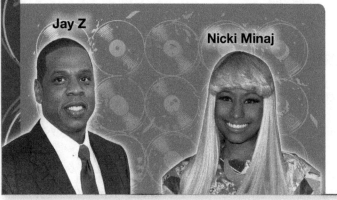

Jay Z

Nicki Minaj

B Read the article again. Write *T* (true) or *F* (false). Then correct the false statements.

1. Rap started in a ~~wealthy~~ ^{poor} neighborhood in New York City in the 1970s. _F_

2. Rap was a way for kids in bad neighborhoods to travel to other cities. _____

3. After rap became popular, many of its stars came from rich backgrounds. _____

4. 50 Cent came from a privileged background. _____

5. Rap music is often criticized for its violence. _____

6. Rap and hip-hop have inspired movies and clothing. _____

2 A controversial rap star

A Read the paragraph about Eminem. Underline the topic sentence. Then cross out any information that does not support the topic.

Eminem is one of the most popular and controversial rap stars of all time. He is known for his distinctive style of changing his pace several times within a song without losing the beat. He often uses a lot of bad language in his songs. He has been married and has three children. He is also famous for telling stories in his songs, talking about his own life and childhood, making fun of celebrities, and criticizing politicians. He has short blond hair, and often wears baggy jeans and sweatshirts. Unlike most rap stars who come from New York and Los Angeles, Eminem is from Detroit.

B Write a paragraph about a famous person. Write a strong topic sentence, and add more information and details in supporting sentences.

Unit 10 Progress chart

What can you do? Mark the boxes. ✔ = I can . . . ? = I need to review how to . . .	To review, go back to these pages in the Student's Book.
Grammar	
☐ talk hypothetically about the past using *if* clauses with the past perfect form of the verb and past modals.	98 and 99
☐ use negative and affirmative tag questions.	100 and 101
Vocabulary	
☐ use at least 8 idiomatic expressions to talk about fame.	98, 99, 100, and 101
Conversation strategies	
☐ soften advice and give encouragement using tag questions.	102
☐ use expressions like *It's hard to say* when questions are difficult to answer.	103
Writing	
☐ write a paragraph with a topic sentence and supporting sentences.	105

Trends

Lesson A / Trends in society

1 On the web

Vocabulary | Complete the questions with the words in the box.

financial support	outsource	shortage	unemployment
obsessed	recruit	traffic congestion	✓ wireless Internet access

Images   Groups   News   Local   More>>

SEARCH

Web   Results of **1-100** of about **969,000** for **Washingtonville** *(0.30 seconds)*

Results for current top news stories: **Local: Washingtonville**

Technology news

A local coffee shop is offering free _wireless Internet access_ . The owner says it's necessary to compete with the large coffee shop chains.

Business

Several companies have announced they will _____ their customer service jobs and lay off staff. Local _____ rates are expected to jump 3%.

Increased demand for the latest hybrid cars has created a _____ at local car dealers.

Local companies are expecting to _____ over 600 employees at the annual job fair this year.

Health

Is our culture _____ with dieting and being thin? Dr. Murphy examines the diet craze and the new "designer" diets.

Education

Tuition fees at colleges across the country are rising at an alarming rate. Local financial expert Ken Rose explains what kind of _____ is available.

Local traffic

_____ is expected in the Washingtonville Bridge area again tomorrow. Delays are due to the ongoing bridge repairs.

Page **1** ◁ ▷

2 Current trends

Grammar | Complete the sentences with the passive form of the present continuous or present perfect. Sometimes there is more than one correct answer.

1. Technology companies have developed a tablet with a much tougher screen glass.
   These tablets _are being sold_ (sell) in stores and online right now.

2. Major airlines have now bought a new type of airplane which _____ (develop) to lower fuel consumption.

3. Scientists are exploring ways to make plants like wheat, corn, and tomatoes disease-resistant. These plants _____ (engineer) and tested on farms around the world.

4. Sports clothing companies are trying to incorporate technology into their clothing. Currently, vests, shirts, and pants _____ (create) to help athletes improve their performance by measuring muscle activity.

5. Many companies have now outsourced information technology jobs. These jobs _____ (move) overseas to cut company costs.

6. Research has shown that children in the United States are gaining weight. Several studies _____ (conduct) by researchers and show that 30% of U.S. children are overweight.

3 In the news

Grammar | Write sentences about the headlines using the verbs given. Use the passive form of the present continuous or the present perfect. Sometimes more than one answer is possible.

At last, a cure for the common cold

1. (find) _At last, a cure for the common cold has been found._

The world's oldest building in Japan

2. (discover) _____

New driving tests for next year

3. (schedule) _____

Traffic slow because of strong storms

4. (delay) _____

Plans to hire more teachers

5. (discuss) _____

1 An environmental puzzle

Vocabulary | Complete the sentences. Then write the highlighted letters in order to complete the sentence below.

1. Many fish are dying because of the _t_ _o_ _x_ _i_ _c_ _c_ _h_ _e_ _m_ _i_ _c_ _a_ _l_ _s_ that factories dump into rivers every day.

2. Scientists think that polar ice caps are melting at an ever-increasing rate because of ____ ____ ____ ____ ____ ____ ____ ____ ____ ____ ____ .

3. Garbage that isn't recycled ends up in a ____ ____ ____ ____ ____ ____ ____ .

4. If we continue to use our ____ ____ ____ ____ ____ ____ ____ ____ ____ ____ ____ ____ ____ ____ ____ , like oil and coal, they might run out.

5. I want a car that ____ ____ ____ ____ ____ ____ ____ ____ less gas because gas prices are rising!

6. Due to the lack of rain, we are experiencing a ____ ____ ____ ____ ____ ____ ____ .

7. Scientists have been working on ____ ____ ____ ____ ____ ____ ____ ____ ____ ____ ____ ____ ____ ____ ____ transportation, like electric cars, to cut down on pollution.

8. Some synthetic materials are not ____ ____ ____ ____ ____ ____ ____ ____ ____ ____ ____ ____ .

_____ energy by turning off lights when you leave home.

2 Conservation tips

Vocabulary | Circle the correct words to complete the sentences. Then check (✓) the things you do to help.

1. ____ Use **biodegradable** /(**energy-saving**)/ **global warming** home appliances to cut back on electricity use.

2. ____ Avoid using plastic containers that take years to **consume** / **recycle** / **decompose** in landfill sites.

3. ____ Encourage government officials to pass tougher laws to reduce **air pollution** / **public transportation** / **endangered species**.

4. ____ Take shorter showers and remember to turn off the faucet while you brush your teeth to reduce **nuclear waste** / **water consumption** / **water pollution**.

5. ____ Try to **recycle** / **consume** / **use** plastic, paper, and glass if possible.

6. ____ Buy appliances like refrigerators and air conditioners that **lack** / **decompose** / **consume** lower amounts of energy.

7. ____ Be aware of companies that **protect** / **contaminate** / **conserve** rivers with toxic chemicals, and don't buy their products.

8. ____ If you think you **buy** / **take** / **lack** information on ways to save energy or conserve water, search the Internet for ideas.

3 Environmental awareness

Grammar | **Circle the word or expression that best fits each sentence.**

1. I think the majority of people would prefer to buy organic produce **due to /despite** the high cost.

2. We always turn our heat down a few degrees in the winter **in order to / instead of** save money on oil.

3. Gas prices have gone up **due to / although** oil shortages.

4. We try to recycle plastic, paper, and glass, **although / so that** it's sometimes hard to do.

5. We're experiencing more hurricanes and severe storms **as a result of / because** global warming.

6. I think some people aren't very aware of environmental problems **instead of / because of** a lack of education.

4 It's important because . . .

Grammar | **Complete the sentences with the words and expressions in the box.**

✓because	due to	in order to	in spite of	instead of	so that

1. It's important to keep the world's oceans and seas free of pollution and contamination ___*because*___ we depend on these waters for food.

2. Car companies are beginning to make some cars out of lightweight carbon fiber instead of steel _____ increase gas mileage.

3. Governments need to work together _____ endangered species are protected around the world.

4. Some rain forests are being deforested twice as quickly as previously thought _____ logging activities.

5. Governments should invest in renewable energy _____ the cost.

6. Some people use vegetable oil to run their cars _____ gasoline.

5 About you

Grammar and vocabulary | **Complete the sentences with true information. Use linking words and expressions.**

1. I try to use *less electricity in order to save money each month* _____ .

2. I try not to waste _____ .

3. I always buy _____ .

4. I'm concerned about _____ .

5. I'm not concerned about _____ .

6. I think governments should _____ .

Lesson C   As I was saying, . . .

1 Referring back

Conversation strategies **A** Taya and Yasuo are talking about current trends. Match Taya's comments with Yasuo's comments later in the conversation.

1. A lot of big companies are employing workers like computer programmers overseas because it's cheaper. I'm not sure that's fair. _e_

2. I think we have some of the longest working hours in the world in this country. It's awful. _____

3. The cost of a college education is so expensive. It's not fair that students have thousands of dollars of debt when they graduate. _____

4. I think it's great that people can work more from home now. It's much better for family life. _____

5. I heard they're increasing the retirement age to 70! I mean, do you think people should work that long? _____

a. Like you were saying, not commuting every day can only be good for everyone, especially people with kids.

b. As you said, it's not right that students have to start their careers owing so much money in student loans.

c. Going back to what you were saying about raising the retirement age, I actually think it's a good idea.

d. Like you said earlier, it's not good to do so much overtime. How do people spend time with their families?

e. You mentioned transferring jobs abroad earlier. I agree that it's not good for local workers.

B Look at Taya's comments in part A again. Refer back to each comment she makes and add your own view.

1. _As Taya was saying, I don't think big companies should move jobs overseas._
   I mean, what will people do here to earn money?

2. _____

3. _____

4. _____

5. _____

2 And so on and so forth . . .

Conversation strategies **Complete the conversations with the phrases in the box and more formal vague expressions like *and so forth*, *and so on*, or *etc*.**

> ✓chemical engineers, electrical engineers, more on-the-job experience, good leadership qualities, organizational skills, good people skills,
>
> paid leave, flexible work hours, relax, reduce stress, pursue interests, vision care, dental care,

1. A I think engineering is a great field for students to study. It offers some of the best-paid jobs for students just graduating from college.

   B Yes. Some of the highest starting salaries go to *chemical engineers, electrical engineers, etc.* .

2. A It's too bad that some companies are cutting back on medical benefits.

   B Yeah, I know. My company has cut things like _____ .

3. A I don't think it's fair that companies are encouraging older workers to retire because they make more money than younger workers.

   B I totally agree. Older workers have _____ .

4. A I'm thinking about starting a family, but I'm really nervous about trying to work and raise a child at the same time.

   B I wouldn't worry. Lots of companies offer new parents benefits like _____ .

5. A I think when you're hiring a new employee, you need someone with a good personality. I think personality is the most important thing.

   B I agree, but I also think you should look for someone with _____ .

6. A I think all workers should have at least four weeks of paid vacation a year.

   B Absolutely. I mean, vacations allow people to _____ .

3 About you

Conversation strategies **Imagine you heard these comments in a conversation. Refer back to them and give your view. Use a formal vague expession.**

1. "There should be fines for people who don't recycle."
   As you said, fines would make people recycle, make money to improve recycling programs, and so on.

2. "Global warming is really impacting our climate."

   _____

3. "People should use public transportation."

   _____

Trendy words

Reading | **Match the terms with the definitions. Read the article to check your answers.**

1. cyberchondriacs __e__
2. e-quaintances ____
3. phishers ____

4. wikis ____
5. MOOCs ____

6. selfies ____

a. friends who meet through social websites, but may not be friends in real life

b. people who attempt to steal other people's identities

c. pictures people take of themselves to upload to a social network / networking website

d. web pages that anyone can add to and / or change

✓e. people who are convinced they are sick because of medical information they found online

f. online classes offered by colleges that anyone can attend for free

---

Internet Vocabulary

Dozens of new words enter the language every year. Many of these have emerged to reflect advances in technology and the ways we use it. Some may stick, and others may fall out of use or change their meaning over time. Here are a number of recent additions. How long will they be around with their current meaning? Only time will tell.

▶ **cyberchondriac** A cyberchondriac visits health and medical websites to read about the symptoms of different diseases, illnesses, or medical conditions. Then, like any hypochondriac, the cyberchondriac becomes worried, thinking he or she has the particular symptoms he or she just read about.

▶ **e-quaintance** An e-quaintance is a person who you communicate with exclusively through online interactions like instant messaging at work or Internet dating – an online acquaintance. An e-quaintance might be a person you email for help with computer issues at work or a person who has similar interests as you do on gaming websites.

▶ **phishing** Phishing describes the Internet crime of trying to get someone's personal information (bank account numbers, national identification numbers, etc.) by sending official-looking emails and directing unsuspecting victims to fake websites. When the victim supplies the updated information to these fake websites, the phisher uses the information to take money from the person's bank account, run up credit card debts, or take out loans in his or her name.

▶ **wiki** A website where users can add or modify text is called a *wiki*. Wikis differ from blogs in that any user can visit a wiki page to search for or update information, making it a continuous work in progress.

▶ **MOOC** MOOC is an acronym for Massive Open Online Course, a type of course given by colleges and universities around the world. A MOOC is a class open to anyone who wants to follow along on the Internet. For instance, a student in Japan can enroll in a physics course taught by a professor at an American college through a MOOC for no cost. MOOCs are being made available more and more as online learning has become more popular.

▶ **selfie** A selfie is a picture that a social networking user takes of him- or herself to post on a profile page. A selfie is usually taken at arm's length and sometimes involves a funny face or gesture. Selfies aren't just being taken by teenagers, they're also taken by celebrities, parents, and even grandparents!

2 Trend watch

Writing | **A Use the words and expressions in the box to complete the blog entry.**

| declined | fewer | growing | increasingly | less | ✓more and more |

Blog

Have you noticed that _more and more_ people use their phones for everything? I mean, everywhere you go, you just see people using their phones. Even my grandparents take videos of us with their phones. They never bring their video cameras anymore. It just seems that _____ people are using them these days. I bet the sales of video cameras and things have _____ due to smartphones. I mean, it's just _____ common to use your phone for everything these days. When I go away for the weekend, I don't even take my computer anymore. It's _____ trouble to just take my phone and use that for email and everything. I use it instead of my credit card too now – like the number of stores that let you pay by phone is _____ . So it's really convenient.

B Write a blog entry about a trend you've noticed in your town or city. Use words and expressions from part A.

Blog

Unit 11 Progress chart

What can you do? Mark the boxes. ✓ = I can . . . ? = I need to review how to . . .	To review, go back to these pages in the Student's Book.
Grammar ☐ use the passive of the present continuous and present perfect.	108 and 109
☐ link ideas with expressions like *although*, *due to*, and *so that*.	110 and 111
Vocabulary ☐ use at least 8 new expressions to describe trends in society.	108 and 109
☐ use at least 15 new expressions to discuss the environment.	110 and 111
Conversation strategies ☐ refer back to what someone said with expressions like *As you were saying*, *Like you said*, etc.	112
☐ use formal vague expressions like *and so forth* and *etc.*	113
Writing ☐ use expressions like *increasingly* to describe trends.	115

Careers

Lesson A — Finding a career

1 Words for job success

Vocabulary | **Complete the definitions.**

1. The document that lists your educational history and work experience is your _résumé_ .

2. If you work for a company for a short time to get some work experience, it's called an _____ .

3. Someone who can give you guidance and help you choose the right job is a _____ _____ .

4. A meeting where you are asked about your qualifications by a potential employer is an _____ .

5. The things you are good at are your _____ , and the things you are not good at are your _____ .

6. A questionnaire that helps you see what kind of person you are is a _____ _____ .

2 What you need to do is take my advice!

Grammar | **Fern is having some problems at work. Read her concerns and then use the cues to give her advice. Use *What* clauses.**

1. Fern   I don't feel my boss notices me. I wonder how I can make her see that I'm ready to take on more responsibility and get promoted.

   You   *What you need is a positive attitude.*
                   (You need a positive attitude.)

   You   _____
          (My friend did something really smart. She wrote a letter to her boss.)

2. Fern   I've been working here for over a year. How can I ask my boss for a raise?

   You   _____
                   (I would just ask.)

   You   _____
      (You need to get another job offer and then ask for a promotion.)

3. Fern   I don't think my colleagues take me seriously. How do I get more respect?

   You   _____
           (You should wear formal business clothes.)

   You   _____
          (You need to get additional skills.)

3 The job market

Grammar | **Rewrite the advice below starting with the long noun phrase given.**

1. Try and get a really good degree.

   The first thing to do _is to try and get a really good degree_ .

2. Get some work experience in a successful company.

   One good thing to get _____ .

3. Be determined to succeed.

   The main thing you need to be _____ .

4. Companies are hiring new graduates right now.

   The good news _____ .

5. Work on improving your English.

   The best thing to do _____ .

6. Internships help you get better jobs.

   The good thing about internships _____ .

4 Online advice

Grammar | **Write two answers for the job seekers' online message board. Start one with a**
What **clause and another with a long noun phrase.**

Message Board
JOB-SEEKING ADVICE

QUESTION: **I had planned to work for a law office during my summer break, but they just told me that they don't need me. I need a summer job fast! What can I do?**

Answer: 1. _What I would do is ask your friends and family members if they_
have any temporary jobs available in their companies.

2. _____
_____

QUESTION: **I would love to work at a ski resort for the winter. Does anyone have any ideas about what I could do, and how I can get a job?**

Answer: 3. _____
_____

4. _____
_____

QUESTION: **I don't know what I want to do with my life. Any suggestions for a recent college graduate who hates to get up in the morning?**

Answer: 5. _____
_____

6. _____
_____

1 What's the job?

Vocabulary | Complete the jobs with the vowels *a, e, i, o,* or *u.* Then match them to the areas of work they belong to. Write *A, B, C,* or *D.*

A = Construction industry   *C* = Media and communications
B = Financial services   *D* = Medicine and health care

1. e d i t o r _____ __C__
2. s __ r g __ __ n _____ ____
3. s t __ c k b r __ k __ r _____ ____
4. c __ n t r __ c t __ r _____ ____
5. w r __ t __ r _____ ____
6. p __ d __ __ t r __ c __ __ n _____ ____

7. t __ x __ d v __ s __ r _____ ____
8. c __ n s t r __ c t __ __ n   w __ r k __ r _____ ____
9. p s y c h __ __ t r __ c   n __ r s __ _____ ____
10. __ n t __ r p r __ t __ r _____ ____
11. f __ n __ n c __ __ l   __ n __ l y s t _____ ____
12. t r __ n s l __ t __ r _____ ____

2 What jobs are you suited for?

Vocabulary | Read what each person says about himself or herself. Write one area of work that each person is suited for and one area of work that each person isn't suited for.

advertising	✓ finance	public relations	the travel industry
business management	journalism	publishing	
the construction industry	✓ medicine	telemarketing	

1. My parents wanted me to be a doctor, but I can't stand the sight of blood. What I enjoy most is anything to do with money, like banking and investments.

   Suited for: _____ *finance* _____   Not suited for: _____ *medicine* _____

2. I love words, and I'm a pretty good writer. My friends often ask me to look over their papers for mistakes, and I enjoy that. I don't want a job with too much responsibility, like being involved in the planning or organization of a company.

   Suited for: _____   Not suited for: _____

3. I really enjoy building things. In fact, I helped my dad design and build a barn for our farm last year. I'm not really good at things like reading and writing. I'm more practical. Like, I can't imagine writing articles for a newspaper, for example.

   Suited for: _____   Not suited for: _____

4. I'm very sociable and love going to parties and events. I really like meeting people, and I think I'm a good communicator – I get along well with everyone. I would hate being in an office all day and talking to people on the phone.

   Suited for: _____   Not suited for: _____

5. I'm a homebody, so I don't want a job that takes me away from home a lot. One thing that interests me is how companies promote their products to customers.

   Suited for: _____   Not suited for: _____

3 What's in your future?

Grammar | **Complete the conversations with the future continuous or the future perfect. Sometimes you can use *may (not)* and *might (not)* instead of *will* or *won't*.**

1. Sasha I have no idea what I want to do when I graduate from college next year. I really need to make a decision soon!

    Tia Oh, two years from now, you _might / will be running_ (run) your own business.

    Sasha No, I _____ probably _____ (look) for a job that pays more than $7 an hour. But hopefully, I _____ (not ask) you to lend me money!

    Tia That'll be great! But seriously, two years from now, you _____ (finish) your degree, and you _____ (work) on Wall Street.

    Sasha Hmm . . . maybe, or I _____ (live) on a Caribbean island and _____ (work) on the beach.

2. Malik I can't believe another year has gone by already.

    Jamie I know. It goes by so fast. I wonder what we _____ (do) this time next year.

    Malik Oh, I don't know. We _____ (live) someplace else, and we _____ (take) a luxury vacation!

    Jamie Yeah, right. We _____ (not pay off) our debts by then, and we still _____ (not fix up) this house, and . . .

    Malik Oh, I hope we _____ (finish) it all by then.

4 About you

Grammar | **Answer the questions with true information. Use the future continuous and future perfect.**

1. What do you think your life will be like ten years from now?
    I think I'll be working in another country and making a lot of money!

2. Will you still be taking English classes?
    _____

3. What job do you think you'll be doing?
    _____

4. Do you think you'll have changed jobs more than once?
    _____

5. Where will you be living?
    _____

6. Do you think you'll have gotten married or had children?
    _____

1 The reason I ask is . . .

Conversation strategies | Complete the conversations with the noun phrases and *What* clauses in the box.

> the best thing was (that) what I heard was (that)
> ✓ the reason I ask is (that) what I thought was good was (that)
> the worst part was (that) what I was going to tell you was (that)

1. **Jamal** Didn't you once get a job on a farm in Australia?

   Ryan Yeah, I did. Why?

   Jamal Well, _the reason I ask is_____ I was wondering whether I should try that myself.

   Ryan You know, I picked garlic. It was hard work, and _____ I smelled like garlic every day. I had to take a long shower at the end of the day to get rid of the garlic smell.

   Jamal Hmm. I think I'd prefer to work on a fruit farm.

2. **Ming-li** Did you hear that the department store at the mall is hiring?

   Thalia No, I didn't. Do you know what positions they're hiring for?

   Ming-li Well, _____ they're hiring temporary sales help for the holiday season. I think the jobs last through the middle of January.

   Thalia Sounds good. I'd love to make a little extra money during the school break. I'll check it out next week.

   Ming-li You should probably go sooner than next week. _____ the store is only hiring about ten people.

   Thalia Ooh. You're right. I'll go today!

3. **Tomo** What did you think about the job interview we had with Andy Fowler?

   Celia Well, I kind of liked him. _____ he had some really interesting ideas about promoting our products. I think he'd be successful in our advertising department.

   Tomo Yeah, he seemed good. He had great qualifications, he'd done his research, and _____ he has a positive attitude. He doesn't have much solid experience, though.

   Celia Well, you need to be hired to get experience. Maybe we should give him a chance.

2 I don't know if you saw . . .

Conversation strategies Read the advertisements. Write sentences about the advertisements with
I don't know if . . . and the cues.

> **WANTED: Energetic, friendly waiters and waitresses to work evenings. Call Sergio at the Cactus Bistro for an interview at 888–555–9609.**

1. (see / hire) *I don't know if you've seen the advertisement, but they're hiring*
   waiters and waitresses at the Cactus Bistro.

> Interested in a new job? Visit the Johnstown Technical College job fair this weekend. Local companies want to meet graduates in business management and information technology.

2. (look for / have) _____
   _____

> Need help writing or revising your résumé? Get creative writing ideas from Résumé Express. Call us today at 888-555-4265.

3. (think about rewriting / get help) _____
   _____

> **Announcement**: Lakewood University is now offering a business management degree with an emphasis on advertising and public relations. We are currently taking applications for the fall semester.

4. (hear / get a degree) _____
   _____

3 I need some help.

Conversation strategies Number the lines of the conversation in the correct order.

_____ Maybe you should get some advice somewhere. I don't know if you're familiar with the Job Resource Center, but they can give you tips on how to interview better.

_____ Really? I didn't know you had help finding your job.

_____ I think I *have* heard of it. Is it on Maple Street, near the park?

_____ Oh, yeah. I never would have gotten the job I have right now without their help. The best part was that they gave me a lot of help with things like writing my résumé and improving my interview skills.

_1_ I've interviewed for six jobs in the past couple of weeks, and I still haven't been hired. I really need some help.

_____ Well, I really need to get a job soon, so I'd better check out the Job Resource Center today!

_____ Yeah, it is. When I was looking for a job last year, I met with a career counselor there.

1 After a job interview

Reading **A** Read the article. Then add the correct heading to each section.

Use the Information Highway   What's the Plan?   It Pays to Be Polite

Following Up After a Job Interview

Congratulations! You were contacted to interview for an amazing job – your dream job – and it went really well. The interviewer was encouraging and easy to talk to. The job location is convenient, and the salary is more than you make now! You're beyond happy! However, it's been almost two weeks since the interview, and you haven't heard from the interviewer or a company representative. Why aren't they calling you? And what should you do?

Many job seekers worry about contacting an interviewer after an interview – even people who feel they made a positive impression. However, contacting the interviewer after the interview is the best thing you can do! Following are three polite and professional ways to remind an interviewer why you are the ideal candidate for a job.

_____

Before finishing up an interview, remember to ask the interviewer what the next steps are in the process – this will give you an idea of the interviewer's timetable, and it will give you a time frame for following up if you need to. If the interviewer tells you it will take about two weeks before he or she makes a final decision, it's perfectly appropriate to contact him or her a few days after that deadline has passed with a short, polite note asking if a decision has been reached.

_____

Always, always, always write a thank-you note after an interview – as soon as you can. The main reason for following up is that it keeps you fresh in the interviewer's mind, and shows that you are professional and well organized, as well as appreciative. Employers like that. Further, it gives you an opportunity to restate your interest in the position and remind the interviewer why you are a great choice. But keep it brief!

_____

Finally, try to look upon the interview process as a way of making professional connections. Make sure you are signed up to work-related networking sites and ask the interviewer if you can connect with him or her. Even if you don't get hired for this job, you still have a way to communicate with professionals in the field you want to work in. Who knows, maybe another job will open up at the company and the interviewer will think of you!

B Read the article again. Which statements are true? Which are false? Write *T* or *F*.

1. Waiting for the company to contact you after an interview is the only thing to do. _____

2. One thing you should do at an interview is ask what the next steps are. _____

3. Interviewers like thank-you notes because they show your appreciation. _____

4. Thank-you notes give you a chance to put in writing everything you said at the interview. _____

5. It's appropriate to contact an interviewer on a networking site before an interview. _____

6. An interview for a job you don't get can sometimes lead to other opportunities. _____

2 Please consider me.

A Read the cover letter. Then complete it with the expressions in the box.

advertised on October 28	cover letter	Sincerely
attached résumé	Dear	Thank you for your time and consideration.

○○○   Application Form

Application for: **JUNIOR BAKER**

Upload a résumé   **Submit**

Include a (1) _____

(2) _____ Sir or Madam,

I am applying for the position of Junior Baker, which was (3) _____ . I am currently a third-year student at the Oakland School of Culinary Arts, and baking is my passion.

As you can see from the (4) _____ , I don't have a lot of experience in commercial baking. I had a part-time job in my school's cafeteria. I was responsible for baking bread and rolls for over 200 students and faculty members every weekend. I am a diligent worker, and I think I would be an asset to your company.

I would welcome the chance to speak with you at your convenience. I can be reached at 888-555-2387 from 8 a.m. to 1 p.m. every day.

(5) _____

(6) _____ ,
Melvin Cruz

B Write a cover letter to apply for a job you'd really like to have. Include an opening paragraph, middle paragraph, closing paragraph, and ending.

Unit 12 Progress chart

What can you do? Mark the boxes. ✓ = I can . . . ? = I need to review how to . . .	To review, go back to these pages in the Student's Book.
Grammar ☐ use *What* clauses and long noun phrases as subjects.	118 and 119
☐ talk about the future with the future continuous and future perfect.	120 and 121
Vocabulary ☐ use at least 20 new words to talk about careers.	120 and 121
Conversation strategies ☐ introduce what I say with expressions like *What I read was*	122
☐ introduce ideas with *I don't know if*	123
Writing ☐ write a cover letter.	125

Illustration credits

Chuck Gonzales: 2, 3, 20, 21, 31, 44, 45, 54, 55, 94   **Frank Montagna:** 10, 11, 26, 27, 46, 47, 52, 67, 76, 78, 79   **Marilena Perilli:** 6, 7, 22, 23, 40, 58, 70, 71, 93   **Greg White:** 18, 38, 61, 69   **Terry Wong:** 12, 13, 28, 29, 50, 62, 63, 83, 90   **Q2A Studio Artists:** 59, 72

Photo credits

4 *(top to bottom)* ©Polka Dot Images/Thinkstock; ©Punchstock; ©Ryan McVay/Thinkstock   **5** ©newphotoservice/Shutterstock   **8** ©RON EDMONDS/Associated Press   **14** ©Getty Images   **15** ©Punchstock   **16** *(left to right)* ©Mel Curtis/Getty Images/RF; ©Tim Garcha/Corbis; ©Kaz Chiba/Getty Images   **18** © Tongro Image Stock/agefotostoc   **19** *(top to bottom)* ©Tim Thompson/Corbis; ©David Lyons/Alamy; ©Watt, Elizabeth/agefotostock *(background)* ©Malchev/Shutterstock   **24** ©Jim Arbogast/Getty Images/RF   **30** ©Zero Creatives/Getty Images   **31** ©Westend61/Getty Images/RF   **32** ©Ryan McVay/Thinkstock   **34** ©Punchstock   **42** ©SnowWhiteimages/Shutterstock   **49** ©Sean Gladwell/Shutterstock   **60** *(top to bottom)* ©Andresr/Shutterstock; ©arek_malang/Shutterstock; © Ocean/Corbis/RF; © photomak/Shutterstock   **64** ©ColinCramm/Shutterstock   **66** ©SuperStock/agefotostock   **67** ©George Doyle/Thinkstock   **72** *(books)* ©LanKS/Shutterstock   **74** *(top to bottom)* ©Kevork Djansezian/Getty Images; ©Thinkstock/Getty Images; ©PhotoAlto/James Hardy   **75** *(top to bottom)* ©Kike Calvo/National Geographic Society/Corbis; ©Lane Oatey/Blue Jean Images/Getty Images/RF; ©Digital Vision/Getty Images; ©Punchstock; ©Wayne Eardley/Masterfile   **77** *(top, top to bottom)* ©s_bukley/Shutterstock; ©Helga Esteb/Shutterstock *(bottom, left to right)* ©MGM/courtesy Everett Collection; ©MGM/courtesy Everett Collection; ©20th Century Fox Film Corp/Everett Collection; ©Alexandra Wyman/Getty Images   **80** *(left to right)* ©D Dipasupil/FilmMagic/Getty Images; ©Jason LaVeris/FilmMagic/Getty Images *(diamond)* ©pdesign/Shutterstock *(background)* ©Ezepov Dmitry/Shutterstock   **85** ©Sue Wilson/Alamy   **86** ©Randy Faris/Corbis

Text credits

While every effort has been made, it has not always been possible to identify the sources of all the material used, or to trace all copyright holders. If any omissions are brought to our notice, we will be happy to include the appropriate acknowledgements on reprinting.

The top 500 spoken words

This is a list of the top 500 words in spoken North American English. It is based on a sample of four and a half million words of conversation from the Cambridge International Corpus. The most frequent word, *I*, is at the top of the list.

1. I	40. really	79. see
2. and	41. with	80. how
3. the	42. he	81. they're
4. you	43. one	82. kind
5. uh	44. are	83. here
6. to	45. this	84. from
7. a	46. there	85. did
8. that	47. I'm	86. something
9. it	48. all	87. too
10. of	49. if	88. more
11. yeah	50. no	89. very
12. know	51. get	90. want
13. in	52. about	91. little
14. like	53. at	92. been
15. they	54. out	93. things
16. have	55. had	94. an
17. so	56. then	95. you're
18. was	57. because	96. said
19. but	58. go	97. there's
20. is	59. up	98. I've
21. it's	60. she	99. much
22. we	61. when	100. where
23. huh	62. them	101. two
24. just	63. can	102. thing
25. oh	64. would	103. her
26. do	65. as	104. didn't
27. don't	66. me	105. other
28. that's	67. mean	106. say
29. well	68. some	107. back
30. for	69. good	108. could
31. what	70. got	109. their
32. on	71. OK	110. our
33. think	72. people	111. guess
34. right	73. now	112. yes
35. not	74. going	113. way
36. um	75. were	114. has
37. or	76. lot	115. down
38. my	77. your	116. we're
39. be	78. time	117. any

The top 500 spoken words

118.	he's	161.	five	204.	sort
119.	work	162.	always	205.	great
120.	take	163.	school	206.	bad
121.	even	164.	look	207.	we've
122.	those	165.	still	208.	another
123.	over	166.	around	209.	car
124.	probably	167.	anything	210.	true
125.	him	168.	kids	211.	whole
126.	who	169.	first	212.	whatever
127.	put	170.	does	213.	twenty
128.	years	171.	need	214.	after
129.	sure	172.	us	215.	ever
130.	can't	173.	should	216.	find
131.	pretty	174.	talking	217.	care
132.	gonna	175.	last	218.	better
133.	stuff	176.	thought	219.	hard
134.	come	177.	doesn't	220.	haven't
135.	these	178.	different	221.	trying
136.	by	179.	money	222.	give
137.	into	180.	long	223.	I'd
138.	went	181.	used	224.	problem
139.	make	182.	getting	225.	else
140.	than	183.	same	226.	remember
141.	year	184.	four	227.	might
142.	three	185.	every	228.	again
143.	which	186.	new	229.	pay
144.	home	187.	everything	230.	try
145.	will	188.	many	231.	place
146.	nice	189.	before	232.	part
147.	never	190.	though	233.	let
148.	only	191.	most	234.	keep
149.	his	192.	tell	235.	children
150.	doing	193.	being	236.	anyway
151.	cause	194.	bit	237.	came
152.	off	195.	house	238.	six
153.	I'll	196.	also	239.	family
154.	maybe	197.	use	240.	wasn't
155.	real	198.	through	241.	talk
156.	why	199.	feel	242.	made
157.	big	200.	course	243.	hundred
158.	actually	201.	what's	244.	night
159.	she's	202.	old	245.	call
160.	day	203.	done	246.	saying

247.	dollars	290.	started	333.	believe
248.	live	291.	job	334.	thinking
249.	away	292.	says	335.	funny
250.	either	293.	play	336.	state
251.	read	294.	usually	337.	until
252.	having	295.	wow	338.	husband
253.	far	296.	exactly	339.	idea
254.	watch	297.	took	340.	name
255.	week	298.	few	341.	seven
256.	mhm	299.	child	342.	together
257.	quite	300.	thirty	343.	each
258.	enough	301.	buy	344.	hear
259.	next	302.	person	345.	help
260.	couple	303.	working	346.	nothing
261.	own	304.	half	347.	parents
262.	wouldn't	305.	looking	348.	room
263.	ten	306.	someone	349.	today
264.	interesting	307.	coming	350.	makes
265.	am	308.	eight	351.	stay
266.	sometimes	309.	love	352.	mom
267.	bye	310.	everybody	353.	sounds
268.	seems	311.	able	354.	change
269.	heard	312.	we'll	355.	understand
270.	goes	313.	life	356.	such
271.	called	314.	may	357.	gone
272.	point	315.	both	358.	system
273.	ago	316.	type	359.	comes
274.	while	317.	end	360.	thank
275.	fact	318.	least	361.	show
276.	once	319.	told	362.	thousand
277.	seen	320.	saw	363.	left
278.	wanted	321.	college	364.	friends
279.	isn't	322.	ones	365.	class
280.	start	323.	almost	366.	already
281.	high	324.	since	367.	eat
282.	somebody	325.	days	368.	small
283.	let's	326.	couldn't	369.	boy
284.	times	327.	gets	370.	paper
285.	guy	328.	guys	371.	world
286.	area	329.	god	372.	best
287.	fun	330.	country	373.	water
288.	they've	331.	wait	374.	myself
289.	you've	332.	yet	375.	run

The top 500 spoken words

376. they'll	418. company	460. sorry
377. won't	419. friend	461. living
378. movie	420. set	462. drive
379. cool	421. minutes	463. outside
380. news	422. morning	464. bring
381. number	423. between	465. easy
382. man	424. music	466. stop
383. basically	425. close	467. percent
384. nine	426. leave	468. hand
385. enjoy	427. wife	469. gosh
386. bought	428. knew	470. top
387. whether	429. pick	471. cut
388. especially	430. important	472. computer
389. taking	431. ask	473. tried
390. sit	432. hour	474. gotten
391. book	433. deal	475. mind
392. fifty	434. mine	476. business
393. months	435. reason	477. anybody
394. women	436. credit	478. takes
395. month	437. dog	479. aren't
396. found	438. group	480. question
397. side	439. turn	481. rather
398. food	440. making	482. twelve
399. looks	441. American	483. phone
400. summer	442. weeks	484. program
401. hmm	443. certain	485. without
402. fine	444. less	486. moved
403. hey	445. must	487. gave
404. student	446. dad	488. yep
405. agree	447. during	489. case
406. mother	448. lived	490. looked
407. problems	449. forty	491. certainly
408. city	450. air	492. talked
409. second	451. government	493. beautiful
410. definitely	452. eighty	494. card
411. spend	453. wonderful	495. walk
412. happened	454. seem	496. married
413. hours	455. wrong	497. anymore
414. war	456. young	498. you'll
415. matter	457. places	499. middle
416. supposed	458. girl	500. tax
417. worked	459. happen	

TOUCHSTONE

MARCIA FISK ONG

SERIES AUTHORS

MICHAEL McCARTHY

JEANNE McCARTEN

HELEN SANDIFORD

VIDEO ACTIVITY PAGES

CAMBRIDGE
UNIVERSITY PRESS

Contents

Character descriptions

Touchstone Video is a fun-filled, compelling situational comedy featuring a group of young people who are friends. David Parker is a reporter. His roommate is Alex Santos, a personal trainer. David's friend Gio Ferrari is a student visiting from Italy. Liz Martin is a singer and Web designer. She lives with Yoko Suzuki, a chef. Kim Davis is David's co-worker. She works in an office.

Through the daily encounters and activities of these characters, you have the opportunity to see and hear the language of the Student's Book vividly come to life in circumstances both familiar and entertaining.

This is David Parker.
He's a reporter.

This is Yoko Suzuki.
She's a chef.

This is Alex Santos.
He's a personal trainer.

This is Gio Ferrari.
He's a student.
He's from Italy.

This is Liz Martin.
She's a Web designer
and singer.

This is Kim Davis.
She's David's co-worker.

The Video

Welcome to the *Touchstone* Video. In this video you will get to know six people who are friends: David, Liz, Yoko, Alex, Kim, and Gio. You can read about them on page iv.

You will also hear them use the English that you are studying in the *Touchstone* Student's Books. Each of the four levels of the Video breaks down as follows:

Episode 1	Act 1	Student's Book units 1–3
	Act 2	
	Act 3	

Episode 2	Act 1	Student's Book units 4–6
	Act 2	
	Act 3	

Episode 3	Act 1	Student's Book units 7–9
	Act 2	
	Act 3	

Episode 4	Act 1	Student's Book units 10–12
	Act 2	
	Act 3	

Explanation of the DVD Menu

To play one Episode of the Video:
- On the Main Menu, select *Episode Menu*.
- On the Episode Menu, select the appropriate *Play Episode*.

To play one Act of the Video:
- On the Main Menu, select *Episode Menu*.
- On the Episode Menu, select *Act Menu*.
- On the Act Menu, select the appropriate *Play Act*.

To play the Video with subtitles:
- On the Main Menu, Episode Menu, or Act Menu, select *Subtitles*.
- On the Subtitles Menu, select *Subtitles on*. The DVD will then automatically take you back to the menu you were on before.

To cancel the subtitles:
- On the Main Menu, Episode Menu, or Act Menu, select *Subtitles*.
- On the Subtitles Menu, select *Subtitles off*. The DVD will then automatically take you back to the menu you were on before.

The Worksheets

For each Act there are *Before you watch*, *While you watch*, and *After you watch* worksheets.

For *While you watch* worksheets*:*
- Find **DVD** [0] on your worksheet.
- Input this number on the Video menu using your remote control. The DVD will then play only the segment of the Video you need to watch to complete the task.

We hope you enjoy the *Touchstone* Video!

Episode *1* A Guest from Out of Town

Act *1*

Before you watch

A Deborah is on a business trip overseas and is calling home. Complete the paragraph with the words in the box.

exhausted	jet-lagged	suitcase	unpack
identical	✓ landed	taxi stand	

My flight (1) _____ _landed_ _____ at about noon, but it took a long time to get out of the airport because I couldn't find my (2) _____ . It was hard to recognize because all the bags looked (3) _____ . I'm going to put a colorful tag on it next time! Anyway, then I went to the (4) _____ and waited for a cab, and that took a long time, so by the time I got to the hotel I was (5) _____ ! I just (6) _____ my clothes and then I went straight to sleep . . . at four in the afternoon! I was so (7) _____ ! But I feel fine today.

B Circle the correct verb form.

1. I hear you're a musician. What instrument (**do you play**)/ **are you playing**?
2. I **just love** / **am just loving** sushi! It's my favorite food.
3. We **went** / **were going** to a wonderful party last weekend.
4. Can I help you? **Do you look** / **Are you looking** for someone?
5. Have you **seen** / **been seeing** *Three Nights in Paris* yet? It's great.
6. We've **waited** / **been waiting** for a long time, but we haven't gotten our tickets yet.
7. I **met** / **was meeting** my friend Brian while I **waited** / **was waiting** for the bus.
8. We're here for the weekend. **We stay** / **We're staying** at the Hotel Monaco.

While you watch

A Number the scenes in the correct order.

a. _____

b. _____

c. _____

d. _____

e. _____

f. _____

B Check (✓) true or false. Then try to correct the false sentences.

1. Alex and Connie met in college.   ☐ True   ☑ False
   Alex and Connie grew up together.

2. Alex sent Connie an e-mail to get back in touch.   ☐ True   ☐ False
   _____

3. Connie left on her trip more than twenty-four hours ago.   ☐ True   ☐ False
   _____

4. Connie's flight arrived late.   ☐ True   ☐ False
   _____

5. Connie met another passenger from her flight.   ☐ True   ☐ False
   _____

6. Connie took someone's bag by accident.   ☐ True   ☐ False
   _____

7. Connie wants to rest before they go out.   ☐ True   ☐ False
   _____

8. Connie works as a writer.   ☐ True   ☐ False
   _____

9. Connie goes to meetings all over the world.   ☐ True   ☐ False
   _____

10. Yoko also likes fashion.   ☐ True   ☐ False
    _____

While you watch

DVD 3-4
VHS 00:35
–01:35
VHS 03:51
–04:52

C Listen for these sentences. Circle the one you hear.

1. a. Where's she living now?
   b. Where does she live now?
2. a. She's living in Singapore.
   b. She's been living in Singapore.
3. a. I was traveling for the past twenty-two hours.
   b. I've been traveling for the past twenty-two hours.
4. a. I heard a lot about you.
   b. I've heard a lot about you.

5. a. What do you do for a living?
   b. What are you doing for a living?
6. a. Right now, I work for a magazine in Singapore.
   b. Right now, I'm working for a magazine in Singapore.
7. a. There was just one problem.
   b. There's just one problem.
8. a. I haven't been on vacation in ages.
   b. I haven't had a vacation in ages.

DVD 5
VHS 01:28
–02:22

D What does Connie say exactly? Circle the correct words to complete the story. Notice how Connie uses the present tense to highlight key moments in her story.

Well, it's a funny story. I actually arrived early, but I had to wait for my suitcase. It took forever, but I finally got it . . . Then I (1) **go / went** to get a taxi. So (2) **I rush / I'm rushing** to the taxi stand when suddenly, someone (3) **grabbed / grabs** my arm. I'm so surprised, I scream . . . So I turn around, and it's (4) **this / a** guy from my flight! He doesn't speak English very well, but (5) **he smiles / he's smiling** and pointing at my bag and then at his bag. And (6) **I think / I'm thinking**, "What does he want?" And then I (7) **realize / realized** – I (8) **have / had** *his* suitcase!

DVD 6
VHS 03:58
–04:43

E Watch the video. Complete the conversation with the correct *to* or *-ing* form of the verbs in the box.

be	become	get	make	try	write

Connie Right now, I'm working for a magazine in Singapore.

Yoko Really? That's so cool. Now, how did you end up (1) _getting_ a job like that?

Connie Well, actually, I never intended (2) _____ an editor. When I was younger, I expected (3) _____ a designer. You see, I loved (4) _____ my own clothes. There was just one problem.

Yoko What was that?

Connie My designs were awful! Eventually, I gave up (5) _____ to design clothes and started (6) _____ about them instead. Now I get to travel to fashion shows all over the world.

After you watch

A What can you remember? Write down some things you learned about Connie.

Connie and Alex grew up together.

_____

_____

B Complete the sentences with facts from your own life. Use verbs with *to* or *-ing.* Then compare your sentences with a partner. Ask follow-up questions to get more information.

1. I really enjoy _____ .
2. When I was a kid, I hated (to) _____ .
3. When I was a kid, I always refused to _____ .
4. I started (to) _____ when I was a teenager.
5. I never expected to _____ .
6. I'm considering _____ .
7. I'd like to stop _____ .
8. I've decided to _____ .

"I really enjoy listening to live music."
"When I was a kid, I hated to eat vegetables."

C Work with a partner. Choose one of the pictures and make up a story about it. What do you think happened? Tell the story as if it happened to you. Add as many details as you can. Use the present tense to highlight "dramatic" moments in the story.

"We were camping one summer. It was late one night. It was getting dark, and it looked like it was going to rain. There was a lot of thunder and lightning, so we were pretty nervous. Then, we hear this noise! . . ."

Act 2

Before you watch

A Look at these statements about typical cultural behavior in the United States. Check (✓) the ones that are also true in your country. Then compare your answers with a partner. For statements that are not the same, why do you think things are different in your country?

Greeting and socializing	
☐ It's customary to shake hands when you meet someone for the first time.	1. __a__
☐ You can offend people by not calling before you visit them at home.	2. _____
☐ When you go into someone's home, you don't have to take off your shoes.	3. _____
At work	
☐ Being on time for appointments is very important.	4. _____
☐ You usually address co-workers and your boss by their first names.	5. _____
☐ It's not typical to exchange business cards unless you want to contact the person later.	6. _____
In public	
☐ You can offend people by making loud noises when you eat.	7. _____
☐ Using a cell phone in public is considered rude.	8. _____
☐ It's impolite to talk loudly in public.	9. _____

B Look at the structure of these sentences. Match each sentence in Exercise A to one of the structures – *a, b,* or *c.* If there is no matching structure, write Ø.

a. **It's . . . + *to* + verb**   <u>It's</u> rude <u>to cut</u> in line.
b. **Verb + *-ing* as subject**   <u>Cutting in line</u> is considered rude.
c. **Verb + *-ing* after preposition**   You can offend people <u>by cutting in line</u>.

C Complete the sentences with the present passive form (*be* + past participle) of the verbs in the box.

✓ call	fill	hold	make	serve

1. My favorite Brazilian dish <u>is called</u> *feijoada.*

2. An omelet _____ with eggs.

3. Usually a hamburger _____ with fries.

4. *Empanadas* _____ with meat, fish, or fruit.

5. The Pan American Games _____ every four years in a different city in North, South, or Central America.

feijoada

empanadas

While you watch

DVD ⑦
VHS 05:19
−09:50

A Check (✓) the topics Connie, Yoko, Alex, and Gio talk about.

☐ clothes	☐ drinks	☐ festivals	☐ foreign films	☐ missing family
☐ customs	☐ a fashion show	☐ food	☐ handicrafts	and friends
				☐ speaking English

DVD ⑧
VHS 05:19
−09:50

B Check (✓) true or false. Then try to correct the false sentences.

1. Connie bought herself a snack.   ☐ True   ☑ False
   <u>Yoko made Connie a snack.</u>

2. Gio recently got back from a trip.   ☐ True   ☐ False

   _____

3. Alex and Connie both love Florence.   ☐ True   ☐ False

   _____

4. Customs in Singapore and the United States are surprisingly different.   ☐ True   ☐ False

   _____

5. Yoko visits her grandparents in Japan.   ☐ True   ☐ False

   _____

6. Yoko would definitely miss family and friends.   ☐ True   ☐ False

   _____

7. Connie and Alex use the telephone to keep in touch.   ☐ True   ☐ False

   _____

8. Yoko loves the food in Japan.   ☐ True   ☐ False

   _____

9. Connie would miss the fashion shows in Singapore.   ☐ True   ☐ False

   _____

10. Before he can visit art galleries, Alex needs some new paintings.   ☐ True   ☐ False

    _____

While you watch

DVD 9
VHS 06:14
–07:44

C Where do these customs occur? Check (✓) all the places that are mentioned. Then answer the question.

Alex

Connie

Yoko

Gio

Where do you . . . ?	the U.S.	Japan	Singapore
1. do business in English			
2. shake hands			
3. bow			
4. take your shoes off indoors			
5. eat food on the street			

6. What Italian custom does Gio mention? _____

DVD 10
VHS 08:07
–08:58

D Listen for these descriptions and complete them with the active or passive form of the verbs. (You will use some verbs more than once.)

call	come	eat	fill	hold	know	make	serve

1. *Connie* There's this one dish that I _**eat**_ for breakfast all the time.
   It **'s called** _kaya toast_. It's a jam that _____ with coconut
   and egg, and it _____ on toast. It's so delicious.
2. *Yoko* I like this Japanese treat that _____ _manju_. Usually it _____
   with this delicious sweet bean paste. Every time I _____ it, I
   remember my trips to Japan!
3. *Connie* My favorite one _____ the Singapore Fashion Week. It _____
   every fall. It's so exciting. Designers _____ from all over Asia to show
   their clothes. It _____ as *the* event for young designers.

DVD 11
VHS 06:14
–08:25

E Listen for these sentences. What do the people say exactly? Circle the correct expressions.

1. **To be honest / To tell you the truth**, things in Singapore are surprisingly similar to the United States.
2. **Actually / In fact**, doing business in English is the rule.
3. In Italy, it's **customary / the custom** to kiss on the cheek.
4. You can offend people **by eating / if you eat** in public.
5. I know that if I lived abroad, I'd **certainly / definitely** miss my family and friends.
6. Oh, yeah. **To be honest / In fact**, I still do.
7. That's **certainly / definitely** how we keep in touch.
8. I'd **absolutely / really** miss the food.

After you watch

A What can you remember? Write down four things you learned about Singapore from Connie.

<u>A lot of things in Singapore are similar to the United States.</u>

_____

_____

_____

B Think about advice you would give a tourist visiting your country. Complete the sentences. Then discuss your answers in small groups.

1. It's customary to _____ when you meet someone.
2. It's polite to _____ .
3. You should(n't) _____ when you go to someone's home.
4. It's impolite to _____ .
5. You can offend people by (not) _____ .
6. _____ in public is considered bad manners.

"It's customary to kiss on the cheek when you meet someone."

C Answer the questions to describe a food you love from your country. Then compare your description with other students.

1. What's it called? _____
2. What's it made with? _____
3. What's it filled with? _____
4. What's it usually served with? _____

"I love a dessert called pumpkin pie. It's made with pumpkin, of course.
You add in eggs, sugar, milk, and cinnamon. It isn't filled with anything,
but it's usually served with whipped cream on top."

Episode **1** *A Guest from Out of Town*

Before you watch

A Match each description to the correct picture. Then complete the chart with words from the descriptions.

1. ____   2. ____   3. ____

a. This man has a more casual look. He's wearing a wool sweater and baggy pants. His sunglasses are very trendy.

b. This man is wearing a vintage look, which is the "in" thing these days. The jacket and pants are a little fitted, but not too much. The leather boots are very stylish.

c. This man is wearing a more formal business suit. It's nicely tailored. The floral tie looks terrific with the striped shirt. It's a classic look.

Clothing	Style or look	Pattern or material	How clothes fit
	casual	wool	

B Rewrite these sentences as negative questions. Use the words in parentheses.

1. That dress is a little too formal, I think.
   (you / think) <u>Don't you think that dress is a little too formal?</u>
2. Maybe the color is too bright.
   (be) _____
3. I think those shoes are a little expensive.
   (you / think) _____
4. Maybe that jacket is a little baggy.
   (be) _____
5. That outfit is a little boring.
   (you / think) _____

While you watch

DVD 12
VHS 09:55
−14:21

A Check (✓) true or false.

1. Alex spends as much money as Connie does.   ☐ True   ☑ False
2. Connie wrote an article about men's fashion.   ☐ True   ☐ False
3. Alex thought the article was helpful.   ☐ True   ☐ False
4. Alex spends a lot of time thinking about what to wear.   ☐ True   ☐ False
5. The first outfit Alex tries on has a classic look.   ☐ True   ☐ False
6. Connie doesn't like the second outfit as much as the first.   ☐ True   ☐ False
7. Connie doesn't think the third outfit is a popular style.   ☐ True   ☐ False
8. Liz doesn't like the outfit Connie and Alex chose.   ☐ True   ☐ False
9. Gio thinks Alex's outfit looks Italian.   ☐ True   ☐ False

DVD 13
VHS 09:55
−12:07

B Circle the sentences that express Connie's opinions.

1. a. Alex needs to look trendy when he visits art galleries.
   b. Alex needs to dress well when he visits art galleries.

2. a. Guys should pay more attention to their appearance.
   b. Guys should spend more money on their clothes.

3. a. It takes a lot of work to look good.
   b. You can look good without a lot of work.

4. a. Your clothes should make you feel comfortable.
   b. Your clothes should always look neat.

5. a. Your style should fit your personality.
   b. Your style should fit your salary.

6. a. Men in ties look more formal.
   b. Men in ties look more professional.

DVD 14
VHS 10:16
−11:27

C Listen for these parts of the conversation and complete them. Notice how Alex summarizes what Connie says.

1. *Connie*   If you want to make a good impression when you start visiting art galleries, you need to dress well.
   Alex   _____ I may have to _____ a little more _____ .
   Connie   Maybe a _____ . But you don't have to go _____ . . . .

2. *Connie*   What matters is that you look good and you feel confident and comfortable.
   Alex   Hmm. _____ you need a _____ that fits your personality.
   Connie   Exactly.

While you watch

DVD 15
VHS 11:27
–13:18

D Listen for what's said about Alex's outfits. Cross out the expression in each list that <u>isn't</u> mentioned.

1. Alex's first outfit
bright
polyester
silk
striped
too formal

2. Alex's second outfit
flared
pattern
tight
vintage

3. Alex's third outfit
fit well
perfect look
professional
stylish
trendy

DVD 16
VHS 09:55
–13:00

E Match the questions with the responses.

1. This place looks a little expensive, don't you think? _____
2. Now, did you read that article I wrote about men's fashion? I e-mailed it to you a few weeks ago. _____
3. A look? Like what? _____
4. I don't know. Isn't it a bit too formal? _____
5. But isn't the color a bit too bright? _____
6. Don't you like it? _____
7. And the pants fit perfectly, don't you think? _____
8. And don't you just love this jacket? _____

a. Not at all.
b. Maybe.
c. Well, it's all right.
d. Really? I don't think so.
e. Uh, no. I'm sorry.
f. Isn't it kind of trendy?
g. It could be anything, really.
h. No, actually, I think maybe they're a little tight.

After you watch

A What can you remember? Describe the three outfits that Alex tries on.

Outfit 1: <u>It's a classic style.</u>

Outfit 2: _____

_____

Outfit 3: _____

_____

B Work in pairs. Read the words in the box. Add as many words as you can to each category. Then compare your lists as a group. Who added the most words?

Clothing	Fit or cut	Materials	Patterns	Styles
jeans	baggy V-neck	leather	striped	vintage

C Work in pairs. Take turns describing what other students in the class are wearing.

"Maria is wearing a pretty trendy outfit. She has on low-rise jeans and a leather belt, a light-green V-neck T-shirt, and a cotton sweater with a hood."

D Work in pairs. Discuss these questions. How similar or different are your answers?

1. What kind of clothes do you wear to work or school?
2. What kind of clothes do you wear on weekends?
3. Do you think you have a unique style or look? If so, what is it?
4. Which famous person do you think has the most unique style?

Episode **2** A Barbecue

Act 1

Before you watch

A Read the sentences. Then choose the expression that is closest in meaning to the underlined word or words.

a. become comfortable with
b. have time off in order to relax
c. have the opportunity to do something
d. leave with permission
e. not make progress on
f. prepare
g. recover from disappointment
h. understand

1. When I was on vacation in Egypt, I <u>got to</u> ride on a camel! _c_
2. I've been very busy, so I'm taking a break. I want to <u>get away from it all</u> for a while. _____
3. If I take the week off, I'll <u>get behind on</u> my work. _____
4. If you move to the city, you'll have to <u>get used to</u> the noise. _____
5. When I found out that I didn't pass the exam, it took me a while to <u>get over it</u>. _____
6. At first I didn't understand the problem, but now I <u>get it</u>. _____
7. How late do you have to work? Can you <u>get off</u> a little early? _____
8. Just give me ten minutes to <u>get ready</u>. _____

B Match the two parts of the sentences.

1. It's supposed to rain today, _e_
2. I'd like to see that movie _____
3. I'm supposed to go to work today, _____
4. The children need to go to bed soon _____
5. We were supposed to meet at 10:00, _____
6. Brian isn't here yet, _____

a. because it's supposed to be really funny.
b. but I think I'll call in sick.
c. but nobody showed up until 12:30!
d. and he was supposed to be here hours ago.
e. so you'd better bring an umbrella.
f. because they're supposed to be asleep by nine.

C Look at these meanings of *be supposed to* and the examples given from the left column of Exercise B. Then look at the <u>right</u> column and find one more example of each. Write the <u>letter</u>.

In this sentence, *be supposed to* means . . .

1. "They say"   _1_   _____
2. *have to* or *should*   _3_   _____
3. what was expected but didn't happen   _5_   _____

While you watch

A Check (✓) the correct people.

Who . . . ?	Alex	Connie	Gio	Kim	Liz
1. has been pretty busy					
2. is going to Los Angeles soon					
3. can't remember					
4. is having a barbecue					
5. wasn't invited					
6. is excited					
7. has to work on the day of the barbecue					
8. is going to the barbecue with Liz and Yoko					
9. didn't have Gio's number					
10. doesn't have directions to the party					

B Circle the correct answers.

1. Gio has been studying hard because it's his last _____ of classes.
   a. week   b. month

2. Liz might be recording a CD for Big _____ Records.
   a. Time   b. Stuff

3. Liz could be moving to L.A. next _____ .
   a. week   b. month

4. Liz can't celebrate with Gio because she's going to _____ .
   a. Los Angeles   b. the barbecue

5. Tomorrow is supposed to be a _____ day.
   a. beautiful   b. rainy

6. Alex asks Liz to give Connie a ride because he's _____ .
   a. not feeling well   b. supposed to work

7. David was supposed to pass on the _____ to Gio.
   a. directions   b. invitation

8. Liz _____ bring napkins and cups.
   a. is supposed to   b. was going to

9. Yoko was going to make _____ , but she didn't have time.
   a. cookies   b. a cake

10. _____ is meeting them at the barbecue.
    a. Alex   b. David

While you watch

C Listen for these questions. Circle the one you hear.

1. *Liz* a. Have you done anything fun?
   b. Have you gotten to do anything fun?
2. *Liz* a. So, you've been pretty busy?
   b. So, have you been pretty busy?
3. *Gio* a. So, what happens next?
   b. So, what's going to happen next?
4. *Gio* a. Kim's having a barbecue tomorrow?
   b. Is Kim having a barbecue tomorrow?
5. *Liz* a. Um, are you going to Kim's barbecue tomorrow?
   b. Um, are you going to go to Kim's barbecue tomorrow?
6. *Alex* a. Do you mind giving Connie a ride to the party?
   b. Would you mind giving Connie a ride to the party?
7. *Yoko* a. So you talked to Gio, and he's going to go?
   b. So you talked to Gio. Is he going to go?
8. *Yoko* a. Alex is meeting us there, right?
   b. Alex is going to meet us there, right?
9. *Liz* a. Um, Yoko, you have the directions to Kim's place, right?
   b. Um, Yoko, do you have the directions to Kim's place?

D Listen for these sentences and complete them with the expressions in the box. Write the letters.

a. get away from it all	c. get going	e. get off	g. getting ready
b. get behind	d. get it	f. get over	h. get used to

1. I've been pretty swamped. I don't want to __b__ on anything.
2. I really want to relax and _____ for a few weeks.
3. I can't believe you might be moving away, Liz. I just can't _____ the idea.
4. I can't _____ it, either.
5. But I don't _____ . I'm sure it's a mistake.

6. I'm just one of those people who spends ages _____ .
7. That's OK. We weren't ready, either. But we really should _____ .
8. He had to work this morning. He managed to _____ a little early, but . . .

After you watch

A What can you remember? Answer the questions.

1. What did Liz think when she heard that Gio did not have an invitation to the barbecue?

_____

2. What did Liz do about it?

_____

3. What would you do if you were in Liz's situation?

_____

B Put the lines of the conversation in order. Then practice with a partner.

_____ At a tech company downtown. It's a much better job.

_____ That's really good news. So . . . let's go and celebrate!

_____ Oh, yeah, much happier. The people are really nice, and the money is better, so . . .

_____ No, I didn't! Congratulations. Where are you working now?

_____ Oh, pretty good. Did you hear that I got a new job?

__1__ So, how have you been?

_____ That's great! So you're happier there?

C Find examples of the following uses of *so* in Exercise B.

Find an example of *so* . . .

1. to start a topic: _So, how have you been?_____

2. to check understanding: _____

3. to let the other person draw a conclusion: _____

4. to close a topic: _____

D Work with a partner. Ask and answer the questions. Use statement questions to check your understanding of your partner's answers.

1. How often do you get together with your friends?
2. Have you gotten to do anything fun recently?
3. How long does it usually take you to get ready to go out?
4. Where would you go to get away from it all?

How often do you get together with your friends?

Well, I see people from work a lot.

So you have lunch together and things like that?

Episode 2 A Barbecue

Act 2

Before you watch

A Match the statements with the responses. Then practice with a partner.

1. I'm exhausted! __c__
2. I watched that movie last night. _____
3. I didn't like it very much. _____
4. I don't have any money with me. _____
5. I'm not hungry. _____
6. I often stay up late at night. _____

a. So do I. I like to watch late-night TV.
b. Neither do I. Let's find an ATM machine.
c. So am I. Let's take a break.
d. Neither am I. I had a big lunch.
e. So did I. Did you like it?
f. Neither did I. I thought it was boring.

B Read the sentences, paying attention to the underlined events. Write *1* above the event that happened first and *2* above the event that happened second.

1. By the time we got to the theater (2), the movie had already started (1).

2. Sam was exhausted because he had driven all the way from Los Angeles.

3. Hannah couldn't find her bag. Then she realized she had left it at school.

4. I didn't go to the party because I had forgotten all about it.

5. I hadn't seen Ted in years, but I recognized him immediately.

6. Marcia had been on vacation for a month, so she looked great.

7. We went to the meeting because they hadn't told us it was canceled.

8. James had lived in New York for a year, so he knew the city quite well.

While you watch

DVD 22
VHS 18:58
−23:20

A Choose the best title for each scene.

a. Gio's Story	c. Two Different Superstitions	e. Yoko's Story
b. I Hope He's OK	d. Where's Alex?	

1. _____

2. _____

3. _____

4. _____

5. _____

DVD 23
VHS 18:58
−23:20

B Circle the correct answers.

1. Alex is bringing **hamburgers** / **hamburger buns** to the barbecue.
2. Kim has already made **hamburgers** / **chicken**.
3. Kenny is someone who Yoko **grew up** / **worked** with.
4. Yoko will call her friend **right away** / **later**.
5. When Connie calls Alex, **his voice mail** / **he** picks up.
6. Gio first met Enrico Turroni in **Italy** / **the United States.**
7. Yoko **had** / **hadn't** heard Gio's story before.
8. **David** / **Connie** is superstitious.
9. Gio's superstition is about a lucky **number** / **nail**.
10. **Alex** / **Yoko's friend Kenny** suddenly arrives.

While you watch

DVD 24
VHS 19:39
–22:27

C Listen to the stories. Number the events in the correct order.

Yoko's story

_____ Kenny moved.

_____ Kenny called.

_1_ Kenny worked at a restaurant.

_____ Yoko thought about Kenny.

_____ Yoko threw away Kenny's number.

Gio's story

_1_ Gio and Enrico grew up together.

_____ Enrico walked in.

_____ Gio talked to a professor.

_____ Enrico's family moved away.

_____ Enrico transferred to another school.

DVD 25
VHS 19:22
–22:32

D Match the sentences with their responses.

1. I'm pretty hungry! _____
2. I just got a message from him! _____
3. I love it when that happens. _____
4. I'm not really thirsty. _____
5. You're a little superstitious, huh? _____
6. And who walks in but Enrico Turroni – this guy I grew up with! _____
7. I've never heard this story before. _____
8. Hey, guys! Come get some food! _____

a. Wow! What a coincidence!
b. Ooh! Let's eat.
c. Oh, not really.
d. Yeah, so am I.
e. Wow! That's amazing!
f. Neither am I.
g. So do I.
h. Yeah, neither have I.

DVD 26
VHS 20:46
–23:20

E Work with a partner. Complete the summaries about the superstitions. (There is more than one way to complete some items.) Then watch the video and check your answers.

wood

1. Connie says "_____ on wood" when she doesn't want something to _____ .

salt

2. Connie _____ some salt over her shoulder because it's _____ to spill salt.

nail

3. Gio talks about an _____ superstition about _____ a nail in your _____ .

After you watch

A **What can you remember? Answer the questions.**

1. What three superstitions are shown or talked about in the story?

   _____

   _____

   _____

2. Do you know any similar superstitions?

   _____

   _____

   _____

3. What do you think happened to Alex?

   _____

   _____

   _____

B **Match each sentence with the follow-up sentence that repeats the idea.**

1. My new computer cost a fortune. _e_
2. The man at the store was really unhelpful. ____
3. I couldn't carry the box because it was so big. ____
4. Another salesperson helped me. She was really nice. ____
5. I thought I'd met her before somewhere. ____
6. It turned out I went to elementary school with her. ____
7. It was so strange. ____

a. It was really huge!
b. Just really weird.
c. She was really familiar.
d. He didn't help me at all.
e. It was really expensive.
f. Very helpful and friendly.
g. We were in fifth grade together.

C **Think of a coincidence, something strange, or something lucky that happened to you. Answer these questions.**

1. When was it? _____
2. Where were you? _____
3. What was the situation? What happened first? Next? In the end? _____

   _____
4. How did you feel? _____
5. What do you think now? _____

D **Work in pairs. Take turns describing your experiences. Repeat some of your ideas (as in Exercise B) to make your meaning clear.**

A *This happened about ten years ago. I was living in Canada at the time.*
B *Uh-huh.*
A *It was a bad winter. Really cold, and snowy. . . .*

Episode 2 A Barbecue

Act 3

Before you watch

A Read the sentences. Write each of the underlined expressions in the chart.

1. Police work hard to <u>catch criminals</u>.
2. <u>Shoplifting</u> is against the law.
3. When you <u>get a ticket</u>, you have to <u>pay a fine</u>.
4. A police officer can <u>pull you over</u> if you're <u>speeding</u>.
5. If you get a lot of speeding tickets, you could <u>lose your license</u>.
6. It's illegal to <u>jaywalk</u> in this city, and they strictly <u>enforce the law</u>.
7. You could be <u>sentenced to community service</u> if you get too many tickets.

What police do	Crime	Punishment
catch criminals		

B Complete the sentences with the passive (form of *be* + past participle) of the verbs in the box.

allow   arrest   ✓catch   change   sentence   stop

1. The criminal _was caught_____ by police yesterday.
2. People shouldn't _____ to talk on their cell phones while driving.
3. People who shoplift should _____ to community service.
4. The legal age for driving should _____ .
5. If he doesn't pay his speeding tickets, he could _____ .
6. My brother _____ for speeding last week.

While you watch

A Circle the correct answers.

1. Alex was late because he got _____ .
   a. lost   b. stopped

2. Alex tried to call _____ .
   a. Kim   b. Connie

3. Driving and talking on your cell phone _____ allowed.
   a. is   b. is not

4. Alex received two fines for a total of _____ .
   a. $175   b. $200

5. If Alex gets stopped again, he could _____ .
   a. lose his license   b. pay another fine

6. Alex has never _____ a police officer before.
   a. talked to   b. been stopped by

7. They're putting security cameras in _____ .
   a. malls   b. cars

8. The idea is that criminals won't _____ .
   a. commit crimes   b. know they're being videotaped

9. The cameras help _____ .
   a. save money   b. reduce crime rates

10. Liz thinks you shouldn't _____ the cameras.
    a. worry about   b. notice

11. David is worried the cameras will be _____ .
    a. misused   b. stolen

B Listen to Alex's story. Number the events in the correct order.

_____ He left work late.

_____ He was pulled over.

__2__ He was busy.

_____ He got a ticket for talking on the phone while driving.

_____ He remembered that he needed to buy hamburger buns.

__1__ He went to work.

_____ He got on the phone.

_____ He got a ticket for speeding.

While you watch

DVD 29
VHS 24:58
−27:37

C Who states these opinions? Watch the video and check (✓) the correct names.

	Connie	David	Gio	Liz	Yoko
1. Going five miles over the speed limit is a minor offense.					
2. People who speed a lot should be punished.					
3. Security cameras are an invasion of privacy.					
4. They make you feel safe.					
5. They help the police catch criminals.					
6. Being filmed makes me uncomfortable – it's weird.					
7. People shouldn't be spied on.					

DVD 30
VHS 23:25
−25:56

D Match the underlined words and the things they refer to.

1. Oh, you won't believe <u>it</u>. _____
2. Here <u>they</u> are, by the way. _____
3. Is <u>that</u> against the law? _____
4. <u>That</u>'s a pretty expensive fine. _____
5. So <u>that</u>'s another hundred dollars. _____
6. <u>That</u> really doesn't sound fair. _____
7. Don't worry about <u>it</u>. _____

a. how Alex could be punished
b. talking on your cell phone while driving
c. being late
d. the reason Alex is late
e. the hamburger buns
f. the speeding ticket
g. seventy-five dollars

DVD 31
VHS 25:56
−27:53

E Listen for these sentences. Circle each sentence you hear.

1. *David* a. Well, basically, it's to help reduce crime.
   b. Well, actually, it's to help reduce crime.
2. *Yoko* a. The point is, no one should be allowed to watch you without your permission.
   b. The thing is, no one should be allowed to watch you without your permission.
3. *Liz* a. Well, for two reasons. One, they help reduce crime rates.
   b. Well, there are two reasons. One, they help reduce crime rates.
4. *Gio* a. I guess that's true.
   b. I guess that's right.
5. *David* a. Um, well, in the first place, I think most people are basically honest, so . . .
   b. Um, well, first of all, I think most people are basically honest, so . . .
6. *Liz* a. Oh, you've got a point there.
   b. Oh, I've never really thought of it that way.

After you watch

A Look at Exercise E of *While you watch* on page 23. Note the expressions to give views and organize ideas. Add at least two more expressions to each category.

Giving main ideas	Introducing a list of ideas	Responding to opinions
Well, basically . . .	For two reasons. One . . .	

B Check (✓) if you agree or disagree with each statement. Then choose three statements and write reasons for your opinions.

	Agree	Disagree
1. Security cameras should be used in public places to reduce crime.		
2. Someone who gets more than one speeding ticket in a short time should get a serious punishment.		
3. There should be a law against driving and talking on a cell phone.		
4. The age for getting a driver's license should be raised.		
5. Shoplifters should always be arrested.		
6. Community service is a good punishment for most crimes.		

Reasons

1. _____

2. _____

3. _____

C Work in small groups. Have conversations about your opinions. Use expressions from Exercise A.

"Basically, I don't think security cameras should be used in public places because they are an invasion of privacy."

Episode 3 The Big Move

Act 1

Before you watch

A Read the reported speech sentences. Write the direct speech.

1. Emma asked how many people he had invited.
   How many people did he invite?
2. Paula told Emma that she would be right back.
   _____
3. Matt said that he was having a good time.
   _____
4. Scott asked Mary if she had seen any good movies recently.
   _____
5. Kathy asked Jim if he would give her a ride home later.
   _____

B Read the sentences. Choose the expression that is closest in meaning to the underlined word(s).

a. agree to do	c. busy, not available	e. throw out
b. bring success or good results	d. finish (something)	

1. Sorry, I can't see you this afternoon. I'm <u>tied up</u> in meetings until five. _____
2. OK, everyone! Let's <u>wrap</u> it <u>up</u>. Time to go home! _____
3. Starting a company is a big investment, but it often <u>pays off</u> in the end. _____
4. I cleaned out my closet last night. I'm <u>getting rid of</u> a lot of my old clothes. _____
5. I'm willing to <u>take on</u> some extra work. I really need the money. _____

C Match the sentences with the responses. Then practice with a partner.

1. Where is Sam? The meeting starts at 9:00! _____
2. Why did Kate have to leave early today? _____
3. The boss doesn't look happy today! _____
4. Why didn't Ron come to the party last week? _____
5. Rosa never e-mailed me back. _____

a. Uh-oh, something must have happened.
b. She might not have gotten the message.
c. I don't know. He might have forgotten about it.
d. She must have had an appointment.
e. I'm not sure. He may have been sick.

While you watch

DVD 32
VHS 28:06
–32:24

A Circle the correct answers.

1. Liz and Yoko went to get _____ .
   a. coffee   b. a truck
2. Liz is moving to _____ .
   a. New York   b. Los Angeles
3. Last month, Liz _____ .
   a. made a demo   b. recorded an album
4. The record company wants Liz to _____ .
   a. make a demo   b. sing in clubs
5. Liz _____ working in Web design.
   a. has stopped   b. will continue

6. David is _____ about Liz moving.
   a. worried   b. depressed
7. Liz has more _____ than Yoko has.
   a. time   b. stuff
8. Yoko is moving _____ town.
   a. out of   b. across
9. All the friends will _____ Liz a lot.
   a. miss   b. visit

DVD 33
VHS 28:28
–28:57

B Circle the correct words. (You may need to watch the video more than once.) Then answer the question.

1. Why does Gio think Liz and Yoko are late?
   He's pretty certain that Liz and Yoko got **tied up in traffic** / **lost**.
2. What does he say about the truck?
   He thinks the truck may not have been **running properly** / **ready**.
3. What does David say about the situation?
   He thinks it's **suprising** / **rude** that they haven't called.
4. What does Alex say?
   He thinks it's possible that they forgot their **driver's licenses** / **cell phones**.
5. Why else do you think Liz and Yoko might be late?

   _____

While you watch

DVD 34
VHS 28:06
–32:24

C Who says these things? Watch the video and check (✓) the correct names.

	Alex	David	Gio
1. I never get up this early.			
2. Well, moving day can be pretty crazy.			
3. How did all this happen so fast?			
4. Anyway, suddenly, the next thing I hear she's moving out there!			
5. Do you know what she's doing about her Web design business?			
6. After all, this is a once-in-a-lifetime opportunity for her.			
7. I really hope this pays off for her in the end.			
8. All of her stuff is going into storage for now.			
9. Yoko must have been kind of upset when Liz told her she was leaving.			
10. But Yoko knows it's Liz's dream to record her own album.			
11. Where's the truck?			

DVD 35
VHS 29:50
–32:03

D Check (✓) the words and expressions that are used to describe Liz.

☐ not taking on new work   ☐ tough   ☐ upset
☐ confident   ☐ thinks before acting   ☐ can't afford the apartment
☐ determined   ☐ doesn't have much stuff
☐ risky   ☐ keeps everything

DVD 36
VHS 29:20
–30:19

E Listen for these sentences. What does Gio say exactly? Circle the correct words.

1. *Gio* Basically, it did happen pretty fast. Liz **told** / **was telling** me that the record company called her a week after she got home. They **asked** / **were asking** her when she could come out to L.A. to record an album, and she told them that **she could** / **she'd** come right away.

2. *Gio* Yeah, and Liz **told** / **was telling** me that the company is getting her a manager and everything. **Apparently** / **Evidently**, they want her to start singing in clubs out there . . .

3. *Gio* Um, **Yoko said** / **according to Yoko**, Liz wrapped up all her projects last week. **Apparently** / **Evidently**, she's not taking on any new work for now.

4. *Gio* Uh-huh. She **told** / **was telling** me that she was determined to succeed.

After you watch

A What can you remember? Answer the questions.

1. What has happened to Liz recently? How is her life changing?

   _____
   _____

2. Do you agree with David that Liz is taking a big risk? What would you do in Liz's position?

   _____
   _____

B Use the expressions in the box to report the following lines from the story. (You may or may not choose to "shift back" verb tenses.)

> David / Gio / Alex said . . .
> David / Gio / Alex was saying . . .
> According to David / Gio / Alex . . .

1. David: "It all seems a little risky."

   David said it all seemed a little risky.
   OR According to David, it all seems a little risky.

2. Gio: "Liz is not the impulsive type at all."

   _____

3. Alex: "Liz always thinks before she acts."

   _____

4. Gio: "All of Liz's stuff is going into storage for now."

   _____

5. Alex: "Yoko has to move across town."

   _____

C Write some things that people have recently told you about these topics. Then choose two pieces of news and tell a partner about them. Say why this information is interesting or important to you.

Write some news about someone's . . .

1. job: _____
2. plans: _____
3. family: _____
4. possessions: _____

"Apparently, my friend Shaun is unhappy with his job. He told me that he's looking for a new one. I'm a little worried that he won't be able to find one."
"Gina said that she was going to China this summer. I'm really excited for her."

Act 2

Before you watch

A Complete the sentences with the words in the box.

| ✓ faucet | inspect | screwdriver | security deposit | showerhead | water damage |

1. The _faucet_____ in the kitchen won't stop dripping! Can you help me fix it?
2. I just got a new dresser, and I need a _____ to put it together.
3. Before you move into your new apartment, you should _____
   it carefully. You need to make sure that nothing is damaged.
4. I think our roof is leaking. There is some _____ on the ceiling.
5. *A* This new _____ is supposed to cut our water use in half.
   B But I like to take baths.
6. If I rent this apartment, I have to pay the first month's rent and a _____ .

B Match the sentences.

1. Our TV and VCR aren't working. _d_
2. My watch strap is broken. _____
3. There's a stain on the carpet. _____
4. I don't like the color of this room. _____
5. The faucet won't stop dripping. _____
6. These windows are very dirty. _____

a. They really need washing.
b. Do you think the knob needs to be replaced?
c. It really needs replacing.
d. We need to get someone to fix them.
e. Let's have someone paint it soon.
f. I'm going to have it cleaned next week.

C Use the words in parentheses to complete each sentence with a past modal.

1. I had a reservation for dinner tonight, but the restaurant said it was for next week.
   Someone _must have made_____ (must / make) a mistake.
2. I feel really bad because I yelled at my brother. I _____ (should not / get)
   angry at him.
3. I got a bad grade on my test. I guess I _____ (could / study) harder for it.
4. I was late for work this morning. I _____ (should / leave) home earlier.
5. Kathy said she would call me right back, but that was over an hour ago! I guess she
   _____ (must / forget).

While you watch

DVD [37]
VHS 32:29
−37:12

A Number the scenes in the correct order.

a. _____

b. _____

c. _____

d. _____

e. _____

f. _____

DVD [38]
VHS 32:29
−37:12

B Watch the video and number the sentences in the correct order.

_____ Maybe I can fix it.

_____ So, where do you want this?

_____ Is everything OK?

_____ There was a bit of a mix-up.

_____ I should get that fixed before the landlord comes.

_____ Ooh. What happened here?

_____ . . . why don't we help you with your boxes?

_____ I should have known that.

While you watch

DVD **39**
VHS 32:29
−37:12

C Circle all the correct answers. (One, two, or three answers are possible.)

1. The rental company had a reservation for the _____ .
   a. morning   b. afternoon   c. evening

2. Liz got upset because she was _____ .
   a. stressed   b. frustrated   c. tired

3. _____ can help in the afternoon.
   a. Alex   b. David   c. Gio

4. They are going to move Liz's boxes _____ .
   a. into the living room   b. upstairs   c. downstairs

5. There is _____ on the floor.
   a. paint   b. a stain   c. water damage

6. The light _____ .
   a. isn't turning on   b. was flickering   c. is too bright

7. The _____ in the bathroom needs to be fixed.
   a. sink   b. toilet   c. shower

8. Yoko broke _____ .
   a. her nail   b. the picture   c. the lightbulb

9. Alex didn't _____ .
   a. use a towel   b. turn off the water   c. try to fix anything

DVD **40**
VHS 34:05
−36:03

D Watch the video and match the sentences with the things they refer to. (You will use some things more than once.)

1. The landlord got someone to come in and fix it. _____
2. Yoko says the landlord should have it repaired. _____
3. It needs to be screwed in tighter. _____
4. It keeps dripping. _____
5. It might need to be replaced. _____
6. It's loose. _____
7. Maybe it just needs tightening. _____
8. It needs to be taken down. _____

a. the floor
b. the knob on the faucet
c. the lightbulb
d. the picture
e. the refrigerator
f. the showerhead

DVD **41**
VHS 36:30
−36:53

E Listen to this conversation. What do the characters say exactly? Cross out the extra letters and words.

Gio   OK. ~~Have you~~ got that end?

Yoko   Just a second. Ow! That hurt!

Gio   Are you OK?

Yoko   Yeah, I'm fine. I just broke a nail.

David   Do you need help?

Yoko   No, I think we can handle it. Thanks
         anyway. OK.

Gio   Are you ready?

Yoko   Let's try it again. Uh-huh.

Gio   1, 2, 3, lift.

After you watch

A What can you remember? Answer the questions.

1. What repairs have been done in the apartment?

_____

2. What does Yoko need to do before she moves out?

_____

3. What should the landlord do?

_____

B Look at the picture. Write six sentences about what needs to be done.

1. <u>The hole in the wall needs fixing / to be fixed.</u>
2. _____
3. _____
4. _____
5. _____
6. _____

C Write some sentences about things that need to be done in your home. Use your own ideas and the words in the box.

clean	fix	lamp	repair	tighten	wash
faucet	floor	lightbulb	replace	walls	window(s)

_____

_____

_____

Tell a partner about what needs to be done. Which of the jobs above would you do yourself? Which would you have done?

"The windows are dirty. They need to be washed. I'll probably do that myself."
"The walls in the living room need painting. I'm going to hire someone to do that."

Act 3

Before you watch

A Read the money tips. Underline the words and expressions related to money. Then put them in the chart.

Money tips from our readers

I always <u>have a monthly budget</u>, and I stick to it. I keep track of all my money. And I always make sure to put some money away for a rainy day.
– Keesha, Phoenix, AZ

You should never borrow money from a friend. But if you do, always pay the loan back quickly!
– Ralph, Tampa, FL

If you're having money problems, it may help to give up some things. You don't want to get into debt – it's too hard to get out of it!
– Michael, Los Angeles, CA

Don't charge too much on your credit card. It's much better to pay in cash.
– Cindy, Denver, CO

Things you should do	Things you shouldn't do
have a monthly budget	

B Match the sentences with the responses. Then practice with a partner.

1. It's hard to stick to a budget sometimes. _____
2. What did Lucy ask you? _____
3. I want to go on vacation, but I don't know if I can afford it. _____
4. I used to be more of a spender than a saver, but I'm trying to change my spending habits. _____
5. What did he say when you asked him to pay back the money? _____

a. I had a similar experience. I had to learn how to keep track of my money.
b. I know what you mean. It *is* hard.
c. He was like, "No problem. I'll write you a check right now."
d. That's like when I went to Italy. I didn't have a lot of money, so I stayed in youth hostels.
e. She asked me if I was going to buy a new car soon.

While you watch

DVD 42
VHS 37:17
−41:38

A Check (✓) true or false. Then try to correct the false sentences.

1. Yoko hates moving. ☑ True ☐ False
   _____

2. She's moving into a one-bedroom apartment. ☐ True ☐ False
   _____

3. Yoko's parents are helping her. ☐ True ☐ False
   _____

4. David thinks it's easy to save money. ☐ True ☐ False
   _____

5. Yoko will be living with a new roommate. ☐ True ☐ False
   _____

6. David has had trouble paying his bills before. ☐ True ☐ False
   _____

7. Gio had to give up a few things. ☐ True ☐ False
   _____

8. Yoko spends about eighteen dollars a month on coffee. ☐ True ☐ False
   _____

9. The friends are going out for coffee. ☐ True ☐ False
   _____

DVD 43
VHS 37:37
−40:17

B Who does or has done these things? Check (✓) the correct people. For some answers, more than one person will be checked.

Who . . . ?	David	Gio	Yoko
1. needs / needed to buy things for a new apartment			
2. hasn't put enough money away for a rainy day			
3. is more of a spender than a saver			
4. tries to set aside money each month			
5. has / had a monthly budget			
6. got into debt			
7. was spending too much money			

While you watch

DVD [44]
VHS 37:17
−41:38

C Listen for these sentences. Match the sentences with the responses.

1. Are you almost ready for your move? __a__
2. What's your new place like? ____
3. I don't know how I'm going to be able to afford everything. ____
4. So are you going to be OK – moneywise, I mean? ____
5. I'm sure you'll be able to pay it back quickly. ____
6. Do you have, um, a monthly budget or anything? ____
7. Oh, no. So, what did you do? ____
8. So, you were saying . . . about giving things up? ____
9. That's like, seventy dollars a month. ____
10. It'll save us some time and money. ____

a. I guess so.
b. I hope so.
c. I think so.
d. Oh, uh, not really.
e. Sounds good.
f. That's like when I moved.
g. Yeah, well, speaking of coffee . . .
h. Well, it's a studio apartment.
i. I had to change my spending habits.
j. Wow! Yeah. Just from making one small change.

DVD [45]
VHS 37:17
−39:42

D Who says each sentence and what does it refer to? Circle the correct name and then match the sentence to its topic.

1. "But still, it was stressful!"
   (Gio)/ **David** / **Yoko** says this about ____ .

2. "Oh, that's really generous of them."
   Gio / **David** / **Yoko** says this about ____ .

3. "I wouldn't worry about it too much."
   Gio / **David** / **Yoko** says this about ____ .

4. "It makes me a little nervous."
   Gio / **David** / **Yoko** says this about ____ .

5. "I had one in the past. . . . I just could never stick to it."
   Gio / **David** / **Yoko** says this about ____ .

a. a monthly budget

b. living and paying rent alone

c. moving

d. taking money

e. loaning money

DVD [46]
VHS 39:23
−40:17

E Listen to this conversation. What do Yoko, David, and Gio say exactly? Complete the sentences.

David What did Gio say?

Yoko He (1) _____ whether or not I had a monthly budget. And I don't.

David Oh. Yeah, having a budget is (2) _____ . I learned that a few years ago when I had some money problems. To make a long story short, I got into some real (3) _____ and had trouble paying my bills.

Yoko Oh, no. So, what did you do?

David I had to change my spending (4) _____ – learn how to (5) _____ of my money. That kind of thing.

Gio Exactly. I had a (6) _____ experience. When I moved here and went back to school, I realized I was (7) _____ too much money. So, I had to give up a few things.

After you watch

A What can you remember? Answer the questions.

1. Why is Yoko worried about money?

_____

2. What is Gio's advice to Yoko?

_____

3. What are some other ways that Yoko can save money?

_____

B Work with a partner. Choose one of the situations and role-play a conversation.

Situation 1

Student A: You are a student. You don't have a budget, you spend a lot, and you charge a lot to a credit card. You don't think you need to worry about money right now – you can think about it after you graduate. Explain this to your friend – Student B.

Student B: You are a student. You keep track of money, pay your bills, and don't buy things you can't afford. You are worried about your friend – Student A. Give your friend advice about money and tell him / her to be more careful. Start like this: *I'm worried about you. . . .*

Situation 2

Student A: You have a budget and usually stick to it. You need to buy a car for a new job, but you can't quite afford it. A good friend – Student B – has a lot more money than you. You want to ask your friend to loan you the money to buy the car. Explain your plan to pay the money back. Start like this: *I have a favor to ask you. . . .*

Student B: Your friend – Student A – wants to borrow some money. You have enough to loan the money. Ask questions to find out how and when your friend will pay the money back. Then decide whether you will loan the money or not.

C Work in small groups. Write down the best advice anyone has ever given you about money. Then compare your advice. Who has the best advice?

_____

_____

_____

_____

_____

_____

_____

_____

"My grandmother told me to put aside a little money every week. She said . . ."

Episode **4** Follow Your Dream

Act 1

Before you watch

A Complete the definitions with the words in the box.

bad press	making a name
celebrity	✓ media
downhill	producer
dropped out of sight	the headlines
gig	up-and-coming

1. The _media_____ is a word used to describe
   TV, radio, newspapers, and the Internet.
2. A person who is famous is often called a _____ .
3. A person who provides money for a movie or a recording is a _____ .
4. An informal word for a performance or a concert is a _____ .
5. A person who is becoming well known is an _____ star.
   People often say this person is _____ for him or herself.
6. A person who is in the news a lot at the moment is in _____ .
7. Someone who is not in the news any more has _____ .
8. A person who has unflattering things written about him is getting _____ .
   After that, his career might go _____ .

B Match the sentences and the tag questions.

1. It's a beautiful day, __g__   a. do we?
2. It's not five o'clock already, _____ b. doesn't he?
3. Tom Richards lives in Hollywood, _____ c. doesn't she?
4. He got married last year, _____   d. didn't he?
5. You haven't seen his new movie yet, _____ e. didn't she?
6. Liz sings jazz, _____   f. is it?
7. She moved to Los Angeles, _____   g. isn't it?
8. We should get to the concert early, _____ h. have you?
9. We don't have enough time, _____   i. couldn't you?
10. You could call a taxi, _____   j. shouldn't we?

While you watch

DVD 47
VHS 41:43
−46:41

A Circle the correct answers. For some items, both answers are correct.

1. Yoko hasn't talked to Liz because **Liz / Yoko** has been busy.
2. David is reading a celebrity magazine for **fun / research**.
3. Luke Richards is in **the headlines / a new movie**.
4. Before she moved to L.A., Liz was working as a **Web designer / singer**.
5. Liz has already **performed in some big clubs / recorded her first album**.
6. David and Gio say that Liz was discovered by a **producer / club owner**.
7. Liz has met some **up-and-coming stars / interesting musicians**.
8. Liz is looking for **a new manager / new songs**.

DVD 48
VHS 41:43
−46:15

B Who says these things? Check (✓) the correct names.

	Alex	David	Liz	Yoko
1. It's a little strange being here without Liz, though.				
2. Um, it's about how the media has changed the nature of fame.				
3. Whoa! Everybody come here a minute.				
4. Now Liz is living her dream.				
5. It sounds like her career is already taking off.				
6. Well, we're all at the park today, and we miss you so much!				
7. It says that you're an up-and-coming star . . .				
8. But I'm a little concerned about next month.				
9. But, you know, nobody really knows who I am yet.				

DVD 49
VHS 42:19
−44:04

C Watch the video. Then check (✓) Liz or Luke to answer the questions.

	Liz	Luke
1. Who is someone to watch?		
2. Who is doing a lot of volunteer work?		
3. Who was in the right place at the right time?		
4. Who has dropped out of sight?		
5. Who got a lot of bad press?		
6. Who is making a name for him / herself?		

While you watch

DVD 50
VHS 41:43
–43:11

D Listen for these sentences. Circle the ones you hear.

1. a. It's great to just hang out in the park, isn't it?
   b. It's been great to just hang out in the park, hasn't it?
2. a. You must really miss her.
   b. You really miss her, don't you?
3. a. He completely dropped out of sight for a while.
   b. He kind of dropped out of sight for a while, didn't he?
4. a. You guys have seen it, haven't you?
   b. You guys haven't seen it, have you?

DVD 51
VHS 45:08
–46:41

5. a. The one in *Wow Magazine*?
   b. That one in *Wow Magazine*, right?
6. a. So, everything's going OK?
   b. So, everything's going OK, isn't it?
7. a. You should talk to your manager, don't you think?
   b. You should talk to your manager, shouldn't you?
8. a. I mean, are you going to be recording your album soon?
   b. I mean, you're going to be recording your album soon, aren't you?
9. a. I mean, can't you sing some of your old songs?
   b. I mean, you could sing some of your old songs, couldn't you?

DVD 52
VHS 41:43
–45:34

E Listen for these sentences. Match the sentences with the ones that follow them.

1. How's she doing in Los Angeles? _____
2. What's happening in the celebrity world? _____
3. So, what's he up to these days? _____
4. What is it? _____
5. It's amazing, isn't it? _____
6. It's not too early to call, is it? _____
7. Sounds pretty great, doesn't it? _____
8. He's supposed to get you gigs and get your name out there, right? _____

a. Oh, no!
b. There's something in here about Liz!
c. Yeah, it does!
d. I don't know!
e. Uh, not much.
f. I mean, it's pretty lucky that she was singing in the club that night.
g. Well, this article says he's doing a lot of volunteer work now.
h. Yeah. And he is.

After you watch

A What can you remember? Answer the questions.

1. What has Liz been doing in Los Angeles?

   _____

2. What is she worried about?

   _____

3. What do you think will happen?

   _____

B Add tag questions to complete the conversation. Then practice with a partner.

A Look at this. . . . Tom Richards has a new movie out.

B Tom Richards? He won an Oscar this year, (1) _didn't he_____ ?

A Yeah, he did. And now he's made another movie.

B That's not the one about the horse ranch, (2) _____ ?

A Yeah, they filmed it in Australia.

B Oh, it looks a bit like California, (3) _____ ?

A Yeah, I guess so. . . . You've been to Australia, (4) _____ ?

B Yeah. I went a couple of years ago.

A You went to Sydney, (5) _____ ?

B Uh-huh. . . .

A That's where Tom Richards lives, (6) _____ ? You could have gotten his autograph while you were there!

B Oh, come on!

C Complete the sentences with your own information. Then compare with a partner.

1. If I had / hadn't met _____ ,

   I would / wouldn't have _____ .

2. If I had / hadn't gone _____ ,

   I would / wouldn't have _____ .

3. If I had / hadn't been _____ ,

   I would / wouldn't have _____ .

Episode 4 Follow Your Dream

Act 2

Before you watch

A Match the words in the box with the definitions.

an analyst	contacts	a degree	a loan	a salary
an award	✓ a corporation	humanitarian	a résumé	worthwhile

1. a large company: _a corporation_
2. a document that summarizes your education and
   work experience: _____
3. a title given by a university: _____
4. a person who examines facts and gives an opinion: _____
5. a prize for an achievement: _____
6. money that is borrowed and must be paid back: _____
7. regular pay you receive for a job: _____
8. people you know who can help you find a job: _____
9. concerned with improving the lives of other people: _____
10. meaningful, useful, or valuable: _____

B Complete the conversation with expressions from the box.
Use correct capitalization.

✓ the best thing to do	what I mean	what the job involves	what we should do
the good thing about that	what she's been doing	what we really need	what you're saying

A What do you think of hiring Penny for the job?

B Hmm. I'm not sure that that's (1) _the best thing to do_ .
   She's pretty green.

A What do you mean, exactly?

B Well, (2) _____ is that she's a
   recent college grad and has only been at her current job for a year.
   (3) _____ is someone with more experience.

A I understand (4) _____ , but I
   think Penny is someone who can grow with the company. Plus, if you look at
   (5) _____ , it's very similar to
   (6) _____ at her current job.

B Well, I think (7) _____ is to hire someone
   else to manage the project, but hire Penny for the assistant position.

A That makes sense. (8) _____ is that we
   can give her a chance.

While you watch

DVD [53]
VHS 46:46
−50:56

A Circle the correct answers.

1. Gio has finished his _____ .
   a. exams   b. job search
2. A company in _____ is interested in Gio.
   a. town   b. Chicago
3. _____ is more important to Gio.
   a. Making a lot of money   b. Doing something worthwhile
4. Alex has heard of _____ .
   a. the company in Chicago   b. East Cliff Bank
5. Henry Willets works as _____ .
   a. an analyst   b. a stockbroker
6. After Gio sent his résumé, he followed up with _____ .
   a. a phone call   b. an e-mail
7. Alex's friend got a job by _____ a lot.
   a. interviewing   b. calling
8. Yoko knows Henry Willets because _____ .
   a. he's a customer   b. she uses East Cliff Bank
9. Yoko says the next time she sees Henry she'll _____ .
   a. talk to him   b. call Gio

B Who does these things? Check (✓) the correct names.

DVD [54]
VHS 46:46
−50:56

Who . . . ?	Alex	David	Gio	Kim
1. hasn't said congratulations yet				
2. hasn't made any decisions yet				
3. asks Gio where he'd like to work				
4. asks if the bank won an award				
5. thinks Gio should go for it				
6. thinks Gio should talk to everyone he knows				
7. thinks companies don't like you to call them				
8. asks Yoko if she knows Henry Willets				
9. says it never hurts to ask friends for help				

While you watch

DVD 55
VHS 47:11
−48:47

C Watch the video and check (✓) the correct answers.

Which company . . . ?	Company in Chicago	East Cliff Bank
1. did Gio send a follow-up e-mail to		
2. does humanitarian work		
3. is a big corporation		
4. is interested in Gio		
5. gives small loans to poor people		
6. offers a great starting salary		

DVD 56
VHS 46:46
−49:16

D Who says each sentence and what does it refer to? Circle the correct name.
Then match the sentence to its topic.

1. "Why don't we start anyway?"
   (Alex) / Gio says this about _____ .   a. East Cliff Bank

2. "It feels pretty good to finally be done."
   Alex / Gio says this about _____ .   b. getting a job at East Cliff Bank

3. "I have a couple more to go."
   Alex / Gio says this about _____ .   c. eating lunch

4. "Isn't it here in town?"
   Alex / Gio says this about _____ .   d. finishing exams

5. "I think you should go for it."
   Alex / Gio says this about _____ .   e. getting personal contacts

6. "But I am not very comfortable asking
   my friends for help like that."
   Alex / Gio says this about _____ .   f. going on interviews

DVD 57
VHS 47:43
−49:45

E Listen for these sentences. Match the two parts to complete them.

1. I guess what I'm saying is _____   a. talk to everyone you know.
2. What his department does is _____   b. give small loans to poor people all over
3. I think what you should do is _____   the world.
4. Something a friend of mine did was _____   c. work for Henry Willets.
5. I need to do more if I want the chance to _____   d. interesting.
                                           e. I want to use my business degree to do
                                              something worthwhile.

After you watch

A What can you remember? Complete Gio's notes about the two jobs.

Company in Chicago

One advantage: _____

One disadvantage: _____

East Cliff Bank

One advantage: _____

One disadvantage: _____

B What would you do if you wanted to work at a particular company? Rank each of these suggestions from 1 (very useful) to 5 (not useful at all).

1. do research about the company and the work that it does   ____
2. call the company regularly to ask if there are any positions available   ____
3. send an e-mail to ask if there are any positions open   ____
4. send a résumé by e-mail   ____
5. write a letter or e-mail saying why you would like to work for the company   ____
6. contact the president or the CEO of the company directly   ____
7. develop a personal contact at the company   ____
8. volunteer to work at the company for free (an internship)   ____

C Give a friend advice about getting an interview at a particular company. Complete the sentences using the ideas in Exercise B and your own ideas.

1. The first thing you should do is _____
2. The advantage of that is _____
3. Another important thing is _____
4. The main reason to do that is _____
5. Something a friend of mine did was _____
6. What I would do is _____

D Work in small groups. Compare your answers to Exercises B and C above. Do you agree with the advice?

Before you watch

A Match the words in the box with the definitions.

ban	gallery	mayor	quality of life
✓ construction	livable	pollution	restless

1. the process of putting up new buildings and structures: <u>construction</u>
2. unable to relax or stay in one place: _____
3. something that makes air or water dirty: _____
4. a room or building where art is shown: _____
5. the leader of a town or city: _____
6. the level of comfort and enjoyment of a group of people: _____
7. to forbid something officially: _____
8. enjoyable to live in: _____

B Use the words in parentheses to complete each sentence with the passive form of the present continuous or present perfect. (Pay attention to time words in the sentences.)

1. *A* Four new apartment buildings <u>have been built</u> (build) in the past year.
   B Oh, that's good. People need more places to live.
2. *A* Hundreds of trees _____ (plant) around the city recently.
   B Oh, I've noticed. They look beautiful!
3. *A* The old City Hall _____ (tear down).
   B Oh, that's too bad. It was a historic building.
4. *A* Private cars _____ (ban) from the city center permanently.
   B Really? Has it helped with traffic?
5. *A* Several new office buildings _____ (put up) in the next year.
   B Oh, do we really need more office buildings?
6. *A* A new house _____ (build) next door to mine right now.
   B That's nice.

While you watch

DVD 58
VHS 51:01
−55:49

A What topics are mentioned? Circle the correct topic in each pair.

1. a. the mayor's plan
   b. the mayor's election
2. a. building parks
   b. planting trees
3. a. new construction
   b. new city jobs
4. a. crime
   b. pollution
5. a. writing a novel
   b. shooting a movie

6. a. finding money
   b. winning the lottery
7. a. opening a restaurant
   b. opening a gym
8. a. learning a language
   b. teaching art
9. a. running a company
   b. running a gallery
10. a. good friends
    b. a good job

DVD 59
VHS 51:36
−52:47

B Listen for these sentences. Match the two parts to complete them.

1. What I heard is that _____
2. Well, it'll be great to have more trees – especially because _____
3. Even though all this new construction is good for the city, _____
4. The reason I ask is, you know, _____
5. Well, what I was going to say was _____
6. So instead of driving everywhere, _____

a. a lot of older buildings have been destroyed.
b. the noise and pollution are getting pretty bad.
c. they want to plant fifty thousand new trees over the next five years.
d. so many new buildings are being put up.
e. people would use public transportation or walk.
f. that part of the plan is to ban private cars from the city center on weekends.

While you watch

DVD **60**
VHS 51:01
−55:49

C Listen for these sentences. Match the underlined words and the things they refer to.

1. I wish there were more places like <u>this</u> in the city. _____
2. <u>It</u>'s supposed to help make the city more livable. _____
3. <u>It</u>'s a shame because some of those buildings were historic. _____
4. See, I think <u>that</u>'s great. _____
5. <u>That</u> sounds good, David, but, um, how are you going to pay your bills? _____
6. But <u>it</u> may be hard. _____
7. <u>That</u>'d be cool. _____
8. <u>It</u> was fun. _____

a. the mayor's plan
b. banning cars
c. the park
d. writing a novel
e. running a gallery
f. destroying buildings
g. going to the park
h. owning a restaurant

D Watch the video and complete the conversations with the correct form of the verbs in the box. (You may need to add auxiliaries *be* or *have*.)

be	go back	run	work
change	graduate	teach	write

DVD **61**
VHS 52:47
−53:34

Kim Do you know what you're going to do in ten years? Or even five years?

Gio I don't even know what I'm doing tomorrow.

Kim No, seriously. What do you guys think you'll be doing? Where do you think you'll
(1) _____ ?

David In five years? To be honest, I have no idea. I suppose I'll (2) _____ jobs again. You know how I get restless. Or maybe I'll have quit (3) _____ and I'll (4) _____ a novel.

DVD **62**
VHS 54:16
−54:54

Alex And hopefully, in five years, I'll (5) _____ with a degree in fine arts. So, maybe I'll (6) _____ art to kids, or . . .

Kim Or you might (7) _____ a gallery or something.

Alex Yeah. That'd be cool!

Gio You want to go back to school, Alex? That's funny. I will have finally graduated, and you'll (8) _____ .

After you watch

A What can you remember? What is one thing each person says about what he or she will be doing in five or ten years?

1. David   *Maybe he'll have changed jobs again.* _____
2. Gio   _____
3. Yoko   _____
4. Alex   _____

B Think about a city or neighborhood you know well. Write three or four sentences about what is being done and what has been done to improve the city or neighborhood. Use the categories in the box to help you. Then compare answers.

apartment buildings	cars and traffic	public services
bike trails	houses	roads and transportation
buildings (old and new)	public areas	trees and parks

_____

_____

_____

_____

"About fifty new trees have been planted in my neighborhood, and a new park has been created. A bike trail is being built to cross the city."

C Work in small groups. Discuss these questions.

1. What is something new you will be starting in the near future?
2. What is a project you'll be working on in the next six months?
3. What is something you will have finished in the next year?
4. What do you think you'll be doing in five years?
5. What is a dream you would like to have accomplished in ten or twenty years?

Irregular verbs

Base form	Simple past	Past participle
be	was/were	been
beat	beat	beaten
become	became	become
begin	began	begun
bite	bit	bitten
bleed	bled	bled
blow	blew	blown
break	broke	broken
bring	brought	brought
build	built	built
burn	burned/burnt	burned/burnt
buy	bought	bought
catch	caught	caught
choose	chose	chosen
come	came	come
cost	cost	cost
cut	cut	cut
dig	dug	dug
do	did	done
draw	drew	drawn
dream	dreamed/dreamt	dreamed/dreamt
drink	drank	drunk
drive	drove	driven
eat	ate	eaten
fall	fell	fallen
feed	fed	fed
feel	felt	felt
find	found	found
fight	fought	fought
fly	flew	flown
forget	forgot	forgotten
forgive	forgave	forgiven
freeze	froze	frozen
get	got	gotten
give	gave	given
go	went	gone
grow	grew	grown
hang	hung	hung
have	had	had
hear	heard	heard
hide	hid	hidden
hit	hit	hit
hold	held	held
hurt	hurt	hurt
keep	kept	kept
know	knew	known
lead	led	led
leave	left	left
lend	lent	lent
let	let	let
lie	lay	lain

Base form	Simple past	Past participle
light	lit	lit
lose	lost	lost
make	made	made
mean	meant	meant
meet	met	met
pay	paid	paid
prove	proved	proven/proved
put	put	put
quit	quit	quit
read	read	read
ride	rode	ridden
ring	rang	rung
rise	rose	risen
run	ran	run
say	said	said
see	saw	seen
sell	sold	sold
send	sent	sent
set	set	set
sew	sewed	sewn/sewed
shake	shook	shaken
shine	shone	shone
shoot	shot	shot
show	showed	shown/showed
shut	shut	shut
sing	sang	sung
sink	sank	sunk
sit	sat	sat
sleep	slept	slept
speak	spoke	spoken
speed	sped	sped
spend	spent	spent
spill	spilled/spilt	spilled/spilt
spring	sprang	sprung
stand	stood	stood
steal	stole	stolen
stick	stuck	stuck
strike	struck	struck
swim	swam	swum
take	took	taken
teach	taught	taught
tear	tore	torn
tell	told	told
think	thought	thought
throw	threw	thrown
understand	understood	understood
wake	woke	woken
wear	wore	worn
win	won	won
wind	wound	wound
write	wrote	written